Dr. Barrington O. Burrell

∽ Live out Your Passion, and Die Empty ∽

This book is the autobiography of a modern-day servant of God – the story of a man destined to bring the miraculous power of the Divine into the lives of many thousands of people. From his early years growing up in Jamaica to his extraordinary and moving conversion, and from his hardships as a young immigrant in 1960s London to his expanding role in the Church, Bishop Burrell recounts the battles he has faced and the victories he has won, and tells of the signs and wonders that have followed his ministry and the Divine mission that has taken him around the world. Bishop, preacher, counsellor, youth leader, inspirational teacher and author, Dr Burrell gives his own account of a life lived in the service of the Lord.

~Joe Tapsell

"Cheating Death" is the fantastic story about a boy who grew up humbly in Jamaica and became an outstanding man of God in the United Kingdom. He has spread the gospel in this contemporary generation and demonstrated the miracle-working power of God to countless people from country to country. Bishop Burrell takes us through the early years of his childhood to the apex of his ministry, as well as the personal struggles against all odds baffling the medical profession, and the triumphs that have inspired his well-crafted work and thrilling narrative. The transparent and uncompromising way in which he expresses himself in this book will provoke creative thinking and inspire godly aspirations for effective Christian living. His practical experiences are weaved into theology and his profound faith in God authenticated. This is interesting reading: survival, endurance, perseverance or divine intervention – whatever you are into, get into cheating death, get more out of life.

~Rev. David Livingstone

Infographic

Timeline of My Life

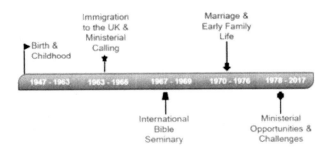

"If you live long enough, you'll make mistakes. But if you learn from them, you'll be a better person. It's how you handle adversity, not how it affects you. The main thing is never quit, never quit, never quit" William J. Clinton.

Cheating Death

·❖· The Autobiography of ·❖·

Dr. Barrington O. Burrell

Grosvenor House
Publishing Limited

This book is published by
Grosvenor House Publishing Ltd
Link House
140 The Broadway, Tolworth, Surrey, Kt6 7Ht.
www.grosvenorhousepublishing.co.uk

Dr. Barrington O. Burrell Publications
Tel: +44 07878 615686
E-mail: Barrington_ob@yahoo.co.uk

KJV

Scripture quotations marked KJV are from the Holy Bible, King James Version
(Authorized Version). First published in 1611. Quoted from the KJV Classic
Reference Bible, Copyright © 1983 by The Zondervan Corporation.

NKJV

Scripture quotations marked NKJV are taken from the New King James Version.
Copyright © 1982 by Thomas Nelson, Inc. Used by permission. All rights reserved.

NIV

Scripture quotations marked NIV are taken from the Holy Bible, New
International Version®. NIV®. Copyright © 1973, 1978, 1984 by International
Bible Society. Used by permission of Zondervan. All rights reserved. [Biblica]

Any people depicted in stock imagery provided by Thinkstock are
models, and such images are being used for illustrative purposes only.
Certain stock imagery © Thinkstock.

A CIP record for this book
is available from the British Library

ISBN 978-1-78623-851-1

CONTENTS

CONTENTS

DEDICATION

To God my heavenly Father and Jesus Christ my wonderful LORD: all that I am, all that I have achieved and all I will ever be, I owe to You. The Apostle Paul affirms, "I can do **all things** through Christ who strengthens me" (Philippians 4:13, NKJV). In other words, I can take on the world and its challenges through the strength of Christ and overcome.

To my beloved wife Maxine of over forty–seven years. We have complemented each other's life like ackee and salt-fish or peas in a pod. Through it all you have stood by me steadfastly and supported me sincerely. Indeed, you have been my tower of strength. Thank you! I love and appreciate you greatly. God bless you my darling.

To my spiritual leaders, mentors, friends and esteemed colleagues who have made significant contributions to my growth and development, I owe much gratitude, respect and deep affection. Many thanks, and God bless you abundantly.

To our daughter Lorna Mae and son Robert Charles Burrell, our three handsome grandsons, two beautiful granddaughters and one adorable great granddaughter, who fill our lives with great joy and a sense of humble pride. I love you.

ACKNOWLEDGEMENTS

I am grateful to the six churches cited in this book for allowing me the privilege of serving them over a period of forty-seven years, and for the opportunity to engage with them via various mediums through which I have gained vital experience and accumulated invaluable knowledge.

To all those who have stood with me and supported me faithfully. Thanks for your prayers and encouragement, especially during my times of difficulty.

I am grateful to Professor Clinton Ryan who read the original manuscript and wrote the foreword. Your comments and encouragement have been well received and deeply appreciated.

Thanks to Genesis Gamra for his advice and invaluable technical support, and to Dwain Williams for assisting with designing the cover and logo on page 327.

The image on page 65 was acquired from Shutterstock. com, and is subject to Shutterstock's Privacy Statement, standard licence, and Website Terms of Use.

FOREWORD

In "Cheating Death", Dr Burrell tells his story with honesty, frankness and transparency, which he believes is what God expects of him. Some of the experiences which he has shared with us in this book are of such magnitude, he said, "Only God Knows how I survived. I am a walking miracle and a mobile reservoir of God's unmerited favour."

An autobiography can have the most positive influence or impact on one's life, but can also be problematic for a Christian author, especially when he is a long-standing and well-known Bishop of his organisation. It is all the more challenging when the denomination has undividedly and unreservedly affirmed him as a man of God with a unique sense of calling and anointing for ministry and mission and as an uncompromising God-bearer.

The difficulty is to decide which events and experiences to record for public consumption and which to leave out. An autobiography of this nature will be controversial, but can be used as a tool for the education of younger ministers and a warning to older members of the clergy.

Some of the details that the author has included are almost unbelievable and others will be hard to accept as having occurred in a Pentecostal church, but they have all helped to inform the author's Christology and have enabled him to develop his ministerial strategies for success.

The author is confident that he was preordained and predestined to live a life of faith, and to serve God's purpose in his own generation. He is of the firm conviction that nothing seen or unseen, heard or unheard, can deter him from God's Sovereign and Ordained Plan for his life, not even demonic attacks or the threat of premature death.

-Professor Clinton L. Ryan, Th.D.

PREFACE

This is a practical non-fiction book, which gives a factual narrative of my life. There is no perfect time to begin writing one's own story, and it is not easy to know where or when to start, but this is my personal contribution to the history of the human race. With a mixture of deliberate confidence, pride, humility, integrity, transparency and clarity, I embark on the awesome task of writing this volume without fear or favour, vindictiveness or ill will. The six churches that I have had the privilege to pastor, the global missions and the experiences gained since my early childhood, all define the time frame of this book. It's the ongoing journal of my journey with God – making particular reference to the milestones in my life.

Through my shrewd efforts in small, but specific roles in the Church, my willingness to cooperate with those who are over me in the LORD, and through having respect for my elders, rather than an arrogant attitude, I have set goals in my humble way and succeeded. I realised early that "Life with a goal is a life that is whole."[1] Benjamin Franklin is reported to have said, "If you fail to plan, you are planning to fail."[2]

My Mother taught me that respect and good manners go a long way in life. Therefore, I have endeavoured to practice basic courtesy and etiquette. Many people's lives are curtailed because of bad manners. Paul instructed Timothy, "Don't let anyone look down on you *[or limit you]* because you are **young**, but set an example for the believers in speech, in conduct, in love, in faith and in purity" (1 Timothy 4:12, NIV).

In other words, "Make yourself an example or a pattern to other believers, and retain respect." The best way to ensure this is to give respect to your elders. Paul says that Timothy is to exercise wisdom, and not to rebuke an older man harshly *[regardless of whether the man is right or wrong]*, but to entreat him as a father *[or as your father]*. (See 1 Timothy 5.1.) Remember: what you sow you reap. If you disrespect the elderly and you are a parent, your child or children may disrespect you in turn.

15 Ways to gain respect and retain it:

- Don't expect respect, or beg for it; you must earn it!
- Earn respect by giving it. Respect others even if you don't like them.
- Practise humility; don't act through pride or arrogance.
- Demonstrate good manners and be willing to help others.
- Don't let your emotions get the better of you. Check your impulsive reactions.
- Lead by example and people will listen and follow you.
- Keep your word and be punctual.
- Don't waste other people's time.
- Show others that you genuinely care about their well-being.
- Make people feel significant, accepted and appreciated.
- Be compassionate and sympathetic with others.
- Sincerely compliment the work of others.

- Don't gossip about others.
- Show yourself to be friendly and wear a smile.
- Dress appropriately for each occasion.

We've often been told, "Self-praise is no recommendation." This idiom was instilled in me as a youngster. People say, "If you praise yourself, others will think that you are boastful and will not respect you or have a high opinion of you." As plausible as this may seem, I think it is not always true. If you don't eulogise yourself at times, you may miss great opportunities, and may possibly develop low self-esteem or inferiority complex.

Self-aggrandisement is the exaggerating of one's own achievement or power; going out of one's way to praise oneself; and stretching the truth to create a false sense of importance. People don't generally like anyone who speaks too highly of themselves habitually, but on the other hand, if you don't "sell" yourself well, no one will "buy" you. For example, when you go for employment, even if you have an excellent CV, if you fail to convince the interviewer of your suitability for the work, it's unlikely that you'll get the job.

You know yourself better than anyone else does. Therefore, you should demonstrate self-confidence. Celebrate who you are, your uniqueness and what you have achieved. Acknowledge where you have come from, where you are now and where you are aiming to be in the future. This is not conceitedness, arrogance or self-centredness; it is self-appraisal or self-evaluation, which is absolutely necessary for growth and self-development.

Everyone who has lived a full life has something noteworthy to tell the world, whether your story is crowned with great accomplishments or tarnished by disaster. You can communicate this by different means; electronically, via social media networks, phone or simply by writing it. Sharing your story in a written format is called an "autobiography," which offers us unique and sometimes surprising insights into the lives of those we think we know from their public personas.

This book is by no means my complete autobiography, but rather a synopsis of the deadliest situations that I have faced, and some of the key features of my life. It shares intriguing first hand insights that will enable the readers to understand the "other," unseen side of me. Furthermore, my story, transcribed herein, is as challenging as it is rewarding, inspiring and interesting. It's like a Lifebook, which is an encapsulated view of my personal life and experiences: the little ones and the big ones, my joys and sorrows, my trials and tribulations, but most importantly, a chronological account of events depicting how I have overcome the hardships of life, and stood where others have fallen. Another fascinating feature of this book are the historical factors of early Jamaican life and British culture in the 1960s–1980s. It reveals some of the idealism, the intellectualism, the music and traditional beliefs.

The evolution of life, with all its vicissitudes (or changing circumstances), presents us with many challenges; the finality of death being the ultimate. When I was a young teenager, I heard my late pastor, the Rev. E. G. Kelly-Wright speak about how he cheated death. I am not sure that I fully understood what he meant at the time, but ever since, the term has resonated powerfully in my mind although I had no premonition that one day the same sentiment would be echoed by me.

Over the years, I have come to the realisation that in the midst of life, there is death, and I have always been a prime target. During my childhood days and throughout my adult life, death has chased me on various occasions, down difficult roads and in diverse ways, but I have escaped triumphantly by the grace of God.

Scripture says, "Don't be afraid. Stand firm, and you will see the deliverance of the LORD, which He will accomplish for you today. For the Egyptians whom you see today, you shall see again no more" (Exodus 14:13, NKJV). Ultimately, even death itself will be destroyed. One day, I will say farewell to this life; close my eyes in death, and go to inherit the astonishing future prepared for me by Jesus Christ, but until then my heart will go on singing and my lips will keep on praising God. I concur with the words of the song writer, "When I think of the goodness of Jesus and what He has done for me, my soul cries out hallelujah, thank God for saving me."[3]

Today, my life epitomises the paradox of a living martyr and the victory of a wounded soldier. The battle scars don't matter anymore. My medical consultant has told me that I am one of the most complex cases he has ever treated, but "through many dangers, toils and snares I have already come!" I fully endorse the words of the Apostle Paul, "I have been crucified with Christ: it is no longer I who live, but Christ lives in me; and the life which I now live in the flesh I live by faith in the Son of God, who loved me and gave Himself for me" (Galatians 2:20, NKJV).

Life Must Precede Death and Resurrection

Christ is the source and fountain of life, but He subjected Himself to death, came back from the dead, and never died again. This gives us hope for tomorrow. We can face death with the confidence that Jehovah has the final say. The Apostle Paul writes, "If in this life only we have hope in Christ, we are of all men the most miserable" (1 Corinthians 15:19, NKJV).

Our generation has undoubtedly seen more scientific and technological advancements than any other, yet the more breakthroughs we witness, the more the world plunges into moral degradation and the more the mortality rate escalates.

"Who knows whether [*we*] are come to the Kingdom for such a time as this?" (See Esther 4:14.)

There is an apparent contradiction in the Words of Christ: "I am the resurrection and the life. He who believes in Me, even though he may die, he shall live. And whoever lives and believes in Me shall never die. Do you believe this?" (John 11:25–26, NKJV.) Here, Jesus is talking about two different experiences: a physical and a spiritual death. So, there is a spiritual and a physical dimension to life and death.

Quite simply, death is the termination of human existence on this planet, and can be a frightening experience if we are not prepared for it, but even if we are, it is still a shock when it comes. But all it takes for life to slip away is for the heart to stop beating for a couple minutes, the blood congeals, the eyes closed, the brain shuts down, every other organ cease functioning and life has ended. As gruesome as this may be, it is the process of death.

The demonic forces or spirit of death, under assignment, pervades our world, and is personified as an evil monster, which parades the path of life, flies in the air, travels the high-ways, and lurks in the back alleys. It visits homes, parks, hospitals, and all sociological classes of people: black and white, rich and poor, educated and illiterate, and moves from prisons to palaces. Death is always active, and never takes holidays or rest periods from its excursions.

Paradoxically, death is one of the most gruesome and dreaded subjects of life. Because of its finality, the grief associated with it, and the void often created by death, people are generally horrified to think, talk or hear about it. Many don't even want to say that someone has died, because it seems too harsh. They prefer to use vague and euphemistic terms like he or she "passed away" or "departed" or "is gone home" or "is no longer with us." Some are fearful of death's attack, while others stand firm and resist its strikes.

Today's world is characterised by increasing frustration and hopelessness in light of the present economic conditions, political upheaval, social depravation, moral collapse and the erosion of Christian values and standards. This sounds quite depressing, but the Bible gives a different perspective. The essence of Paul's message is that if our hope in Christ is substituted by these situations, and He will not raise us from the dead, then we are of all men the most pitiable; but the Christian hope extends beyond what we see, above mortal life and the gloominess of the grave.

One of the earliest lessons all human beings learn, is that life is unfair. The unfairness of life as a whole is universal, and impacts on all humanity. Let's say you have been physically assaulted, lied to and cheated on by your wife or husband, isn't this hard to grapple with? Maybe you have been unfairly dismissed from your employment and are finding it difficult to cope.

Sometimes you are misjudged, misunderstood, misrepresented, marginalised, ostracised or betrayed. No doubt you are often treated as an underdog: overlooked, unrecognised, and frequently undermined and undervalued by those who think they are superior. Maybe you are just a victim of circumstances. I know this might not come as a consolation, but it has not only happened to you my friend, but to millions more. And as if that's not hard enough, you may also have to struggle with the aftermath of sickness and even the pain, loneliness and emptiness of the death of those you love and the contemplation of your own mortality.

Death is a tragedy, but not an extinction or an annihilation. It is an end, but not the ultimate end because Scripture teaches us that there is life beyond the grave. The historical resurrection of Jesus Christ guarantees life after death for those who believe in Him. Over three thousand years ago, Solomon declared that God put eternity in the heart of every person, except that no one can find out the work that He does from beginning to end. (See Ecclesiastes 3:11.) Immortality was a part of God's image in man before the catastrophic fall of Adam (see Romans 5:12).

Most people make no preparation for death, yet it comes to all humanity. The writer of the Hebrews reminds us that we all will die sooner or later (see Hebrews 9:27); and indeed, there is nothing we can do to prevent it, except to try to cheat its premature attacks, and live as long as we can. How is this possible? There are different views regarding the prospect of cheating death.

However, the term "cheating death" is commonly used to describe the way a person avoids a potential death, or possibly fatal event, or who prolongs his or her life despite of considerable odds. This phrase was coined to depict "near-death" experiences or "narrow escapes" from death.

I recall the scenario of an old-time preacher man from Kingston Jamaica named Elder Robb. On his transatlantic flight a storm caused dreadful turbulence and the passengers began to panic and scream hysterically. The man of God cried out, "God, I refuse to die in this way!" Everything calmed down, returned to normality and the airplane landed safely. Flight turbulence is not usually any more dangerous than a car driving over a bump in the road, but fear as well as baggage flying through the cabin can be harmful.

We are in a spiritual war. Therefore, the Bible says, "Fight the good fight of faith, lay hold on eternal life" (1 Timothy

6:12). When we hear the word "fight," we think of using force to try to defeat another person or enemy; it conjures up thoughts of combat, attack, assault, scuffle, perseverance and even pain and sometimes death. Although Paul's admonition to Timothy here may be taken out of context, the principle is still relevant. We must get radical and "fight" sin," fight demons, fight sicknesses, fight diseases, fight our arch enemy – Satan; fight our last enemy – death and claim our inheritance in Christ.

Many people say you can't cheat death; when your time comes you just have to go. Some ask, "Can any man really outwit nature? Or can we change destiny?" "Can we postpone our time when death calls our number?" We certainly can, and have done many times, even without realising it. If you have survived a massive heart attack, a major sickness or a disaster of some kind, then you have cheated death – otherwise you could have been a victim of death.

For instance, a heart attack is life-threatening. Its purpose is to kill you. I have had three heart attacks, and but for good, rapid medical care and the benefit of divine miracles I would have died. This is a fact: death viciously attacked me, and I survived! From a spiritual perspective, my heart attacks have become my trophies of God's grace and mercies.

Some may say, "that's because your time wasn't up," but if I was living in an undeveloped country where good medical care was not accessible, I could have died and the same people would have said, "Your time had come." This is utter confusion. Is my time on this planet determined by my geographical location or adverse circumstances? Is your time up because you lack proper medical treatment? How does one know when one's time has come?

Surely if God is ready for me, He doesn't have to fight me

with heart attacks, which I may or may not survive. He can simply serve me a summons from the portals of heaven.

Furthermore, the mortality rate in any given period or of any particular population is too simple a tool to calculate God's immeasurable immortality and eternal life of humanity. God is sovereign and our lives are under His control. "Jehovah is not the God of the dead, but of the living" (Luke 20:38).

Our arch enemy the devil is constantly trying to kill us, so we have to do something about it. We must resist sickness and disease and everything that is orchestrated by Satan to shorten our lives, and by so doing "ward off " or "cheat death." Many people are known to overcome terminal illnesses. A terminal illness is a disease that cannot be cured or adequately treated medically and that is reasonably expected to result in the death of the patient within a certain period.

Les Brown, a renowned motivational speaker, cheated death. He was diagnosed with prostate cancer, but conquered it. Cancer is probably one of the most feared words in the human vocabulary. After the initial shock, Les began to think about how he was going to deal with this disease. He pondered, "Do I have cancer or does cancer have me?" He thought about all the many things he had to do to restore his health, and became involved in the process, but even more importantly, he had a mindset which said, "I am more powerful than cancer." Today, Les Brown is cancer-free.

Bishop Miller, someone I helped mentor, collapsed in his Church office one day, and while his deacons were mourning his passing, his spirit left his body and on the way to heaven encountered the LORD, who said to him, "You can either come with me or go back to finish the work." He felt good about his assignment and went back into his body, and having had three heart attacks, today he is doing great work for God.

However, many people have survived hospitalisation and prolonged their lives in critical situations by "healing themselves" of cancer or other terminal (or life-threatening) sicknesses and diseases in the face of chronic or dangerous medical prognoses and often without the use of conventional medicines. And, there are those who have narrowly escaped death, perhaps from a major accident, a gunshot or a knife wound to the chest. All these people may be described as having "cheated death."

Many people have taken the matter to another level and talked about their out of body (OBE) experiences. While the stories are all different, and often have no cause at all, some claim to have floated away into some sort of oblivion before regaining consciousness. Others talk about being in a bright light, and feeling a tranquil peace in a heavenly environment. Whatever the case, they all seem to have avoided death.

However, some view these incidents as "astral travel" or a "fight or flight" response, which is a natural reflex of someone confronted with a potentially fatal danger. Some scientists say OBE might be a trick of the mind, but many who have had these experiences say that they have had positive impacts on their lives. These mysterious episodes are spontaneous occurrences, which cannot be scientifically, medically or biblically explained, but we must trust God even when we don't understand.

Life does not always make sense to us. Some things are just too deep for the human mind to fathom. You may or may not have had any of these experiences, but you can be assured of God's protection in the face of critical circumstances, adversities, sickness and ultimately death.

In summary, this book reveals the story behind the man. It primarily recounts my practical contacts and observations of facts or events associated with the six churches I pastored in the New Testament Church of God (UK), and international missions. Some of the experiences may have impacted on my life "for better or for worse," but my transparency and frankness throughout will help the reader to know me on a personal level.

It is my prayer that you will be positively impacted, encouraged, and motivated to live a dynamic lifestyle in spite of the odds or setbacks you may face. It is no secret what God can do; what He has done for me and for others He'll do for you. I hope that you and future generations will enjoy reading my story as much as I have enjoyed writing it.

INTRODUCTION

There are many notions cited in this volume that will help to illustrate the incredible concept of escaping death. However, the perspective of this book "Cheating Death" goes beyond the medical, physiological, and psychological dimensions to embrace the supernatural and miraculous phenomena. The first death that one can cheat is the death of sin, but this is possible only through Christ. "We know that we have **passed from death to life**" (1 John 3:14; John 5:24; Ephesians 2:1). The human demise in sin has been nullified by the eternal effect of the death and resurrection of Jesus Christ, "who has abolished death and brought life and immortality to light through the gospel" (2 Timothy 1:10, NKJV).

Scripture says, "With God all things are possible" (Matthew 19:26). The Apostle Paul affirms, "I can do **all things** through Christ who strengthens me" (Philippians 4:13, NKJV). In other words, I can take on the world through the strength of Christ and overcome its challenges. Now a lot of people don't understand this principle; they go around wallowing in self-pity, self-abasement and self-condemnation and wonder why they don't maximise their potential in life.

I have navigated my way through the good times and bad times, down in the valley and up on the mountain top. I have been thrown, as it were, into the fiery furnace and the lions' den. I have lived in the midst of death, and have cheated death in more ways than one. I have fought in the physical, spiritual, and metaphorical arenas of life and won. Like the Apostle Paul, I encountered the perils of my own country-men, the perils of false brothers and sisters in the Church, and the perils of religious potentates (leaders).

Hezekiah too cheated death, and God extended his lifespan. He was twenty-five years old when he became king, and he reigned in Jerusalem twenty-nine years (2 Kings 18:2). "In those days Hezekiah was sick and near death" and Isaiah prophesied to him, "Thus says the Lord: "Set your house in order, for you shall die and not live." Hezekiah turned his face to the wall and wept bitterly as he interceded: "Remember now, O Lord, I pray, how I walked before You in truth and with a loyal heart, and have done what is good in Your sight" (Isaiah 38:3–5, NKJV).

In response to Hezekiah's supplication, God expanded his mortality beyond the boundaries of life and death, and granted him fifteen-years extension on this planet. (See Isaiah 38:1–5, NKJV.) He was one of the first individuals to cheat death. What God did for King Hezekiah, He can do for you today. Another man in the Bible who may be said to have cheated death was Enoch who never died. Death is normally the transition to another state, but he short circuited death.

The Bible says, "Enoch walked with God: and he was not; for God took him" (Genesis 5:24), and the writer of the Hebrews confirms, "By faith Enoch was translated that he should <u>not see death</u>; and was not found, because God had translated him: for before his translation he had this testimony, that he pleased God" (Hebrews 11:5). Enoch lived a God-fearing life in this world, but he cheated death in the process, and God miraculously transported him to heaven.

The Prophet Elijah was a Tishbite from Gilead – a man

with natural infirmities, who suffered afflictions like other humans do (James 5:17). He had a very ordinary lifestyle and was described as "a hairy man wearing a leather belt around his waist" (2 Kings 1:8). His name means Jehovah is God. Elijah was a courageous man of prayer and remarkable faith (see 1 Kings 18:36–37). He had a passion to do God's will, and was obedient to his mandate.

However, nothing much was known about Elijah except that he appeared and delivered a message to King Ahab (1 Kings 17:1). Following a period of three years and six months without any rain, there was a severe famine. God instructed Elijah to hide himself by a brook called Cherith where he could get water. God also directed ravens to bring him bread and meat every morning and evening until the stream dried up.

After some time, God purposefully told Elijah to go to Zarephath where a widow would accommodate him at her home. God does some unconventional things at times that make our traditions look like chaff in the wind. Furthermore, there would be a bountiful supply of oil and meal miraculously provided for Elijah, the widow, and her son. When the lad became very ill and died, Elijah was used by God to raise him from death.

Elijah did not die a human death, but like Enoch he too short circuited death and was supernaturally taken to heaven. One day Elijah was with Elisha; "Then it happened, as they continued on and talked, that suddenly a chariot of fire appeared with horses of fire, and separated the two of them; and Elijah went up by a whirlwind into heaven" (2 Kings 2:11). Elijah's disappearance was more mysterious than his first appearance. Yet he is immortalised in Hebrews chapter eleven, called the "Hall of Faith" or the "Faith Hall of Fame" – a portrait gallery of people who believed God and triumphed in faith.

The Apostle Paul cheated death. Jewish antagonists "stoned Paul and dragged him out of the city, supposing him to be dead" (Acts 14:6, NKJV), but he got up and continued his assignment. His life was constantly exposed to severe trials and great dangers. He was continually threatened with death. Paul said, "I have fought with *[wild]* beasts of Ephesus" (1 Corinthians 15:32), speaking metaphorically of the fierce enemies he encountered among men. He was a living martyr – a perpetual sacrifice for the faith he professed.

Paul told the Corinthians that he had experienced "stripes above measure, in prisons more frequently, in deaths more often. From the Jews five times I received thirty-nine stripes *[or 195 blows]*, three times I was beaten with rods, once I was stoned; three times I suffered shipwreck, a day and a night I have been in the deep; in journeys often, in perils of water, in perils of robbers, in perils of my own country-men, in perils of the Gentiles, in perils of the city; in perils in the wilderness, in perils in the sea, in perils among false brethren, in weariness and painfulness, in sleeplessness often, in hunger and thirst; in fasting often, in cold and in nakedness" (2 Corinthians 11:23–27).

Evidently, the devil cannot kill some of us. If he could, he would have done it long ago, but he can't because God has not given him any authority over His covenant people. The lives of believers are "hidden with Christ in God" (Colossians 3:3), and no power from hell can pluck them out of His safe-keeping. Therefore, I decree that I will not die, but live, and declare *[or manifest]* the works of the LORD. (See Psalm 118:17, NKJV.) The LORD has taught me many hard lessons, but He did not let me die.

As a pastor for over forty-seven years, one of the things I observed is the diversity of our vocation. A pastor has to serve different people in various contexts. It is for this reason that his work is complicated and challenging, but he has to love people and serve them sincerely regardless of their ethnicity and whether or not they love him. This is hard, but it gives the true pastor a deep sense of fulfilment and contentment.

In the course of my life, there have been many momentous occasions, but perhaps one of the most unusual things occurred at my Church one Sunday afternoon in December 2008 when a visiting lady introduced herself to me after the service as Bunmi (Olubunmi). I had never heard a name like this before. She told me that she was from Nigeria and she was returning home shortly.

Having said that she put her twenty-year-old son's hand in mine and said intentionally, "This is my son Toni (abbreviation of Oluwatoni), I am leaving him in your hands..." Wow! I looked at her, perhaps somewhat mystified, but then without any hesitation, prevarication or discussion with my wife said, "Okay." Toni and I exchanged telephone numbers and we began communicating. This was the dawn of a new day for him and a new experience for me.

Ever since, I received this stranger into my life and treated him as my own son, and he called me "Dad." I cared for Toni, and introduced him to the Church as my new son. I had no qualms about it, and I warned the girls at Church to keep their eyes off him or else they would have to deal with me, but later I realised that Toni was not quite as innocent as he looked. I really should have warned him to stay away from the girls.

Toni recommitted his life to the LORD Jesus Christ, and I baptized him in water. He soon received the baptism with the Holy Spirit. Despite his struggles, Toni had a genuine love for the LORD, and he was very teachable. What stood out conspicuously about him was his good manners, humility and respect. He was very truthful and transparent. To me, he was like an open book. On a few occasions, he said to me, "You know me better than I know myself." The LORD assigned me to him, and I had the mandate to guide him through that difficult phase of his life.

I took Toni with me on various occasions to visit my mother, and she also loved him. She often said to me, "He's a nice young man, make sure you take care of him." Toni loved Mom too, and sometimes went to see her even in my absence. Our meetings at Mom's were always filled with laughter and jubilation, and Toni himself enjoyed a good laugh.

Toni used to fast and pray a lot. Somehow, when we were together at Mom's she could always discern when he was not eating and asked him, "Why?" She usually said that I should get him something to eat. This became a standing joke between Toni and me, so much so that we would come to expect this comment from her. Mom had a way of saying things that would make us laugh, even when she was serious. There was never a dull moment around my mother.

Owing to Toni's laid back attitude, I had to be very firm with him at times in order to pull the best out of him, but I did it with love and understanding, and he always reciprocated with appreciation and respect. A strong bond was established between us and our relationship solidified. This provoked jealousy from some people who felt that I was giving him preferential treatment, but they really didn't understand God's purpose in all of this, and they couldn't drink from the same cup.

Furthermore, they would not have submitted themselves to the strict discipline to which Toni was subjected, but his own good attitude reflected in his gratitude, and demonstrated his fortitude, which determined the altitude of his success. "Toni's response to my rod of correction was, "Thank you Dad, I am going to change," and he did. To his parents' amazement,

Toni's life was miraculously transformed. Generally, he became more mature, punctual, reliable, dependable and responsible, and endeavoured to live a spiritually balanced life.

Toni was a part of my family and we spent a lot of time together. He was particularly helpful to me during the time of my physical and health challenges, for which I am grateful. He successfully completed his PR degree at **London Metropolitan University,** married a Jamaican girl named Nardia and relocated to Canada.

Soaring from Survival to Success

SECTION ONE

THE EARLY BEGINNINGS

The journey began, when as a tiny foetus in my mother's womb, Satan tried to kill me, and that journey continues today with enduring convictions. When Mom was expecting me, the obstetrician told her that either she or the baby would die, both couldn't survive the pregnancy so he advised her to have an abortion. Obviously, my mother defied his advice, and I am glad she did. We praise God for the doctors, but their report is not the gospel of Jesus Christ. It's not over until God says so!

Whose report will you believe? Mom believed the LORD's and lived to be almost ninety-four years old, retaining good health for most her life and maintaining the faith for which she died. A faith that is not worth dying for is not worth living for. By the grace of God, I am still here carrying the torch to places my mother has not been, and telling the story she has not told. No matter what the devil does to the flesh or what anyone might say, Jehovah has the final say!

Jeremiah records, "Before I formed you in your mother's womb **I knew you**, before you were born **I set you apart** *[sanctified you]*; **I appointed you as a prophet** to the nations…

You must go to everyone I send you to and say whatever I command you. Do not be afraid of them, for I am with you and will rescue you," declares the Lord. Then the Lord reached out his hand and touched my mouth and said to me, "I have put my words in your mouth" (Jeremiah 1:5–9, NIV). This implies four sacredly designed principles and concepts:

1. God knew me before I was conceived in my mother's womb. He has absolute knowledge of me: past, present and future.

2. My birth was not a mistake or an accident; it was preordained by the Creator of all things, and my destiny was predetermined.

3. My assignment on this planet preceded my birth, and Satan couldn't abort neither my birth nor my purpose.

4. My mandate is not a human appointment, but a divine commission orchestrated by God to enable the purpose for which I came into the world.

Therefore, I was born by the will of God in Jamaica on 25 August 1947 to Lucille Delphena Burrell (née Whyte) and Walter Christopher Burrell, at the *Victoria Jubilee Hospital (VJH)*, North Street, Kingston, and was named Barrington Orlando Burrell. I was presented to the LORD in Christian dedication on 4 January 1948 at the Church of God, 89 Beeston Street, Kingston.

Victoria, Jubilee Hospital, Kingston

Although the majority of Jamaican families have an African background, they are of a multi-ethnic composition from India, China, the Middle East and Europe, but each group has its unique customs, traditions and values. The original inhabitants of Jamaica are believed to have been the Arawak, an indigenous Indian tribe called Tainos. They came from South America over 2,500 years ago, and named the island Xaymaca, which meant "land of wood and water".

A male and female Taíno are depicted in the Jamaican Coat of Arms standing on either side with the motto across the shield: "OUT OF MANY ONE PEOPLE". In 1494, Christopher Columbus (1451–1506) "discovered" Jamaica – an island, which has probably been inhabited from as early as 600 to 650 A.D., with the second wave of natives arriving between 850 and 900 A.D., long before his birth. Was Columbus a discoverer or a wayfarer?

I do not know the origin and etymology of my full name, except that Burrell is English, Scottish and northern Irish. My first and middle names were chosen by my godmother Hazel McLarty (née McLeod), affectionately known as Aunt Hazel.

I was later called Barry and Mass Barry as a term of endearment, and this stuck with me.

I am the first of three siblings. My sister Audrey, our younger brother Paul and I form that trilogy. I never knew any grandparents because they died before I was born, but I met my great grandfather (Mom's granddad) on his deathbed, and I was terrified of him. He was a white man from Scotland, and had white hair, a white moustache and blue eyes. His name was Archibald Campbell and he was affectionately called Papa Archie.

My Great Grandfather (Papa Archie)

Growing up, I was not a fat child, but as people say, "Contentment is great gain." Today, I reflect on my early beginnings with a deep sense of gratitude and cheerfulness. My earliest memories as a child go back to when I was about three years of age. I was a quiet but active and curious child – a little chatterbox, who was not afraid to ask dozens of questions, even the most embarrassing ones. I remember asking one of my female neighbours if she had a penis as well; she told me "Yes" and I believed her.

On another occasion, I heard a male voice in her bedroom, and curiosity led me to ask her, "Mrs Thorpe, who is that man talking in your room?" She replied, "Mr Thorpe, my love." She knew very well that if she had told me the truth, when her husband came home, I would have told him. As a result of being such a "parrot" (one who talks a lot, and has a mimicking ability), it was felt by some that I would grow up to become either a barrister or a parson; hence, I was nicknamed "Parson" by some, and "Barrister" by others.

Childhood days have usually had many fond memories for me, like spending time with my loved ones, playing my favourite games or having a treat such as sweets, spicy popcorn, peanuts, ice cream and chocolates. "At other times, I might recall eating a lot of mangoes, enjoying a swing, or chasing the chickens, cats, dogs, and rabbits around the place, and even riding a donkey or playing the role of a daredevil." But there were also numerous challenges and vulnerabilities. I was a normal young toddler facing the same kind of events and developments that other children my age often experienced. When I was just over three years old, a strange phenomenon happened, which is printed indelibly on my mind.

I saw a duppy man. "**Duppy**" is a **Jamaican** Patois word of Northwest African origin meaning ghost or spirit – a zombie or a malevolent spirit which is the dismal reanimation of a human corpse, according to a spooky Jamaican superstition. A duppy can appear in different shapes or forms of animals and humans. The commonly known term, "duppy man" is used in Jamaican culture to reference an evil spirit of the dead in the form of a man. However, a duppy does not really exist, except in the Jamaican collective imagination. Death returns you to the dust in a totally unconscious state. The Bible is crystal clear on this matter. Dead is dead! However, for me, this was a dramatic experience, to say the least.

I was still living in Kingston, and often climbed the stairs of our next-door neighbours' home to collect cotton reels from a dressmaker. Her husband had died, and the overwhelming spectacle of the funeral cortege unfolded: a number of mourners all dressed in black and white, and a black hearse driving off slowly with his coffin placed on the inside, garnished with an elaborate array of flowers. But all that paraphernalia really didn't mean anything to me. I had no perception of death.

Sometime later, I was about to climb the stairs as I often did, and I saw the man standing at the top, just as I had known him before he died. I was delighted to see him, but obviously he was not pleased to see me. He was very serious, and he made an unwelcoming gesture with his hand indicating that I should go away. So I went to my mother reluctantly and communicated to her what had happened. She immediately reacted frantically with anxiety and anointed me with (mentholated) bay rum, fearing that the evil imposter might have harmed me. No doubt, the incident made such an impression on me because it was generated in an emotionally charged situation, compounded by Mom's reaction.

Even the disciples of Christ thought He was a ghost when they saw Him walking on the Sea of Galilee; they were terrified and "cried out for fear." (See Matthew 14:26–28, NKJV.) Most Jamaicans are familiar with duppy stories. We have heard of ghosts attacking or haunting people like one on youtube CVM News: "Duppy bax the yute inna the night, drag him foot and tump him up…" In other words, a young boy is being pushed, pulled around and bullied allegedly by a ghost which caused distress to his family.[1]

As I matured, I found the scenario most hilarious because there is no such thing as a duppy. As a matter of fact, I have deputised for or played the role of a duppy; hiding in the bushes at night and frightening the saints on their way from church. They spoke in tongues and rebuked me, of course not knowing what or who they were reprimanding, and at the time I found it funny.

Furthermore, I cannot conceive any reason why people should be afraid of the dead; they cannot hurt anyone. When a person dies that is final as far as his or her existence on this earth is concerned. The perceived duppies are demons (unclean spirits or fallen angels) that assume the form or appearance of the dead, but they have no power over the life of a believer. Not everyone can see a "duppy," only rare people who are born with a caul (or cowl) over their eyes or Spirit filled believers, and it is believed that they cannot harm those who can see them.

Shortly after the above incident, my mother and I relocated to live in a district called Desire, in the Parish of Clarendon where I spent most of my childhood. My brother joined us later. Being the first child, my mother would not allow me to eat cooked food like yam, breadfruit and bananas because she felt they would give me a big belly. So, when she thought I was old enough to eat them I tended to refuse them, but I loved meat, eggs, porridge and any food that was roasted. At the same time, I used to eat dirt and suffered from constipation as a result. Some children eat dirt or sand out of natural curiosity about their environment, but I believe my dirt-eating propensity was probably related to nutritional deficiency of calcium, iron or zinc in my body.

Mom became worried as most mothers would and took me to the doctor, thinking I was ill. After an examination, the doctor said to her, "He is a healthy child." Then he asked me why I wouldn't eat. I promised him that I would begin to eat and he gave me some tablets, which I now presume were appetisers.

Consequently, I ate my first piece of cooked food when I was almost four years of age. This was how it happened: my cousin Winston tricked me by putting a piece of food in a spoon and covering it with a piece of meat. I ate it thinking it was just meat, and the rest was history. I kicked the habit of eating dirt long before my primary school years, and became a lover of food until this day.

I grew up in an average nuclear family of three: my mother who "fathered me," my brother and I. (My dad was delinquent as far as his fatherhood responsibilities were concerned. I believe he loved his family and would do whatever he could to physically protect us, but he never demonstrated his love or care in a practical and meaningful way.)

According to an article published in the Jamaica Gleaner on Sunday 26 May 2013, "Over 80 per cent of Jamaican children are born out of wedlock. The majority of these used to not even have their father's name on their birth certificate, the most basic association with a father."[2]

The sociologists say, "Children without fathers in their lives are more likely to commit crime, drop out of school, abuse drugs and live in poverty," but it doesn't have to be that way! My brother and I were raised by our mother in the country and my sister by my godmother in Kingston, but we all enjoyed the benefits of a loving home and a good, healthy family background. We have never committed any crime, never dropped out of school and we are not living in poverty. President Barak Obama was brought up by a single mother and only saw his father when he was a toddler and again when he was ten years of age.[3]

I had a very strict, but God-fearing upbringing, which helped to prepare me for who I am today. My mother, who became a believer at age fifteen, taught me the principles of godliness and the Christian values that kept me over the years. She was a good woman. I have often said that if my mother has not gone to heaven, I don't believe there's anyone on this planet who will.

Hurricane Charlie Hits Jamaica

Our family had not long moved to Clarendon, and we were still in the process of adjusting to our new environment when Hurricane Charlie hit the Island. This Hurricane was the deadliest tropical cyclone of the 1951 Atlantic hurricane season. Charlie swept mercilessly across the island with ferocious winds of up to 135 mph (215 km/h). It was forecast in The Gleaner's headline of 17 August 1951, but Jamaica was still not prepared for the onslaught, which pounded Jamaica that same evening and devastated the country.

Although I was only about four years of age, I remember it very clearly. Our country style house, which was built primarily using timber and zinc was almost blown down. It was left standing at a treacherous angle. We had to vacate in the night to the neighbour's house amidst lashing rain and gale force winds – very hazardous weather conditions indeed.

Several sheets of zinc were blown off the next door's house, and almost every room was drenched with water. Apparently, there was only one dry room in which all of us converged for the night. The adults were crying out to God for mercy, but the children were having the time of their lives.

According to the Jamaica Gleaner, Hurricane Charlie hit Jamaica leaving 154 dead, 20,000 homeless, and causing 16 million pounds sterling in damages.[4] Some were struck by lightning, many livestock were damaged or killed, and local agriculture was devastated. The hurricane pounded the island for about 24 hours. Many trees were uprooted, houses wrecked, and there were major floods and landslides everywhere, yet I personally enjoyed the momentum. All of us could have been killed before the next day dawned, but we little ones didn't understand that. It is true what they say: "Young birds don't know a hurricane."

My Primary School Days 1950s–1960s

In the early 1950s, at the age of 5–6 I went to infant school in Water Works after which I attended the *Frankfield Primary School* (we called it big school). The Principal was Mr Austin C. Pyne, a close friend of Sir Clifford C. Campbell (1892–1991), who was the first native Governor General of Jamaica and who visited the school when I was a student there. In 1946–1955, statistics showed a rise in the cost of living for food, clothing, rent, fuel etc., and although schooling was inexpensive, for many it was still unaffordable.

I started writing with slates and pencils – a thin piece of slate, which is a stony substance used as a medium for writing (or a pencil). Slate is a very fragile material that breaks easily. I began using small slates measuring 4x6 inches (10.16 x 16.24 centimetres), then progressed to big slates 7x10 inches (17.78 x 25.4 centimetres), and to exercise books.

Slates were cleaned with a piece of cloth or slate sponge or the deep-red flower of a shrub named Hibiscus, commonly known as choeblack or in the "Creole version" of shoeblack (shoe black), as it is called in Jamaica. The crushed flower is used as black shoe polish. The plant is widely grown in tropical and subtropical regions of the world, but recognised as Haiti's National Flower. It is used to make a refreshing drink which has several medicinal purposes.

In order to get to and from school, I had to cross two rivers, the Peckham River and the Rio Minho River, usually by stepping on stones specially arranged for this purpose. My school shoes were carried in my hands for about two miles to the second river where I would wash my feet and put them on. I wore my shoes on the historic asphalt road to school and back in the afternoons. Sometimes I cheated by wearing my shoes until I was nearly home, but it never took my mother long to notice how clean my feet were, and figured out what I had done. This often led either to a caution or a physical chastisement.

In the 1950s, tourism was in its infancy and the bauxite mining and aluminum processing industries had not yet been fully established in Jamaica. Agriculture was the main livelihood in Jamaica's economy. Farmers cultivated a lot of sugar cane, bananas, coconuts, citrus, coffee, cocoa, vegetables, tobacco and Irish potatoes on their farms.

On 2 June 1953, Queen Elizabeth II was crowned in Westminster Abbey, and the whole commonwealth joined together in celebrating her coronation. She was not only Queen of the United Kingdom, but also Queen of Jamaica. I was only a little school boy just under six years of age, but nevertheless this was a very special occasion. At that time, many Jamaican children respected the Queen and held her in high esteem.

In those days, we used the old British (pre-decimal) currency system called pounds, shillings and pence ("**£sd**" or "LSD"). Four farthings made a penny (1p), twelve pence made a shilling (1s or 1/-), two shillings equalled a florin (also called a "two bob bit" (2/-); two shillings and six pence was a half crown (2/6), five shillings made a crown; twenty shillings made one pound (£1), and a guinea was 21 shillings. My daily school lunch money was one and a half pence (1½d), which I often spent at a Chinese restaurant, on penny bread and half-penny syrup.

By 1930, there **were** four thousand Chinese immigrants in **Jamaica.** By 1931 the government had stopped issuing passports in an effort to reduce the "*Chinese Invasion*" as it was called then. By 1954, there were over one thousand commercial establishments owned by the Chinese in Jamaica.[5] These Chinese were noted for their business acumen, and for the caring and nurturing of their children, placing great emphasis as they did on education and family life, all of which have had a positive impacted on the Jamaican society up to the present.

Over the years, the Chinese became integrated in many professions such as law, medicine, business, retailers, civil servants and teachers, while others remained wage earners in the banking and manufacturing sectors. Jamaican Chinese are greatly admired for being hardworking, diligent and courteous.[6]

The average mother did not go out to work, and her primary role was domestic, while many fathers, especially in the country areas cultivated the land or did farming. Cooking at my home was traditionally done on wood fires. The only cooking oil I knew was the pure organic extra virgin coconut oil, which my mother usually made herself. Coconut oil was used extensively for its health benefits, but also for skin care and all hair types and textures, and it was affordable.

Before going to school in the mornings, I frequently had to look for firewood and carry the bundles home on my head. There were no water pipes or reservoirs in the community and rainwater caught in the typical rain barrels did not last very long, especially outside the rainy season. The spring from which we drew water was a couple of miles away and on alternate days, I also had to fetch a five-gallon tin of water on my head.

A heavy weight was carried without causing extra pressure on the head beyond what was reasonably expected by using dried banana leaves to make a kata (a word of African origin, which is a wrap or cushion worn on the head for carrying heavy loads). On some weekends, I used to transport breadfruit on a donkey and carry a basket of mangoes on my head for about five miles to sell at *Cave Valley Market*, St. Ann Parish. In addition to the above, I had to assist Mom in shining the floor with a coconut brush and bees-wax.

If these chores were not executed when required, the penalty was a physical punishment, which I have always resented. Whereas, some people have said that the beatings did them good, it brought the worst out of me. I probably did a lot of naughty things for which I deserved a good flogging, but my mother never knew about them. Parents generally don't know what their youngsters get up to, although they often think they do. Children and young people are very adventurous and only God truly knows them. Sometimes it is good for us adults to reflect on our own childhood and adolescent days and make some confessions.

A Christian mother strongly vouched for her daughter's character, and asserted that she wouldn't do certain inappropriate things, but I knew that the girl was far from being innocent.

Often, the things that Mom flogged me for were trivial. If I had just been given some guidance, and it had been explained to me why I was wrong, most likely I would have complied.

The other extreme, when children are idolised and can do no wrong in their parents' eyes, is even worse, especially if the child is a female. An undisciplined boy will behave badly, but as every parent knows, the girl's behaviour can be twice as bad. An over-protective mother is a danger to her son, and an over-protective dad is an enemy to his daughter. Such children are likely to fall victims of their parents' attitude who may reap a negative harvest from the seeds they have sown.

However, it's important to note that a child is never bad; no one is born bad, but one's behaviour may be bad. A behaviour is a response to stimulus that each individual has learned either from their environment or by being taught. So, incorrect behaviours will require changes during the process of one's development. Therefore, each child has to learn what is acceptable or inappropriate behavior, and this brings training into focus.

The Bible says that whoever **spares** the **rod** hates their children, but that the one who loves their children is careful to discipline them. (See Proverbs 13:24; 23:13.) The emphasis here is not on the rod, but the correction. I do believe that children should be flogged moderately at times as a means of discipline, but they should not be beaten up or abused – and if they are – the parents deserve a beating themselves.

Children learn more from example than by beating, slapping or hitting them. This is certainly not the best way to try and correct or discipline them. Furthermore, parents who fight and quarrel with each other create an unhealthy climate for the training and development of their children, who are likely to become like them.

All human beings, for the most part, are gregarious (they like the company of others), but this sociable need is more prominent in young children, and this can either be good or bad. Some adult lives are plagued with discontent and failures from the past, but I am extremely grateful for my upbringing and the kind of childhood I was privileged to have had. From a winner's perspective, a failure is a lack of success, which indicates that there is a way to succeed, but a negative mindset only perceives frustration and collapse.

School is one of the places where you have many friends and foes. School-age children can be very unkind to each other and behaviour of this kind has had devastating effects on many. It may take the form of bullying and even when perceived as such, may impede people's healthy development and lead to personality disorders, and emotional and mental health issues in later years.

On the other hand, good friendships provide children with the capacity to develop emotionally, ethically and morally. However, for one reason or another some children find it difficult to make friends. Maybe they are shy or just not of a friendly disposition. The wise King Solomon says, "The man who has friends must show himself friendly" (Proverbs 18:24). Today, dogs are raised to be people-friendly; how much more important it is for friendliness to be instilled in young children.

I was privileged to have grown up in a tightly–knit community, and had many school friends. We knew each other very well and often travelled to and from school together. We were good play-mates who shared the same classroom, and bathed in the Rio Minho River together. This is the longest (92.8 kilometers or 57.7 miles) and probably the most dangerous river in Jamaica. We also got up to some mischievous things as well, but cherished one another's lasting friendship.

School started at 9 o'clock, and once the assembly bell rang, the headmaster would go to the school gate to greet the late-comers with a cup of "hot milo." Milo was a thick leather strap with which he "disciplined" the children. My friends and I used to leave home early in the mornings "for school." To the displeasure of my Mom, I left my breakfast on many occasions. Our parents thought that it was due to our love for school, but no, we just wanted to go "swimming" in the river.

Since we had no clock to tell us the time we depended solely on a certain morning bus, which became our timepiece. This meant that if the bus was late, we were also late for school. At the first sign of the bus, we would hurriedly navigate the task of putting our clothes on wet bodies, and would run about two miles straight to school. By this time, all the river water from our heads came running down like sweat, our clothes were soaked and we were physically exhausted. Teacher would often feel sorry for us because of our "keen interest in getting to school on time."

Primary schools in Jamaica had a 1–6 grading system. When I was in second class (Grade 2), my teacher was Mrs Elliston. One day I went for a reading lesson unprepared. The teacher asked me, "Where is your reading book?" I told her that I had forgotten it at home. She was furious and with that she stormed back to the cupboard for a guava whip and gave me the worst beating of my life; the memory of which I'll carry to my grave. She said, "It's better you had told me that you didn't have a book than to say you forgot it; that's lack of interest!" I didn't agree with her rationale but that made no difference to her. This kind of aggressive and cruel punishment was not only unprofessional, but illegal and she could have lost her job if I had reported the incident.

There was a fictitious character in our reading book called Mrs Reece, and because her name sounds like a Jamaican swear word, many children hesitated to say it when reading. I can remember Mrs Elliston becoming angry and beating them to "say the name, it's not a bad word, say it!" Her sternness stood-out more than her aptness to teach. Amidst widespread fears that several children were brutally beaten in school, many adults still believed that good teachers beat their pupils and that children had benefitted from the beatings.

As a school child, if you misbehaved on the road or if it was thought that you were misbehaving, any adult could spank you, and then report it to your parents who would give you another flogging without asking any questions. Whatever the situation, the best interests of the child were paramount. Some parents did their best to go beyond what the teachers could provide in order to develop their children. Illiteracy may have inhibited some parents' ability to become involved in their children's education, but many did their best to help with their homework.

Many upper middle class children were taught not to talk the local Patois (Patwa or Patwah), also called Jamaican Creole by linguists (an English-based creole language with West African influences). They had to "speak properly," and although Patois was not a language taught in school, we all understood it and most spoke it, even some of the elite. In most cases, words are spelt in Patois or Creole dialects as they sound. The individual sound depends on one's heritage, and the area in which one lives; so no two dialects sound the same.

Having had the experience of living in both urban and rural Jamaican communities, this gave me a taste of the diverse cultural flavours. Jamaicans love music and dance, but they have a great sense of humour which is reflected in their creole language. Someone has said, "Jamaicans are the funniest people on earth," but they are very creative, especially when it comes to coining their own terms and sayings. Consider the following six typical examples:

1. "Yuh gi mi sponge fi go dry up de sea."
   You are giving me an impossible task to do.

2. "Dem gi We water fi carry Inna basket."
   This means you were given a raw deal.

3. "Wen mi a fi yu age mi couldn't do dat."
   When I was your age I couldn't do that.

4. "A bucket wid hole in a de bottam nuh have no business a riverside."
   One shouldn't put one's self in a situation that does not concern one. In other words, mind your own business.

5. "Good fowl gone a market, sensei fowl seh him waa go too."
   Someone less suitable wants to imitate the action of an able individual. Don't be a copycat.

6. "Cockroach nuh business inna fowl fight."
   Don't get involved in what doesn't concern you; it may consume you.

I still speak Patois even now because it gives me a sense of identity with my people and culture, but I know when and where to use it. It's amazing how some Jamaicans can be so "stush" and polished in their elocution until you offend them – and then they automatically switch to Patois. You wouldn't believe they were the same individuals.

People versus Persons

Jamaicans tend to use the word persons rather than people. In modern or formal English, people is the plural of person, but "persons" is also the plural of person. Over the years, there seems to be a confusion regarding the use of the two terms. Is it just a matter of preference, or do we need to differentiate between the context in which they are used? Both people and persons mean more or less the same thing although they are derived from two different Latin words.

"Person" derives from *persona,* which denotes an individual. On the other hand, "people" comes from *populum*, meaning two or more persons sharing a culture or social environment. Nowadays, "people" is used in preference to persons as the plural form of person, and the frequency of the Jamaicans' use of "persons" is old-fashioned, even though the legal and some very formal texts still use persons as the plural form.

This complexity is further compounded by the plurality of the word people to peoples. For example, one can use "peoples" to denote different cultural groups of individuals in a given context, but "people" is the correct contemporary plural of person, and should be used in most cases in place of "persons."

It is interesting to note the different variations of the Jamaican greeting in Patois: "Wah gwaan," which means "how are you doing?" Jamaicans frequently use the term "goodnight" to express greeting at night. Rather than saying good evening, they say goodnight. However, if one is adhering strictly to Jamaican etiquette and customs, one should use the appropriate salutation for the time of day. "Goodnight" is not an acceptable form of greeting. As a matter of fact, it is customarily used when one is leaving or going to bed. It actually means goodbye. It may also be used to wish a person a pleasant night as in, "Have a good night!"

Along with its language and culture, Jamaica is distinguished by the richness and diversity of its natural environment. The island is blessed with many tropical fruit trees, loaded with gorgeous fruits in their season. The star apple is one of the few fruits that do not fall from the trees when ripe, but it is delightful to eat. Not only were the fruits growing on the hillside or near the roadside always attractive, but tempting to hungry school children. On our way home from school in the afternoons, the boys in particular took pleasure in stoning the star apple trees, the mango trees, the guava trees, and the cashew trees in an effort to get the fruit.

One day, problems emerged when some of the stones went astray and chopped my uncle Mack's yam vines off the stick. (A variety of hardwood or bamboo sticks were used to provide support for the climbing **yam vines**.) He became very angry and the lads were terrified. Generally, I was respected as a leader among the boys and often got them out of trouble. On this instance, I decided to chat the case for them if the fees were right. I charged them a few ripe mangoes and they agreed to pay me.

I went to my uncle and apologised profusely for what had happened, and explained that it was unintentional. I told him that the boys were not stoning his yam deliberately. They were just trying to get some mangoes and did not envisage any damage being caused to his yam, and I assured him that it wouldn't happen again. Guess what – my apology on their behalf was accepted! I got them off the hook and was rewarded handsomely, but the boys also learnt their lesson.

Christmas was a special time of commemoration and celebration with impressive seasonal lights, multiple coloured bulbs, the singing of Christmas carols and the traditional Christmas expressions with a distinct Jamaican flavour. And, of course, there was the historic performance of the John Canoe (or Jonkonnu) traditional festival. Because of their outrageous costumes, the John Canoe evoked a mixture of fear and excitement in the onlookers.

As a young child, I was very afraid of the Jonkonnu, probably because I associated them with the flying saucers or the dreaded blackheart man. Flying saucer was a Jamaican term for aliens or UFOs. I understand that UFOs were sighted in the skies with astonishing frequency. These are unidentified, mysterious objects seen in the sky for which it is claimed no orthodox scientific explanation can be found, often supposed to be a vehicle carrying extra-terrestrial beings into the human atmosphere. While Jamaicans were generally comfortable with their appearances, children were convinced that they might take them away.

Most children grew up hearing about this blackheart man, one of the scariest Jamaican fables. We were told that we must be careful of strangers who might walk up to us and offer us sweets, or invite us into their cars or homes. These blackhearts were believed to hang out in the lonely countryside or gullies. Tradition had it that they might also show up at public places like schools and parks, and would even abduct children and take their hearts out. So, we were constantly on the lookout for the terrifying blackheart man.

I had a strong aversion to these things and was obviously scared, but was too young to distinguish between a flying saucer, a blackheart man and a Jonkonnu. As far as I was concerned, they were all one and the same. My worst nightmare was one day when the John Canoe were passing by my house in Kingston, and I ran inside and hid under the bed. This created quite an alarm because I fell asleep and was missing for hours. It was feared that someone had kidnapped me, and everyone became worried. What a relief it was when I woke up and reappeared in my state of shock and nervousness.

However, the main feature of Christmas for us children was the toys, which we always looked forward to receiving. Living in the country, Mom was unable to afford as many gifts as she would have liked, so we had to save our own Christmas money. Surprisingly, this was not too difficult to do.

We used to pick up rat cut cocoa and coffee beans from the cultivation. The average number of cocoa beans in one pod is around 40, but the actual number of beans can vary between 20 and 60 or thereabouts. Rats nibbled or cut through the pods and sucked the syrup off the beans, then spat them to the ground. Ironically, we were grateful to the rats for contributing towards our Christmas money. We dried the accumulated beans and sold them by the pound to those who buy the quality beans for exportation.

Sorrel drink is common at Christmas time, and is indigenous to Jamaica as it is to other parts of the Caribbean, India and Hawaii. It is made from the sorrel plant and sweetened with sugar or syrup, and flavoured with cinnamon, ginger, cloves and Jamaican White Rum or brandy. This positive sight with its traditional identity usually occupied its place in almost every home. It has been said by some Jamaicans that "Christmas" is not Christmas without the delightful and familiar taste of sorrel.

However, nowadays, sorrel drink is sold in many countries throughout the year, and has excellent health benefits. It is high in vitamins and minerals with powerful antioxidant properties. It helps to reduce the chances of heart disease and stroke, thinning the blood, lowering high blood pressure, bad cholesterol and detoxifying the entire body (seriously, Google it). Now that I am more health conscious I drink a glass of sorrel almost every day.

By the time I became an adolescent, I had earned myself another nickname. Because I procrastinated and did a lot of my work at night, which should have been done in the daytime, I was called Nicodemus. This was the name of a Jewish ruler, who went to Jesus by night. (See John 3:2.) Nicknames are common in Jamaica.

Almost everybody has a nickname or a pet name. Some nicknames are associated with one's occupation. Others are just endearing names chosen by relatives or lovers, while a few are based on incidents that have occurred in one's life. It is not unusual to know a person by one name, and for them to be known by another in an official capacity.

Aldeam Facey explains, "In the lower and middle class Jamaican society, where bureaucracy and hierarchy fail to prevail, where regular informal conversations form the basis of relationships, Christian names are seldom used. In lieu of the Christian name, a name descriptive of a physical characteristic, occupation or some other defining personal trait is used. This is done because these names are much easier to remember and often-times they are very funny."[7]

In the late 1950 and 60s, for socio-economic reasons, the Jamaican diaspora was concentrated in three countries – the United States, Canada and the United Kingdom. The U.S. imported (or exploited) a significant number of farm workers from Jamaica and elsewhere on seasonal visas to cut sugar cane. The 1961 census in Great Britain showed that of some 200,000 West Indians in England, fifty percent were from Jamaica.

For most of us living in the country, the luxury of a TV was out of the question. I recall when the first radio came into our district. It was bought by a returnee farm worker from the United States. It was an oblong shape like a large car battery, and the external aerial was a tall bamboo pole with a broken bottle-neck on the top. People used to gather nearby to listen to the radio, and this made the owner feel important – he could now wear American clothes, flash a few dollars and own a radio.

There was no electricity in our community and we had to use other means of illumination at night. Sometimes the moon was quite helpful, but the most common was a bottle lamp. This was simply made by putting kerosene oil (paraffin) into a bottle and making a paper or cloth wick, which was lit to generate a glowing flame, like an Olympic torch.

The "Walking Dead" Drama

One day my mother sent me to the shop, which was about two or three miles away from our home. As per usual, I played marbles until it was late before starting out on my journey. Obeying Mom's instructions was something that "Nicodemus" had to do or else he would have been physically punished. Mom often said, "A man yuh a tun?" (One would think it was a crime to "turn a man," but what I think she meant was "If you are too big to obey my instructions, you have to leave my house or face the consequences of your actions like a man".) So I got a bottle lamp and off I went.

Amazingly, on my way to the shop I saw another duppy man! A man with fair complexion was walking towards me. As he approached me closely, his legs grew extremely tall such as I have never seen, and he stepped over a precipice. "I was shocked, and petrified. My head felt swollen, my heart pounding and my body shaking and sweating. I was involuntarily glued to the spot and couldn't move for a while," but I still had to pluck up the courage to carry out my duty. When I returned home, and described to Mom the man who I saw and explained what had happened, she said, "His horse fell over that precipice with him, and he broke his neck and died." I nearly died too! The devil is a liar.

Even at this young age, I endeavoured to be caring, positive and practised good principles. Coming home from school one afternoon, I was speaking to one of my cousins about his inappropriate behaviour that day. Unbeknown to me, my uncle Mack was in a tree nearby and overheard the conversation or perhaps he was eavesdropping.

Later that evening, he said to his wife, "I heard Mass Barry giving Mass Ancil some good counselling." I don't remember ever having a fight in my life, but I was always giving good advice and constructive criticism. I never allowed my peers to influence me in the wrong way. I always felt that they never knew anything that I didn't know, and if I wanted to learn anything it had to come from the older folk. I used to hear them say, "New broom sweep clean, but owl broom noe de cahnas," meaning "New broom sweeps cleaner, but old broom knows the corners," and I agreed with them and spent much time in their company.

I used to hate getting my hands dirty. Because of this, when my Mom sent me to dig yam, I usually cleaned my finger nails almost after every handful of dirt, but very seldom did I succeed in digging out a whole yam. I would often break the yam and leave a big piece of it in the ground. Some may say I was lazy, but I don't agree. I just had an aversion to dirty nails. Well, there are those who may say I should have worn gloves. Gloves? Such luxury was not available to me.

We had a piece of fertile land a little way from our home called Gunner, but thieves stole nearly all the yams, bananas, breadfruits and cocoa from that cultivation. One day, while I was there digging up a yam, I heard the dry leaves crackling as though someone was walking on them. I looked around just in time to see one of my mother's cousins tip-toeing with a bent forward body posture as he slowly made progressive strides towards me.

He held a machete in his right hand like a drawn sword ready to make the fatal strike. Suddenly he recognised me, and a gleam of awareness came into eyes. As he glared at me in shock, he muttered nervously, "Lard mi Gad, I would a chap yuh tiday yah!" (meaning, "Lord my God, I would chop you today!") He thought I was a thief. **This was the second deadly satanic attack on my life**. In Satan's mind, I was already dead.

Breadfruit Tree Disaster

This was the third deadly satanic attack on my life. A breadfruit is the large round starchy fruit of a tropical tree, which originated in the South Pacific. It has unique qualities and is consumed when mature, but still firm, and can be used to make a variety of palatable meals and drinks: it can be boiled, steamed, baked, fried, or roasted. A moderately ripe breadfruit tastes like boiled potato or a freshly baked Jamaican hard dough bread, and is sometimes used to make dumplings or a delicious drink.

As a country boy raised by my mother, I was a boy-man. This can be defined in two ways: a man who behaves like a boy or a boy who acts like a man, but I was the latter. I had to climb small fruit trees and assume some manly responsibilities at an early age – assuming some duties that my father was not present to undertake.

One day, I climbed a breadfruit tree and accidentally stepped on a large dried limb (branch), which broke. I fell almost from the top of the tree and just managed to catch hold of the last limb before hitting the ground, and there I was swinging like a monkey from a "banana tree." It was not unusual for men to fall from breadfruit trees and die. If I had fallen all the way to the ground, my life may well have gushed out like the inside of a fallen ripe breadfruit, but God providentially saved me yet another time.

My Religious Background

I grew up in the house of God, and have always been a part of the Pentecostal heritage, although I cannot be classified as a traditionalist. My dad was not a Christian, but my mother was a member of the New Testament Church of God (NTCG) fifteen years before my sunrise. As you may have already deduced, my mother was the greatest source of inspiration and the strongest influence in my life. Thank God for Mom, who taught me right from wrong." She took me to Church regularly, and taught me to say the "Lord's Prayer" at an early age, and to read the Bible daily.

In addition to this biblical model prayer, my mother taught me two other prayers:

1. At nights, I would pray: "In this little bed I lie, heavenly Father hear my cry; Lord protect me through this night and keep me safe till morning light." Amen!

2. In the mornings I said, "Now I wake and see the light, God has kept me through the night, make me good O Lord I pray, keep and guide me through this day." Amen!

God heard those little prayers, because I was sincere. The Bible is right, "Train up a child in the way he should go; and when he is old, he will not depart from it" (Proverbs 22:6). Early training goes a long way in life. The Apostle Paul reminded young Timothy "that from childhood you have known the Holy Scriptures, which are able to make you wise for salvation through faith which is in Christ Jesus" (2 Timothy 3:15, NKJV). Timothy was raised by his grandmother Lois and mother Eunice, who instilled the Word of God in him from his infancy. (See 2 Timothy 1:5.) But training is not converting the child; it's setting the right example for him or her to emulate.

My Mom always tried to get me to give a recitation at Church in line with the custom of the day, but I refused because I was too shy. One week I consented and the Sunday morning when I was called to recite, everybody was excited and waited in great anticipation. They gave me a rousing round of applause as I made my way towards the podium, but to their dismay I walked straight across the platform and out through the backdoor. The Pastor's nephew just couldn't take all that excitement and attention. I was very unassuming and unpredictable, but there has always been a lot more to me than meets the eye.

I never wanted to become a Christian at a young age, and I didn't like to hear my mother speak in tongues; believing it was all nonsense I made a mockery of it. Paradoxically, I used to get saved every night, and backslide in the morning. Why? Because I did not know of anyone who died during the daytime; all the deaths in my community occurred at night, and just in case I died in the night, I wanted to ensure I go to heaven.

Coincidentally, when anyone died, their relatives and friends would often arrange what is called a Nine-Night, which is the customary Jamaican form of a Wake, also called a Dead Yard or a Set Up. This is also a traditional funerary practice in other parts of the **Caribbean**, primarily Grenada, Dominica, Guyana, Trinidad, Haiti and the Dominican Republic, with roots in African religious tradition.

A Nine-Night may last for several nights, but it typically takes place on the ninth night after death occurs, but before the burial. During this time, but especially on the ninth night, the family, friends, well-wishers and even people who were not acquainted with the deceased all gather at the Dead Yard to celebrate the life of the dead loved one, but there is no standardised way of holding the ceremony. It differs from one family to the next.

The Nine-Night is the most celebrated ritual in Jamaica. People don't go to a Nine-Night to mourn, but to celebrate. They sing and dance, eat fried fish and hard dough bread, and drink hot chocolate, coffee or something stronger – most often Jamaican Overproof White Rum. Not only do these events in the neighbourhood often disturb one's sleep, but they can be a bit unsettling and scary because one can tell by the style of singing that someone has died in the vicinity.

Many Jamaicans believe that after one dies the spirit (or duppy) stays in the locality for nine nights before finding its eternal abode. Hence, another common practice is to change the direction of the bedhead, rearrange the furniture and turn over the mattress of the departed loved one to prevent the spirit from recognising the room and from wanting to stay when it comes back, and to help the roaming spirit to settle and find a peaceful resting place in the afterlife.

Some of the deeply rooted rituals in the cultural beliefs and traditions involve turning all pictures, looking glasses and mirrors to face the wall or covering the mirrors to avoid a reflection of the image of the dead and to confuse the departed spirit. Some believe that nailing a horseshoe over their doors or sprinkling salt about the place can ward off evil spirits or bring them good luck, but this is a fallacy.

Sadly, many Jamaican immigrants have taken these customs and beliefs to the UK and elsewhere, but my family and other Christian families don't follow them because they are ungodly and contrary to biblical doctrines. True protection comes from faith in Jehovah, not misleading traditions or unconventional practices.

I used to play church like many adults still do today. Breadfruit leaves were my Bible, and the nearby plants my congregation. I would preach and make altar calls for the "sinners" to repent. As I got older, I would "cut tongues" which I learned from others in the Church. My common phrase "sacka backa tire" was copied from one of the deacons, who I understand was not even filled with the Holy Spirit. Furthermore, I practiced conducting funerals with dead lizards. There was a leader in me struggling to emerge, but this took many years to manifest itself.

In the meantime, I was fascinated by the smoke coming from male smokers' nostrils, and eagerly wanted to enjoy that experience, or so I thought. Hence, I secretly picked a dried tobacco leaf from the plant and rolled a cigar with the veins intact, thinking all the while how great this was going to be. I lit it and took a big puff and swallowed it.

To my amazement and displeasure, the smoke burnt down my throat into my stomach and back up through my nostrils. Well, that wasn't what I had expected, and it was the first and last time I attempted smoking. Please don't smoke: "Tobacco is a filthy weed, and from the devil it does proceed. It stains your fingers, picks your pockets, burns your clothes, and makes a chimney of your nose."[8] The tobacco smell is obnoxious and revolting. I remember having to fumigate my office after a short visit from a smoker.

Coming from a rum–drinking culture, I had occasionally emptied and drank the residue of Wray & Nephew White Overproof Rum bottles, left around the house by my unsaved relatives. It was a killer; the drink burned like fire in my throat and put me off alcoholic beverages for good, especially White Rum. Some call it Jamaica's national drink, others use it to make cakes or rum punch and it serves other good purposes, but the uninitiated can take this as a warning to keep away from drinking rum.

In those days, they used **cookware made of cast iron.** The pots had lids, handles and legs all made from the same material, which allowed them to be used on the stovetop (cooker) and in the oven. They had excellent heat retention properties and the entire pot would eventually become extremely hot, including the iron lid and handles. These went out of fashion in the 1960s–1970s, as Teflon-coated aluminium non-stick cookware was introduced and became more popular.

I came from a poor background, but was still better off than many less privileged people. We were never deprived of anything because God always supplied our needs. I recall my mother putting her pot on the fire and praying for food to come. Before long someone turned up with yam, bananas, potatoes, etc., more than enough to suffice. She cooked a meal seasoned with the grace of God, and I have to say we never went to bed hungry.

I also remember with sincere gratitude and deep appreciation my mother going to shop without any money, but as she walked along the road she prayed that Jehovah Jireh would provide. This reminds me of the great invitation, **"Come, buy** wine and milk **without money** and **without** price" (Isaiah 55:1–3). At that time, there were no postal systems like we have today, but on arriving at the Post Office, Mom asked the postmistress, with a prayer in her heart, "Is there any letter for Lucille Burrell?"

While the Postmistress flicked through the pile of mails alphabetically, she continued praying: "Du mi Gad" (Do my God)…and there it was – a registered letter either from England or America with more than enough money to do her shopping. She went praying, but came back rejoicing. That was faith in action! Don't underestimate the power of a praying mother! Alas, today we have more playing mothers than praying mothers, and society is falling apart.

Our home was well kept, and we were always clean and neatly dressed, so not many people knew our economic situation. My mother taught my brother Paul and I not to take food or drink from anybody. This was because jealousy was prevalent in the community and Mom feared that they might put something poisonous in our food. Paul took it so religiously that he refused food or drink even from our Aunty Mack, who was the Pastor of our Church. As a result, many people felt that we were rich and didn't eat poor people's food.

In reality, I had only one pair of shoes, which I wore to church and to school, but I did have my Sunday best: one's best clothing worn to church on Sunday or on special occasions. Also, my Aunt Glen was an air hostess, and she often brought back fashionable clothes for us from Miami, Florida, USA, which gave the impression that we were affluent.

As a matter of fact, my one khaki (a type of fabric) school uniform was usually washed overnight and ironed in the morning. This led some people to believe that I had many school uniforms and they begrudged me for it. And, because my Mom was naturally very generous, many thought we were financially the richest people in the community, but the only wealth we had was the richness of Christ's love" (Ephesians 3:8).

Whenever it rained, instead of sheltering to avoid getting wet, I had a field day in the rain. In the first place, I would walk through the downpour, and would throw myself into the river with all my clothes on before walking the few miles to my home. Somehow, when you had to dry yourself and change the wet clothes it made the dinner taste much nicer.

Mom's typical dinner was a standard with a few variations: rice and peas, plain white rice, curried goat, beef, chicken, fish, ackee and salt fish, yam, breadfruit, bananas, potatoes, flour dumplings and soup twice a week. When I got home from school, the last thing I wanted to see was any visitor because this meant that my portion would be smaller. Instead of the normal two dumplings, I might only get one or even just a half. However, Mom would often cook for unexpected visitors and this would compensate for any existing capabilities or potential shortfalls.

Sleepwalking and Sleep Talking

Sleepwalking, formally known as somnambulism or noctambulism, is defined as a behavioural disorder that originates during deep sleep, and results in walking or performing other complex behaviours while asleep. It is allegedly more common in children than adults and is more likely to occur if a person is deprived of sleep. To me, this is purely a psychological assumption, which does not correspond to my experience. I was told that "You can startle sleep walkers, and they can be very disoriented when you wake them up. They can also have violent, or confused reactions," but I cannot confirm any of this as I have never been woken up during sleepwalking.

I didn't know when it started, how it happened or when it ended, but I know that I used to sleepwalk up until I was about ten years of age. I understand that there are two types of sleepwalking, both of which are unexplainable, but one type is dangerous. For me, this was a natural phenomenon, which occurred while I was asleep. I was never wandering about looking dazed or confused, but always fully conscious of my environment. I was capable of seeing, hearing and giving rational answers to any questions asked about my condition or activities.

My Mom was scared that I may open doors and go away at night, but I had no fear of any potential danger. One night,

Mom came home from church just in time to find me opening the last door to go out. She asked me a few questions to which I answered rationally. She sent me back to my bed (still asleep), and when I woke up in the morning I retained all that happened during the night, and it all seemed normal to me. In retrospect, I can understand how frightening this must have been for my family, but I had no concern whatever about it.

Some call it a parasomnia that causes people to get up and walk around in their sleep. It appears to me that when scientists cannot explain anything outside their scope or capability, "it is abnormal." Sleepwalking seems to be a hereditary trait, which runs down through some families. Hereditary is the process by which genetic information passes from parents to their offspring. But, what actually causes sleepwalking we do not know, but we do know that genetic traits can be positive or negative.

I can confirm that I know two of my cousins who used to sleepwalk in the same way. One day Howard, the younger of the two got up while sleeping, packed his travelling bag and walked down the stairs with it in his hand. When asked where he was going, he said that he was going to town to take the tram to Kingston. He was told to go back to his bed and he did, still asleep. Munroe, the elder cousin, was a sprinter and he went sprinting down the road one night in his pyjamas fast asleep.

Sleep talking, formally known as somniloquy, is defined as a sleep disorder in which one talks during sleep without being aware of it. I used to talk a lot in my sleep; sometimes I was aware of it, and at other times I was not. It appears there were a lot of "abnormal" things about me. But that's why I am still alive today. The "abnormality" also marked me out as a special kind of person.

It is said that people who talk in their sleep can't keep secrets, but I have never divulged anything confidential in my sleep. Mostly when I wake up, I remember what I said while asleep. Another strange thing about me is that occasionally I have been in a deep sleep snoring, while listening to a conversation, which I have remembered upon waking. The scientists don't seem to have found an explanation for this kind of "abnormality" as yet.

Horrific Demonic Attacks

When I was in the sixth form at school, I used to take evening lessons. One evening, I was followed home by demon spirits. I never saw them, but as soon as I got on the veranda I heard footsteps following me. My mother didn't hear anything, but she picked them up in the Spirit and rebuked them with righteous indignation. The dogs went after them and chased them down to the bottom of the cultivation (which we used to call gully bottom, but it's no longer called that). Just as the **Holy Spirit** is the power of God; **witchcraft** is a power of Satan.

Dabbling with the occult is called obeah (or obia) in Jamaica. "Obeah" is a term used in the Caribbean to refer to contemporary Dabbling with the occult is called obeah (or obia) in Jamaica. "Obeah" is a term used in the Caribbean to refer to contemporary folk magic, sorcery, witchcraft, or voodoo, and originated among the West African slaves, specifically of Igbo. It is a "bad omen" involving magical charms, casting of spells, rituals, fetishes and other evil practices, which initially were directed against the European slave masters.

It was believed that the obeah man (or woman) has the incredible power of divination (or magical power) to cause great harm or death to individuals. He or she sometimes claims to be a herbal bush doctor, whose practice involves using natural remedies, which fall outside of established conventional medicine. This African cultural heritage began to gain popularity in Jamaica after the abolition of slavery and the increasing number of practitioners advanced their evil deeds, usually in secret.

Incidentally, some covetous people decided to work obeah on a few members of my family, either to curtail their lives or to hinder their success. However, they couldn't succeed because my mother and my Aunty Mack were filled with the **Holy Spirit**, and we weren't superstitious. There is no power greater than the power of God, as demonstrated in the biblical story of Aaron, Moses and Pharaoh's magicians or obeah men. (See Exodus 7:1-16.) What Moses had was more powerful than anything the magicians could have produced.

Anyway, every night, we heard as it were the sounds of all the sheets of zinc being taken out from under the cellar of our house and destroyed in the yard, but in the morning, nothing was ever out of place. Drinks on the dining table were often knocked over by invisible hands, and there were strange but faint, almost inaudible movements inside the house. One morning when we woke up, the veranda was messed up with loose dirt (believed to have been grave dirt), a silver three-pence piece and some black thread. Mom swept up everything except the money which we spent, but the disturbance continued.

When something of this diabolical nature occurred, the norm was to engage a stronger obeah man to dispel the bad omen, but instead Mom arranged prayer and fasting at the home. Sister Anderson and sister Lewin from Grantham, Clarendon, who had an anointing to deal with witchcraft (obeah) began to manifest in the Spirit. One asked for a machete and they went under the high cellar. We followed them and they went to one of the main pillars of the house and spoke in tongues while they dug up a silver florin (a two-shilling piece) and gave it to the Pastor. This neutralised the power behind its source. The power of God's Word and prayer can break up every magic spell.

The sisters pointed out other spots under the house where a vial with rotten eggs and black thread among other things were buried, but the Spirit only led them to dig up the florin coin. When they left, I went to dig at one of the places indicated and began to utter "Sacka backa tire," the only unknown "tongues" I could speak, but I did not find anything, and I did not suffer any harm as a consequence.

The disturbances abated somewhat, but still carried on sporadically, until one night my mother had a vision: she was confronted by a man who threatened to kill her because as he said, "Every time I make my plans you mash it up." She rebuked him and chased him away and those problems immediately ceased.

At the time, I didn't understand what that was all about, but in retrospect it gave me an unwavering faith in the power of the **Holy Spirit**, and I now know that no demon can harm me. Jesus has given us the believers "Power over unclean spirits to drive them out, and to heal all kinds of sickness and all kinds of disease" (Matthew 10:1, NKJV).

Yet despite all that I was taught, and what I had seen and experienced, I became an agent of Satan. Even though I played church, preached to the weeds and made altar calls for "the sinners to repent," being a real Christian was out of the equation. I felt that I was too young for that commitment, and wanted to enjoy my youth. I thought that maybe on my deathbed I would consider giving my life to God, but I could never imagine myself living a double standard life. I was a sinner, but not a hypocrite – and there were too many of them already in the church.

I had the gift of the gab and could express myself better than many. In a spirit of positivity, I did not believe in swearing, although my tongue slipped once and I uttered a bad word. I just couldn't see the point in using non-essential or nonsensical words that meant nothing when it was easier to say what I meant and mean what I said. However, I confess that I did try to confuse some of the young Christian girls, who couldn't defend their faith, with a view to turning them away from the Church, and one or two did. Upon reflection, one wishes that history could be reversed, but God is merciful."

We may plan for things to go a certain way, but God has greater plans for our lives. Scripture says, "For I know the plans I have for you," declares the LORD, "plans to prosper you and not to harm you, plans to give you hope and a future" (Jeremiah 29:11, NIV). Let no one define you by your past, but let the dark yesterday give way to a brighter tomorrow.

My Extraordinary Conversion

In July 1963 – when I was approximately sixteen years of age, God rescued me as a branch from the burning. To help you get the whole picture and have a proper understanding of this profound miracle, let me relate what happened. Even as a youth, I had struggled to cope with the Jamaican heat. Jamaica has a tropical climate with warm or hot weather at sea level during the entire year; only in the higher inland regions is the climate more moderate.

Often by about mid-day, the asphalt on the road melted like butter in the sun, and if I was not at school or church I would usually go to shoot birds with my catapult in the cool shady cultivation or go to the stream for a splash in the water – I couldn't swim. (A stream is a small narrow river – a body of water flowing down a hillslope or mountain with current confined within a bed and banks.) It was on one of these occasions that God miraculously transformed my life, and I became born again.

My conversion was momentous, dramatic and historic. Nature itself witnessed this miraculous transformation. It was a hot, sunny day with the classic blue sky canopy, and it seemed to me that I could hear the birds singing and chirping as never before. The trees swayed gently in the cool country breeze as if to welcome me into the Kingdom of God, and the only sounds were this and the natural sound of the soothing waters flowing between the rocks, all of which encapsulated the typical scenic features of Jamaican ornamental landscape.

The cows grazing on the hillside were instinctively unmoved by what was happening. It is important to realise that this was not the work of a man, but that God Himself had orchestrated it for His glory. Prompted by the Holy Spirit, and though "clothed" only in my birthday suit, I knelt on a flat stone in the stream and prayed my way into eternity as the Spirit led me step by step – there was no church and no preacher present, solely the LORD and I.

During my powerful encounter with God, I apparently entered a brand-new day and not only was my life marvellously transformed from that instant, but everything around me was seemingly changed and time stood still. In the tranquillity of the moment all that really mattered was the presence and glory of the LORD. This experience was real! I was truly and wonderfully converted! There are some things in life that cannot be described, they have to be experienced, and I realise that the new birth is one of them.

Even though I did not understand the dynamics of this experience, my becoming a Christian was not the result of the influence or persuasion of my mother or anyone else. I determined my choice of actions that day, and made a conscious decision in response to the moving of the Holy Spirit. The after effect was like getting married and wanting to share the good news with everyone, but I was too shy and didn't have the courage to do so.

At a testimony service on the following Wednesday, I tried to testify about my experience, but nerves got the better of me. I had rehearsed my testimony all day, but when the time came to deliver I had "cold feet" and froze. This can sometimes happen to even the most capable adults if they are new converts.

A couple of weeks later, I was baptized in water amid the cooling fragrance of the morning. This was an experience never to be forgotten. It took place at a stream in Johns Hall very early on a Sunday before the sun rose over the eastern horizon, and some five hundred people had intentionally gathered for this spectacular and momentous event – the occasion of my spiritual burial with Christ (Romans 6:1–6). They came from near and far, as people often do at funerals today.

Many were there to participate; some had come to spectate and others to speculate. They were dubious or uncertain about the whole idea of baptism. Some felt I couldn't live the life and gave me only two weeks; others one month or three months, but I kept the faith by God's grace. (Twenty-two of us were baptized that day, but over a period of time the other twenty-one sadly backslid.)

The norm was for each candidate to give a testimony before being immersed in the water. I was too modest, reserved and timid to conform to this tradition, so I decided to trick them, in a genuine way. While someone was testifying, I muttered a few quick words under my breath that no one heard, and when I was asked to testify, I made the excuse that I testified already.

Although I grew up in the Church, I had no idea that God could speak to any individual living in our generation. I thought that accounts of such events were just Bible anecdotes, and antiquated. To me, the stories of David and Goliath, Daniel, Joseph, Elisha, Peter and John were just good Bible tales, but had no relevance to us today. Funnily enough, I thought places in the Bible like Israel, Jerusalem, and Jericho were now in heaven. In those days, good Bible teaching was a scarce commodity. Many of the preachers and Sunday school teachers never had any formal theological training.

I had a radical experience, which changed the course of my destiny dramatically, and gave me a new perspective of life. One evening, after sunset as it began to darken, I stood on a hilltop in Desire looking down at the village lights. That moment, God said to me intently and inexplicably, "You cannot testify now, but one day you shall preach this gospel and heal the sick." It was like a dream to me, and I couldn't envisage how that would be possible, but it resonated in my spirit.

Nevertheless, the penetrating voice of God was so powerful and had such an impact on my life, I felt like a frozen chicken thawing out as streams of tears bathe my eyes profusely. How did I know it was the voice of God? I don't know, but I knew it with a deep conviction, probably because it was unlike anything I had ever heard – indeed, it was one of the most overwhelming experiences of my life. I kept it to myself like a hidden treasure and never shared it with anyone in Jamaica at that time. Providentially, my life began to gain spiritual momentum, which became evident as I developed.

In 1509, The Spanish Empire began its official rule over Jamaica for 146 years. On 10 May 1655, a large group of British sailors and soldiers landed in the Kingston Harbour. Spanish forces surrendered without much of a fight on 11 May; many of them fleeing to Spanish Cuba or the northern portion of the island.[9] British colonial jurisdiction over the island was quickly established, with the newly renamed Spanish Town – continuing as the capital and home of the local House of Assembly, Jamaica's directly elected legislature.[10]

Jamaica remained a British Colony until it gained independence from the United Kingdom on 6 August 1962, an event symbolised by the raising of the National Flag which signified its new status as an independent and sovereign nation. The country also became a member of the British Commonwealth – an organisation of ex-British territories. This auspicious occasion is noted as a national holiday in Jamaica, and has been celebrated as Independence Day every year on 6 August by Jamaicans at home and abroad.

The flag of Jamaica is one of the country's national symbols – featuring two diagonal gold lines across each other forming four triangles: two black and two green. The black represents the colour, strength and creativity of the people; gold, the natural wealth and beauty of the sunshine, and green, the hope and agricultural resources of the land. The Jamaican people as a whole are very proud of their flag and country.

The National Anthem was chosen after a competition which took place between September 1961 and 31 March 1962. The lyrics of the Anthem were voted for on 19 July 1962 by Jamaica's Houses of Parliament, and the winning lyrics were chosen with an overwhelming majority out of nearly one hundred entries. The Official Anthem, completed only days before Jamaica's independence on 6 August 1962, is the creative work of four people – the winning script was written by the late Rev. Hon. Hugh Braham Sherlock O.J., O.B.E., D.D., LL.D., M.I.B.A, the music was composed by the late Hon. Robert Lightbourne OJ, and the anthem was arranged by Mapletoft Poulle and the then Christine Alison Poulle (now remarried to Raymond Lindo)."[11]

It was on a Monday, and I was in grade 6 at school. This was the 218th day of the year 1962 in the Gregorian calendar (named after Pope Gregory XIII). I was given a special souvenir cup on the first Independence Day in 1962 to mark the occasion, a cup which is still in my glass cabinet unused. Pupils had to assemble in the forecourt of the school and salute the Jamaican flag as it was raised while they sang the National Anthem, "**Jamaica**, Land We Love" – one of the best anthems in the world. The lyrics speak for themselves:

> "Eternal Father, bless our land,
> Guide us with thy mighty hand…,
> Be our light through countless hours.
> To our leaders, Great Defender,
> Grant true wisdom from above.
> Justice, truth be ours forever,
> Jamaica, land we love,
> Jamaica, Jamaica, Jamaica, land we love…"

Norman Manley was voted leader of Jamaica in 1955, but he also served as the colony's chief minister until 1962. According to the Observer's newsroom, Thursday 13 September 2007, "Norman Manley was premier, not prime minister." The Jamaica Labour Party (JLP) won the General

Parliamentary Elections on 10 April 1962. Sir Alexander Bustamante – leader of the JLP, was the first Prime Minister of Jamaica. He served from 6 August 1962 until 27 February 1967. He was made a national hero in 1969.[12] Trinidad and Tobago gained independence on 5 August 1962, and Nelson Mandela began 27 years' incarceration on 4 August 1962.

Immigration to England

The history of slavery, as well as the poor economic conditions, have had an impact on family structure and gender roles, heightening the need for people to seek employment outside their localities, in other parishes and also abroad, especially in the United Kingdom "the mother country," which has distanced many Jamaicans from their homes and families, but nonetheless provided them with some hope of a better lifestyle.

An advert in the Jamaican Weekly Gleaner on 13 April 1948 offered cheap transport on the **SS Empire Windrush** for anyone who wanted to work in the United Kingdom.[13] The passengers embarked at a fare of £28.10s 0d each, and departed Kingston, Jamaica, on 24 May 1948, bound for England. The prospect of travelling to England was one of anticipation, adventure and apprehension, especially for the younger men who eagerly wanted to live and work in the UK.

For many, this dream was materialised when the SS Empire Windrush docked at Tilbury, Essex on 22 June 1948, with 490 men and two women on board, mostly from Jamaica and Trinidad. The ship was en route from Australia to England via the Atlantic, docking in Kingston, Jamaica, in order to pick up servicemen who were on leave.

Some former veterans and comrades also took this opportunity to return to Britain with the intention of re-joining the Royal Air Force (RAF) while others decided to make their maiden journey just to explore life in England. This marked the beginning of large-scale post-war immigration from the Caribbean to England, resulting in an estimated 172,000 West Indian-born people living in the UK by 1961.[14]

Many of the early arrivals were told that England was the "mother country" and that they were all welcome. They were British, but not English. Soon they were met with rejection and racial prejudice tinged with hostility. However, very few of these immigrants intended to stay in Britain for more than a few years.

My mother was not a part of the Windrush Generation. In the autumn of 1962, she made her maiden voyage to England, which was like a journey to an illusion; her misconceptions vaporised and vanished into the atmosphere. But it was a blessing for Mom to be reunited with her sister Ivy and her sister's husband Rev. Austin Gordon, who received and welcomed her in their home at Kensal Rise, London NW10. Like many of the early Jamaican immigrants to the UK, her objective was to improve her economic situation, and of course to better support her children back home.

Upon her arrival in the United Kingdom, she was immediately associated with the Kilburn *New Testament Church of God (NTCG),* which had its base in Kensal Rise. The Church had changed its location from Kilburn, but still retained the prefix to its name. It wasn't long before Mom became a loyal and devoted member of the immigrant Church, with its *International Offices in Cleveland Tennessee, USA.*

In the interim, I was left in Clarendon with my aunt, Pastor McMillan (affectionately known as Mother Mack) and my Uncle Mack. My mother had seven sisters and one brother, and my father had four brothers and one sister. Mom's only brother was married to my dad's only sister, which meant that my uncle married my aunt. Mom worked very hard and sent for me to join her in England at the earliest opportunity.

The next major transition in my life was my emigration to England. This move came approximately two months after my conversion. On 15 September 1963, I boarded a *British Overseas Airways Corporation (BOAC)* flight to the UK, to be reunited with my mother. Mom met me at Heathrow Airport; we got on a *National Express Coach* from there to *Victoria Coach Station*, and took a number 52 bus to my new residence in Kensal Rise. I was wearing an airport tag on my wrist and the bus conductor said to me, "You can take that off now, you won't get lost again."

My first impression had not been too favourable, bearing in mind this was my first time in a foreign country and I had to make conscious efforts to adapt. The English accent sounded a bit strange at first; people frequently completed their sentences with "innits," such as, "You enjoy going to football, innit" or used the term "you alright" as a form of greeting, especially in the London dialect (cockney), but although I never spoke cockney, I was intrigued by it. I loved London, and before long I too became a Londoner.

Initially, life in the UK was a culture shock for me. It was so unlike my lifestyle back home, which was much more laid back and family orientated. This made me keenly aware of the many differences: the social and cultural diversities, the houses with chimneys, the way people dressed, the transportation, the shops and shopping habits; even the Church life was different.

Joining long queues at the bus stops was also foreign to me, but the sight of youngsters eating fish and chips out of brown paper or newspaper on the street was repulsive and difficult to come to terms with. That was probably because eating on the street was frowned on in Jamaican culture. Another disturbing facet of my new life was the many teenage boys and girls hugging and kissing in public; some even swore at their parents. All these things went totally against the grain of my culture and it was hard for me to adapt.

In 1963, the population of Britain had just reached 53.65 million15 (compared to 65,097,000 people in 2015). The 1960s, commonly known as the "swinging sixties" are regarded as the most defining decade of the twentieth century in British history.[16] It was the era of the Mini cars and miniskirts, the Austin Cambridge, the Ford Zephyr 6 and the Consul. They were strong stylish vehicles with good body works and were quite reliable, compared to their successors. This decade introduced a new era of profound cultural, social and economic changes.

In those days, racism was rife in Britain and black people were marginalised, disdained, unwanted and still undermined by the stigma of slavery. Like London and Liverpool, Bristol was a city with global reach whose enormous wealth derived from the international trade of enslaved Africans. It was the birthplace of one of the era's most notorious slave owners, Edward Colston, whose earnings financed Bristol's growth, and who still has a statue in the City and a school named after him.[17]

It wasn't just slavery that marked out Bristol for its racial impact in the UK. In 1963, a small group of Caribbean workers initiated a bus boycott because the local bus company, backed by the unions, refused to employ black or Asian staff.

The brave actions of a few hundred men and women – led by Paul Stephenson, who supported Marvin Rees – not only forced the bus company to capitulate, but also persuaded Britain's Government to begin the process of protecting minorities from blatant discrimination.

In 1965, The Race Relations Act became law.[18] This Act was the first legislation in the United Kingdom to address racial inequality. And it outlawed discrimination on the "grounds of colour, race, ethnic or national origins" in public places, and set up a Race Relations Board (R.R.B.) to investigate complaints. The Race Relations Acts of 1960s–1970s did not eradicate racial discrimination, but were a significant change which marked a turning point in the evolution of the British multi-cultural society.

Other changes were occurring. During the 1960s, pop music was the number one priority for many teenagers. Groups such as the Beatles and the Rolling Stones changed the music scene forever. They were very flamboyant and charismatic and their many female fans screamed, cried and became almost hysterical when they performed.

Teenage fashion changed at an astonishing and unprecedented rate in the 60s. Several youth cults appeared and disappeared. A distinctive music called Rock 'n' Roll had emerged in the late '40s and '50s and was hugely popularised in the '60s along with a new youth cult – the Teddy Boys, and later the Mods and Rockers, all of whom were outrageous and violent. Each group had a distinctive style, and some rode scooters or motorbikes, with black leather trousers, and had longish, greased-back hair in oft-combed waves over the top and sideburns down the cheeks – a hair style that was becoming popular.

They could be extremely dangerous. Going to evening lessons at college and elsewhere at night, I had to be very aware of their presence in society. They often hurled racist remarks at me. I witnessed them attacking innocent people with weapons: bike fenders, bottles, screwdrivers and basically anything they could find. They were notorious for assaulting innocent people, pushing the elderly off pavements, attacking other youths, picking fights at cinemas and dance halls and clobbering bus conductors.

The evolution of the skinheads – another British subculture movement originated among working class youths in London during the 1960s. They were characterised by short haircuts or typically shaved heads, tattooed faces and foreheads.

Their behaviour was racist, aggressive, violent and socially disruptive. They were some people's worst nightmares. Travelling to and from home on foot or by bus or tube was sometimes risky, especially at night. One had to be wary of potential dangers from these idle youths who usually travelled in groups and lurked on the streets.

Tattoos have long fascinated both advocates and opponents of the trendy art, which soon became a popular fashion of the day. What was most intriguing about this trend was probably the permanent patriotic, romantic and religious designs on their bodies. Some would often have tattoos like "I love Cheryl." The only problem was that for many she left long ago, but they still had the indelible tattoos of a broken relationship.

Historically, the hippies were a liberal countercultural movement, which originally began its development as a social youth movement that started in the United States and the United Kingdom during the mid-1960s and which spread to other countries around the world. Rock music was also an integral part of hippie culture. They were nonconformists and everything about them was different. Their characteristic long hair, leather clothing, theatrical behaviour and challenging beliefs had a major effect on culture, influencing popular music, television, film, literature, and the arts.

Female activists demanded more rights for women, whose role in society began to change. In 1961, the birth control pill and other contraceptives were made available in the UK on the NHS for married women only – this lasted until 1967 – and are now taken by 3.5 million women in Britain between the ages of 16 and 49, making it possible for women to plan their careers and have babies when they wanted them. Furthermore, measures were taken to improve the position of women.[19]

The "swinging sixties" had their ups and downs and did not always swing in the right direction. A sliced loaf of bread was unavailable in 1963; three years later a loaf of bread cost 5p, but the pendulum swung to the opposite extreme and morals collapsed. The moral code that prevailed in 1945 broke down under Prime Minister Harold Wilson's Labour Government.

My First Job

Shortly after my arrival in London, I braved the elements of the weather and started my apprenticeship as a motor mechanic engineer at a garage in Kilburn, North-West London. I had to commute by train and bus to work. My wages were £6.50p per week. I further pursued my career by enrolling on an engineering course at **Kilburn Polytechnic College**, which I never completed because I changed my career path.

As an impressionable 16-year-old youth and a born-again believer, I used to worship at work and enjoy my Christianity.

This upset my Irish foreman so badly that one day while I was singing, he shouted at me angrily, "Shut up, you're not in church now!" Suddenly, a response came out forcibly from the bottom of my stomach, "I am not in church, but church is in me." In retrospect, I realised that it was a word of knowledge from the Spirit. Some people are aggravated about God; others gravitate towards God; it depends on what drives them.

The foreman did not dislike me as a person, but there was a spirit in him that was uncomfortable with my worship. I found myself at the mercy of my cruel foreman, who subsequently took me along on a MOT test (a diagnostic test to ensure a vehicle is road worthy), and persuaded me to accompany him into a pub. Being a late arrival from Jamaica where we have rum bars – not pubs, I didn't know what a pub was. He offered me a soft drink, which I accepted and he bought me a gin. I didn't know what a gin was, and I didn't like the environment so I had my tipple quickly and hurried out, but I couldn't hold my drink.

I had never drunk any strong alcoholic beverage before and I gradually realised that I was intoxicated. Dark clouds of sadness obscured the brightness of my day; my melting eyes became blurry and my legs unbalanced. I heard the hosts of hell rejoicing. It sounded like a million voices collaborated in celebration: "I knew you couldn't make it, look what you have done," they said, and I sank in utter despair.

My soul-dissolving sighs of guilt, shame and feelings of condemnation overwhelmed my heart. At such a time as this, not a word of prayer could emerge from my soul. I wondered how I was going to face my family and the Church. I didn't know who to turn to or how to deal with this difficult and unfortunate situation.

Almost devoid of energy, I managed to get home safely, but did not have the audacity or confidence to share my experience. My world was turned upside down and my dreams shattered, but I knew that backsliding was not an option. I spoke with no one and I had no dinner; I simply relied on the mercies of God – and threw myself across the bed in penitence. A surge of thoughts flooded my mind as arrows of anguish pierced my soul, but there was not much I could do except to surrender to God.

Immediately, it was as if I were caught up in a trance. I saw myself at a cross roads and felt that I was in an even bigger predicament. I perceived that if I went to the right or the left there was death, and if I turned back it was death. I don't know where the courage and strength came from, but I made a conscious effort to go forward.

Momentarily, the heavenly sunlight shone through my darkness. I was instantly delivered and restored to my normal self. In hindsight, I realised this was a stepping-stone to greater and better things. Satan "meant evil against me; but God meant it for good" (Genesis 50:20, NKJV).

One was not legally permitted into a pub until the age of twenty-one, and I was only sixteen at the time. Some two or three weeks later, I told my uncle-in-law what had happened and he was extremely angry about the situation. He was a no-nonsense person. He went to my workplace and had an altercation with the foreman and my boss, but decided not to pursue legal action since God had already dealt with it.

Adverse Weather Conditions

The British weather is so unpredictable in comparison to the constant hot tropical climate of the Caribbean. Seeing the snow for the first time was a fascinating experience for me, and the temptation to play in it was irresistible. The white, crystalline snow falling from the clouds in the form of glittering flakes looked somewhat like Jamaican snowball (shaved ice, served with syrup), and I wondered if it was edible. Playing in it was great fun, and all the youngsters found it enjoyable and engaging.

On the other hand, along with the coldness of many people from the British indigenous community came the freezing winters. Emerging from the hot Jamaican summers to the bitter-cold British weather, I had to embrace myself for the grave effects of the winters like many others. The general experience of winter was horrendous, and many including I struggled to cope with the cold weather. Ironically, I didn't like the Jamaican heat, and now I don't like the British cold, but given the choice between the two, guess which one I would choose? That heat? Not necessarily.

The winter of 1962–1963 (also known as the Big Freeze) was one of the coldest and gloomiest winters on record in the United Kingdom. Temperatures plummeted to as low as −200C, bringing blizzards, snowdrifts and blocks of ice which caused grave damage and disruption to commuters. One day on my way to work, I slid on a thin layer of ice and hit the ground. My trousers were ripped almost in two, but apart from that I was fine. I had to return home and change them.

The long severe cold spell caused lakes and rivers to freeze over, and the sea water in some harbours also froze. Shivering and wheezing in the cold with frozen fingers, I often literally pushed my hands into a blazing fire to thaw them out. Today, the Approved Code of Practice suggests a minimum **temperature** of 16°C in a workplace or at least 13°C if your **work** involves rigorous physical effort, but there was no such regulation then. Sometimes I had to put a bottle of hot water into my bosom to keep me warm. That was a recipe for disaster, but I survived.

My uncle Mack in Jamaica used to say to me sarcastically, "My God, Mass Barry, you are too nice; you scorn Massa (Master) God's earth. Your hands mustn't get dirty, go and preach with your aunty!" He was partially right, I didn't like handling dirt, and motor mechanic engineering was too greasy and dirty. So I started to learn the trade of a woodworking machinist, with a small company called Apex Studio, off the Harrow Road in Kensal Green, London.

Electric Shock at Work

This was the fourth deadly satanic attack on my life. One day at work in my new trade, I touched a live electric wire accidentally, and it almost killed me. Some 250 volts surged into my anatomy and shook me without any resistance. With the swift powerful current passing through my body, it felt like I was grabbed violently by invisible hands, but I escaped providentially. When you think that even a standard 9V battery can kill a person, it's a miracle that I am alive.

Talking about cheating death, on another occasion after it rained, I slipped and fell down a wooden and metal stair case at the same company. I ended up in a hospital with excruciating pain, and about five doctors surrounding me. By their demeanour, I guessed they feared the worst, but fortunately my ribs were just badly bruised, not broken. At the time, I was attending the Willesden NTCG.

Between seventeen and eighteen years of age, I was already an active, forward-looking youngster in the Church, and I had potential for the Christian ministry. After I served as Sunday school teacher of the intermediate class for a short time, I was appointed as leader of the *Young People's Endeavour (YPE)*.

It was evident that some people were always in the habit of going to Church late. That is a bad practice and I didn't like it. This doesn't mean that the individuals themselves had negative character traits, but anywhere you find people with too much of a laid-back personality, you find people whose timekeeping is usually poor.

Occasional tardiness (or lateness) may be circumstantial or excusable. However, consistent or habitual lateness not only affects the late-comers' availability to perform their duties, but wastes other people's time. It may also have an impact on what they do and how they deliver in the meeting. On the other hand, being early is advantageous. "The early bird catches the worm," but if everyone is punctual everyone will catch a worm.

So, from this perspective, persistent lateness is bad manners and a lack of respect for the punctuality of others. Good manners are an essential part of Christian behaviour and civilised living, and it's important to teach this principle in the Church by precept and example. Furthermore, what does this casual and carefree behaviour of going to church late say about your attitude towards God's time?

No friends, relatives or anything kept me back when it was time for me to do God's work. I would often leave my dinner so as to be on time for Church. My mother used to be very unhappy about this and tried to persuade me to have dinner first because "You know they are going to be late," as she often said. My ready-made response was: "Mom it is my duty to be on time regardless of who is late."

I deduced that "talking" didn't work with some people, so I proactively took a desperate action, which was unconventional and unpopular, but it worked. I went to Church on time as per usual and conducted service to the empty chairs. By the time the late-comers arrived, I had dismissed the invisible congregation and was on my way home. They soon learned their lesson well. Christians are urged to live a life worthy of the calling they have received. (See Ephesians 4:1.)

Yours Truly 17–18 Years Old

Coming from a very traditional church background, I deviated from many of the old-school traditions that were not conducive to my Christian development or in tune with where I was heading spiritually; but I was mindful not to "throw the baby out with the bathwater." I knew that there were some traditions which we should cling to as a vital part of our heritage, and God gave me the wisdom to avoid confusing the two, and to preserve those useful natural disciplines or principles drilled into me during my formative years.

Unlike the sister who took her hat off in church one Sunday morning and showed the Church her uncombed hair, saying that she didn't have any pride in it, I had pride in my hair. It had to be well groomed for church on Sundays and other special occasions. Anyone wishing to pray for me was welcome to do so, but they couldn't lay hands on my head. To this day, I don't like anyone touching my hair. I avoid putting my hands on anybody's head when praying for them. It wouldn't be right to do to others what I dislike having done to myself.

My trousers were usually well ironed with razor-sharp creases at the front and back; they looked good and I took pride in them too. They were kept laid-out with seams in line to avoid wrinkles, and they had to be handled with care. At one of our national conventions, I heard a renowned preacher say in his sermon, "Your trouser seams are so sharp, you can't even kneel to pray."

That didn't go down well with me. My response was: that's okay, if I can't kneel, I'll stand and pray. I didn't feel that my trouser seams would affect my worship or impede my relationship with God. (I haven't changed much in that regard. I still groom my hair nicely, and owing to my current busy lifestyle, I buy suits that don't require frequent ironing; some are made from travel- friendly, wrinkle-free fabrics.)

Ministerial Call Affirmed and Ratified

As far back as I can remember, I have always sensed the call of God on my life, although I didn't understand the gravity of it. However, I embraced His call at the tender age of sixteen when I had a supernatural intervention. This life-changing experience dramatically impacted on my life, charted my course and shaped my destiny.

God commissioned me to preach the gospel and heal the sick. I had felt that maybe I would consider serving as an evangelist, but I did not want to be a pastor, for reasons of the flesh, I supposed. I grew up among pastors and witnessed first-hand how they suffered unnecessary troubles caused by unscrupulous church members.

As a result, I literally vowed that I would never become a pastor owing to the same selfish motive, but as I got older it became more evident that God's hand was on me. (See Ezekiel 37:1.) The calling takes time to develop and vital training was not a thing of the day. I began preaching at the age of eighteen, and some people in the Church started calling me young preacher.

My First Public Exhortation

My first public exhortation was at Willesden NTCG, but I felt it was a disaster. I was well prepared and my notes were slotted in between the pages of my Bible. Then I was invited on to the platform to deliver my message. During the singing of a chorus I stood there with "the shakes" like someone having a panic attack while I flicked through the pages, but couldn't find my notes or my text.

Trembling and sweating profusely, I asked the congregation to sing another chorus, and I repeated the process to no avail. All eyes were now on me; it was either I faint, exit through the back door or say something quickly. It's one thing just saying something, but it's quite a different matter having something to say. But I managed to quote my text from memory, and spoke extemporaneously by faith for about ten minutes.

I went back to my seat and continued vibrating like someone having a medical tremor for the rest of the service with sweat running down my face and between my shoulder blades, but the people still greeted me as "young preacher." Apparently, they saw something that I couldn't see, although as time progressed, God began to reveal Himself to me. Every time any significant change was about to occur in my life or ministry, Jesus appeared to me and enhanced my relationship with the supernatural. We cannot intellectualise the supernatural, and that is why a revelation of God is paramount.

Supernatural Visitations

1. Whether this was a vision or not, I cannot tell, but at about seventeen years of age, I knew that the Lord Jesus came into my bedroom one night and stood there looking at me graciously. His face was not visible to my natural eyes, and I don't remember Him saying anything to me, but the awesomeness of his presence spoke volume; it can never be erased from my conscious mind. A reverential fear took a hold of me; I could not get off the bed momentarily. My life was changed and for the weeks that followed I felt like the holiest person on the planet, but ultimately it was a humbling experience.

2. Sometime later, Jesus appeared to me again in a vision. This time He was in a white cloud and He said, "Follow me!" How I followed Him through the air I cannot explain, but I know that it was not by any effort on my

part. I was taken up in the clouds instantaneously and transported to a lonely place which I perceived was the Garden of Eden, and He disappeared.

In the stillness of the moment, I heard the authoritative voice of God saying to me, "You shall preach this gospel, and heal the sick." Again, my eyes became a fountain of tears and I was in awe. Up until then, I had never heard of any sick being healed in our generation, and I still thought it was a Bible day phenomenon.

3. On a separate occasion, I saw the Lord Jesus again in another vision. He called me and said, "Follow me, and I will show you your apostolic ministry." Immediately, two gigantic men (who I perceived were angels) appeared – one on my right hand and the other on my left. They did not say anything to me; we just followed Christ, who walked a little distance ahead of us, until He entered a large room and I saw Him no more.

The two men also disappeared mysteriously. I was left on my own in the room, and there were explosions of various miracles. As I observed the mighty works of God, I gained an understanding of the revelation: an apostolic ministry is characterised by miracles, signs and wonders. I came out of the vision with a clear perception of my identity and purpose."

Intriguingly, for many years I have carried an unquenchable passion and a strong anointing to teach the Word of God, yet at no time has God ever told me that I should teach His people. He has commissioned me to preach the gospel, but He opened up my understanding and revealed to me that there can be no good preaching without a high content of sound biblical teaching.

Both preaching and teaching are intrinsically connected. In the greatest sermon on record, the Bible says of the Master Preacher, "He opened His mouth and taught them saying…" (Matthew 5:2). Here is our pattern. Theologically, preaching and teaching are the effective communication of the gospel of Jesus Christ.

The Baptism with the Holy Spirit

In 1964, I attended a national convention at the NTCG, Lozells Road, Handsworth, Birmingham. I was praying at the altar and I heard the resounding voice of God saying, "You shall preach this gospel and heal the sick," and I wept profusely as these words reverberated in my spirit: I felt so unworthy of such an honour.

Another night, I was seeking the baptism with the Holy Spirit in the back hall of the same Church. This experience is also called baptism in the Holy Spirit, or baptism of the Holy Spirit or just Spirit baptism. While I prayed, something strange was happening to me. I felt like a tape recorder was playing deep inside my stomach, and the sound was rising through my throat. As I opened my mouth to say hallelujah, foreign words which I never understood came out. I was made to understand that this was unknown tongues or speaking in tongues according to Acts 2: 4.

The Holy Spirit is not just a powerful influence; He is the third person of the God-head. The baptism with the Holy Spirit is a crisis experience just as our initial experience was at conversion, and comes after salvation and sanctification. It is a supernatural endowment of power from on high, which equips believers for spiritual service. Jesus says, "But you shall receive power when the Holy Spirit has come upon you; and you shall be witnesses to Me" (Acts 1:8, NKJV).

The news of my being filled with the Spirit got back to my home Church in Willesden quicker than a telegram. I went back to Church not knowing that I was under scrutiny. In those days, they had self-appointed "spiritual midwives" who felt they had to certify you filled in order that your claim to be filled with the Spirit might be attested. So, as one can imagine, I was under the watchful eyes of these observers.

It was a Sunday night and they had testimonies as usual. A senior mother of the Church stood up and gave her negative "testimony": "I don't understand these young people nowadays; they say that they are filled with the Spirit, but haven't got the power. I remember when we got filled; we used to jump and knock the benches over and they had to hold us down because we were filled with the power." This dear lady and others were just genuine traditionalists, with a pre-existent, widespread traditional belief, who were overcome by zeal without knowledge, but they meant well.

Nevertheless, I seriously considered, is that it? Obviously, I was not filled with the Spirit in the conventional way, and if what this respectable mother described was truly a manifestation of the power, I really didn't want it. So, I totally dismissed the notion of being filled with the Spirit, and disregarded my experience for over one year.

However, from those early years the LORD began to guide me away from many of the old church traditions and the traditionalists' simplistic way of thinking, telling me that there was a more excellent way and, without understanding the deeper and nobler things of the Spirit, I obeyed and eagerly went in His direction, and in hindsight I am glad that I did. Scripture says, "But when He, the Spirit of truth, has come, He will guide you into all the truth: for He will not speak on His own authority… and He will tell you things to come" (John 16:13, NKJV).

The Holy Spirit has become my personal friend and source of supernatural power. He unveils the truth of God's Word to me and uses me for the ministry to which I have been called. Therefore, He is responsible for all the opportunities that God has given to me and the successes of my ministry.

You see, The Holy Spirit gives us a paradigm shift from self-consciousness to God-consciousness; from our big-church syndrome and glamorised materialism to a place of humility where God's purpose can be manifested and He is glorified. All our accolades, awards and achievements in life, properly contextualised, are nothing but trophies of God's grace.

In summary, the 1960s was a significant decade in the history of my life. It was during this period that thirteen significant things happened to me – I:

- was born again

- was baptized in water

- emigrated to the UK

- started my first job

- received the baptism of the Holy Spirit

- became a Sunday school teacher

- became a leader of the Young People's Endeavour (YPE)

- received my call to the ministry

- gave my first public exhortation

- attended Bible school

- met the dream of my life and started courting

- became District Youth and Christian Education Director

- started pastoring my first Church

I was now maturing and life had begun to take on a new shape and a new meaning. I realised that the past was now behind me and I was moving towards my destiny, but this came with a cost. I began seeing things not only through the eyes of a man, but through the eyes of God, and started to prepare myself to face upcoming challenges and to accept new responsibilities.

The Lion

A symbol of Strength, Courage and Leadership

SECTION TWO

MINISTERIAL OPPORTUNITIES AND CHALLENGES

This section explores a very important aspect of my Church-life and ministry. Life always has its ups and downs, but that's perfectly normal. It is said, "Life is not a bed of roses," but even roses have prickles. There are many challenges and substantially more opportunities which come our way from time to time. For example, there are challenges and opportunities in education, business, investments, relationships, ministries and so on, but we may be assured that in moments of great challenges exist even greater opportunities for us to embrace.

Sometimes, we face our own defining moments – moments that define who we are and our possibilities for success. Our God-ordained opportunities which are intended to propel us into our destiny are often providentially disguised as problems and challenges, so instead of bewailing our challenges let's turn them into opportunities.

Our covenant–keeping God will always be faithful to His people, and when He opens doors of opportunities, no one can close them. He affirms, "I know your deeds. See, I have placed before you an open door that no one can shut. I know that you have little strength, yet you have kept my word and have not denied my name" (Revelation 3: 8, NIV). God knows our actions, so we can't fool Him. (See Revelation 3:15.)

The Bible further states, "Take advantage of every opportunity because the days are evil" (Ephesians 5:16). I look back with a great deal of regret over wasted years and opportunities in my life, but I thank God for those that I have seized wholeheartedly, and for His sustaining grace. The great Apostle Paul says, "So then, while we have opportunity, let us *[not waste our time but]* do good to all people, and especially to those who are of the household of the faith" (Galatians 6:10).

When I was growing up, I had the dream of becoming a police officer, but first I wanted to learn to drive a car. In 1967, I achieved this objective by passing my driving test after 18 lessons, at a total cost of £18. This was about three months before I went to Bible school, and my dream of joining the police force did not materialise because God had other plans for me.

Bible School 1967–1969

In September 1967, God made the way and opened a door of opportunity for me. An unknown person from the USA sponsored me to go to the *International Bible Seminary (IBS)* in Switzerland, where I pursued my theological training. Our theology matters because what we believe about God determines our thinking, shapes our philosophy of life and positively impacts on our lifestyle.

The capital of Switzerland is Bern but the largest city is Zurich, and the country's population in 1967 was 5.992 million Central European people. Switzerland has numerous lakes, villages and historic places of interest. It is also known for its top ski resorts and hiking trails. Hiking is taking a long walk in the countryside or woodlands on trails or footpaths, usually for pleasure or exercise. Some of the students and I explored many of these adventures. The country's main industries are banking and finance, and Swiss watches and chocolate are renowned worldwide.

I went to IBS on a scholarship and had no idea who paid my school fees. This was a great opportunity for me, and indeed, an education in more ways than one. There were eleven different nationalities at IBS, but we had to eat from the same pot, and learn to live together as one family. I often reminisce about this period: they were, for me, the good old days.

International Bible Seminary (IBS), Switzerland, 1968

The first evening I arrived at the Bible seminary, sausages were served for supper. I had never eaten anything like it before so I made the excuse that I wasn't hungry. The following day the leftover sausages were served again – nothing was put to waste. I was very hungry, so I started my sausage–eating life that day; it continued until I returned to England.

In Switzerland, the typical breakfast includes bread, butter or margarine, marmalade or honey, maybe some cheese or cereals, milk, cold or hot chocolate, and tea or coffee. On the rare occasions when we were favoured with the luxury of a fried egg, bacon and baked beans breakfast, that was like a bonus. How I missed my English breakfast!

I was the only black student in the Bible school, and as a matter of fact, I did not meet another black person in Switzerland for the first year. Whenever we had street meetings, I had to preach and large crowds gathered to hear what this "black man from Africa" had to say. When we visited the local hospital, they pushed beds with patients into the assembly hall to hear "this African man." This was a great opportunity for me to preach to them and ministered to the sick.

Being black was an advantage because there were not many of us around. I had a good sense of humour and a natural inclination for entertainment, with an elegant dress-sense, admired by many. I was also at the forefront of many school activities and the centre of attraction; girls were fond of me and so were the children, many of whom had never seen a black person before.

Girls were often puzzled by the texture of my hair, which they found fascinating, and some young children naturally thought my skin was unwashed. A little boy once said to his mother, "Er ist schmutzig," meaning "he is dirty." He obviously thought I needed a bath, but his mum was very embarrassed and tried to reprimand the innocent child.

Another enthusiastic young man joined us at IBS in the second year, and I was his guardian angel. A guardian angel is believed to be an angel that is assigned to protect and guide a person, group, kingdom, or country. So, my role was to make certain that he was safe and treated equitably. In practice, this meant that anyone who offended him had to answer to me. Incidentally, the Dean of the school was disrespectful to him, perhaps unintentionally, but when I was through with him he had to call the young man and apologised to him.

My friend was from a very poor background – a drug addict, who accepted the Lord Jesus Christ into his life on a roadside when Bishop S. E. Arnold witnessed to him in Ghana. He was sponsored to attend IBS by an old lady from the USA. They corresponded throughout his training, and upon his graduation she requested a visit from him, adopted him and willed her entire estate to him. She died shortly after that leaving him a wealthy man. This is a testimony to the goodness and faithfulness of Almighty God.

Winter in Switzerland was usually bitter cold in the truest sense of the term. The teachers had their cars fitted with winter tyres and snow chains, but oftentimes that was not enough to get them by. Sometimes female students had to sit inside the car while some of the males sat on the bonnet to increase the weight and others pushed as they battled with the snow while driving up the steeply hilly sloping entrance to the school.

The colder the weather the drier the snow, and I practiced baptizing a few male students in a four feet deep snow drift. I also enjoyed sledging, but one day the sledge sank into the snow at the bottom of a steep hill behind the school, and I continued rolling in a series of summersaults on frozen, snow-covered ground and gliding on the icy surface cutting up my face and bruising my elbows and arms. This was painful, but skiing was even more dangerous and hospitalised many people. I constantly reminded myself that I was there for study, not for sport or recreation.

The Alpine region of Switzerland is conventionally referred to as the Swiss Alps, an ideal destination for skiing and holidays. Examples of the classic scenery and of the major natural features of the country can be seen driving up the narrow winding roads of the Alps, with blue skies above, white capped mountains below and a sheet of snow spread on frozen ground, and further down the blue-green transparent lakes reflecting the snowy mountains and trees in their glossy waters.

On one occasion, IBS arranged a school trip to the highest peak of the Alps. These are high mountains, and the roads go from beautiful to challenging, but when we reached our destination and beheld the magnificent beauty of God's creation, the entire student body and faculty broke out in Christian praise and worship spontaneously. This was amazing as no one initiated it, and the glory of God was evident. It was a historic moment that left me with sacred memories I will cherish and treasure for the rest of my life.

IBS was located on the outskirts of the District of Rorschach on the south side of Lake Constance (also called Bodensee) in the Canton or City of St. Gallen – about 95.5 kilometres (59.34095 miles) from Zurich. Switzerland is divided into 26 cantons (different regions or states) as of 1979. As well as providing the visitor with breathtaking views of the country's majestic mountain scenery, Switzerland also encompasses wide tracts of sparsely populated woodlands, which provide a good source of food for herds of wild reindeer that roam the woods.

As young men without many opportunities to pursue recreation at IBS, we often occupied our spare time with funny and unusual activities. Sometimes we fought for one apple and literally shook the three-story traditional wooden building or played hilarious pranks on each other, but occasionally we would take a stroll through the woods and strategically position ourselves to chase the reindeer, but we didn't catch any. Those animals were so wild, they would " jump over the moon" if possible and even risk their lives to escape us.

On one occasion, I found the carcass of a deer caught up in the hedge of a ditch. Apparently, it had been thirsty and stretching to get water, but died in the process. This brought home to me what the Psalmist meant by his assertion, "As the deer pants for streams of water, so my soul pants [or cries] for you, O God. My soul thirsts for God, for the living God" (Psalm 42:1). This intimate longing for God is a real and fulfilling commitment that brings deep satisfaction, even in the face of death. Death is the ultimate price that some of God's servants pay for their unquenchable thirst for living water from the wells of salvation. (See Isaiah 12:3.)

Moses Jesus Abraham was the name of one of my Bible school mates from the Middle East. He was a fine young man who truly loved the LORD, but his English often betrayed him. One morning, as he was preaching in the chapel he said, "While the cook was cooking (meaning while the cock was crowing), Peter denied Christ three times." Well, that was the end of his message; his interpreter burst out laughing and so did everybody else. The worst place for that to happen was in a Bible school. From that moment on, Moses became the subject of constant ridicule, although not in a nasty way.

When the Church of God (COG) historian Dr Charles W. Conn visited IBS, I was tremendously blessed. One of the things he said was that he could not be insulted because for anyone to insult him, they had to be above him and no one above him would want to insult him. I got his gist and it resonated with me. We had a little talk and he promised to furnish me with some books from the publishing house upon his return to United States. Thereafter, he invested in my ministry by sending me several excellent books, which are still a part of my study library.

Sister May Terry, a renowned international COG evangelist from America, visited the Bible school on her way to preach in the U.K. While she was preaching one morning in the chapel, her little straw hat that she had bought in town fell off her head.

In the middle of her sermon, she picked up the fallen hat and said, "Brother Barry, they told me that when I get to England I have to preach with a hat on, so I am practising from now but it won't stay on my head." This was quite funny because the NTCG women in England wear beautiful and ostentatious hats coordinated to match their costumes, but Sister Terry was only concerned about keeping her modest straw hat on her head.

Intriguingly, the COG women in Germany did not wear hats, and had traditional dos and don'ts for their hairstyles, which were handed down to the Church by its late founder, Brother Herman Lauster. The wearing of hats was construed as pride. Sister Terry had to make the transition from one culture to the next; I suppose she was trying to do what Paul says, "I have **become all things to all people** so that by all possible means I might save **some**" (1 Corinthians 9:22, NIV).

Later, we went to Germany where Sister Terry was preaching. The German ministers in general did not believe in women preachers. Hence, they received her ministry with a degree of scepticism, but Sister Terry had a powerful voice and could preach to over one thousand people without the use of a microphone. Furthermore, she was an outstanding preacher. One pastor asked her, "Sister Terry, what do you think about the Scripture which says that women should keep silent in the church?" Sister Terry responded, "Have you ever heard a woman sing silent in the church yet?"

Rev. Parnell Coward was the Dean and homiletics teacher at IBS. Some of us students accompanied him on a preaching engagement to France. On the Sunday evening, he made an altar call for believers to receive the baptism with the Holy Spirit, but no one responded. In fact, the people were very offended and asked their Pastor to tell him that if he did it again they would leave the service. The reason was that they were not accustomed to seek the Holy Spirit baptism on a Sunday; that was relegated to Wednesday.

Our homiletics teacher learned a very important lesson, and we all benefitted from it too. He said to us, "Boys, never you go to preach in a foreign field without first gaining an understanding of their culture." This was sound advice and a good education for us. Consequently, I have never gone to preach on the mission field without first researching the history and culture of the people. Sometimes, we must make adjustments and adaptations in order to win the lost at any cost.

I was on my way to Germany for the Christmas holiday with two of my friends when their car broke down in heavy snow. We could have died from hypothermia but for the fact that they had carried a couple of warm blankets in preparation for any eventuality. The breakdown service took quite a while to reach us no doubt because of the weather conditions, but

God was right on time to preserve us. No amount of human efforts can be as effective as God's help.

Going to a Bible school fills a spiritual void, but it is not the most perfect place on earth. IBS, like similar institutions, was only as holy as those who attended it. Obviously, the main interest of the students was to study the Bible, and the faculty members were exemplary, but some students allowed themselves to be overcome by the flesh and were consequently expelled from the Seminary. By the grace of God, I successfully completed the programme and maintained my dignity throughout. Hence, upon my graduation, I received an award as the best-behaved student.

Finally, a recommendation was made by the **Church of God European Council** (consisting of all the national overseers in Europe) without my knowledge or consent that upon my graduation I should be given a church to pastor in England.

The Dean of IBS told me that my National Overseer at the time objected initially because I had "a bad reputation among the ministers in England."

This was surprising to me, but after the European Council meeting, my Overseer visited IBS and I asked him about his allegation. He said, "Well, I should have said something to you before, but do you remember that exhortation you gave at the National Youth Convention in 1966?" Before I could answer, he continued, "Some of the ministers were offended and complained to me about it."

At the said Youth Convention, I spoke about "Cannibalism in the Church". My text was taken from Galatians 5:15, "But if you bite and devour one another, *[watch out]* take heed that you be not consumed one of another." At the time, I thought that I had done well, but in hindsight I guess I didn't exercise a lot of wisdom. After all, I was still just a teenager!

However, I was not talking about NTCG ministers specifically; I was speaking in general terms when I said, "Unfortunately, this spirit of cannibalism has even entered the ministry." Oopsy-daisy! I knew that some feathers were ruffled, but no one said anything to me. I explained to the Dean of IBS what precipitated my Overseer's comment, and he advised me not to take any notice of some of the older folk in the Church, for they were the same in England as those in America. I got the gist of his conversation. We learn as we grow.

I could have been discouraged by the negative attitudes of some of the older ministers and discarded the ministry, but I have learned not to make permanent decisions based on temporary circumstances. The way we perceive things today may be quite different tomorrow. I didn't like the Council's decision to appoint me as pastor, but accepted it as God's will for my life and grew to love pastoring. The devil will fight anything that is orchestrated by God, but he is a liar and a loser.

In the Sexual Offences Act 1967, Parliament in the United Kingdom (citation 1967 c. 60) decriminalised homosexual acts in private between two men, both of whom had to have attained the age of twenty-one. The comments of Roy Jenkins, Home Secretary at the time, captured the government's attitude: "Those who suffer from this disability carry a great weight of shame all their lives."[1] In 1968, a new act enlarged and extended the R.R.B's powers and set up the Community Relations Commission (C.R.C) to help enforce the new laws.

On 30 January 1968, the **Jamaican** House of Representatives voted to decimalise the old **monetary system** by introducing the dollar, worth 10 shillings, to replace the **Jamaican** pound (£). The coins and banknotes went into circulation on 8 September 1969, and has since been the **currency** of **Jamaica**.

The dollar is often abbreviated "J$" or "JMD" – the "J" serving to distinguish it from other dollar-denominated currencies, and it is divided into 100 cents. (On Monday 15 February 1971, Sir Edward "Ted" Heath's Government formally decimalised the pound sterling and abolish the old British currency system. This outraged millions of ordinary Britons, but he saw it as a way of modernising Britain.)

Apollo 11 was the first spaceflight project that landed humans on the Moon. Three American astronauts, Commander Neil Armstrong along with Edwin "Buzz" Aldrin and Michael Collins launched from the Kennedy Space Centre on 16 July 1969 and the first two made the first historic moon landing in their lunar lander named Eagle on 20 July 1969, while Michael Collins piloted the Command Module in orbit. The primary mission objective was to land two men on the lunar surface and return them safely to Earth, thus realising a national goal set by President John F. Kennedy on 25 May 1961.[2] This was a giant leap for mankind, which Armstrong also called "a beginning of a new age."

Some critics say that Apollo 11 Moon landing was fake and that it was a multi-billion-dollar conspiracy hoax staged by NASA with the aid other organisations. They claimed that Apollo 11 did not have to technological capabilities to transmit high quality pictures directly to earth and asserted that the photo shoots shown on TV were edited publicity images released by NASA for the world to see.

There are many unanswered questions regarding the

Apollo programme and the associated Moon landing. However, I do not have the scientific skills or ability to debate this "Moon Hoax Theory." You do your own research and decide for yourself. I am simply giving an overview of what is generally accepted as the facts.

Commander Neil Armstrong and pilot Edwin Eugene Aldrin, also known as Buzz Aldrin stayed a total of about hours on the lunar surface. This spaceflight project was watched on TV by an estimated 530 million people. Given that this was the first time human beings had ever walked anywhere other than on their own planet, this event seen from a scientific perspective was applauded with a sense of great achievement and exhilaration with hope for the future, but the religious community responded in a totally different way. Here the event was met with fear, criticism, scepticism, and often condemnation.

Many Christians felt that homo sapiens (mankind) had gone too far, "flying into God's face" and were invaders of His sacred domain – the heavens. They said that if God wanted us on the moon He would have put us there. As a young believer, I was not sure what to believe, so I just looked on with some degree of trepidation. Some had predicted that when Apollo 11 landed on the moon, it would be the fulfilment of Joel's prophecy, "The sun shall turn into darkness and the moon into blood..." (See Joel 2:31.)

Others felt that the advancement of technology violates God's plan for mankind; the heavens are His throne and humans were put on our planet Earth for a certain time and purpose. On the same topic, someone wrote: "We as humans do not have the right to play God in such a manner. I don't believe in altering God's plan; You are messing with God's work and his plan for you."

Even more intriguing was the fact that Neil Armstrong (5 August 1930–25 August 2012), the man who spearheaded the successful landing of Apollo 11 spacecraft was a Christian. He was president of Charlie Duke Enterprise and an organisation called Duke Ministry for Christ.[3]

Aylesbury Church 1969–1980

In July 1969, I returned to England and was appointed to the pastorate of an emerging branch of the New Testament Church of God (NTCG) in Aylesbury, Buckinghamshire, where I served simultaneously as *District Youth and Christian Education Director* for the Reading District, for the eleven ensuing years. At this time, I was living at 315 North Circular Road, Neasden, London NW10.

On 14 August 1969, I wrote to the Church Secretary, brother Graham, and advised him of my intention to visit the Church in my new capacity on 23 August and to stay overnight to preach for them on Sunday morning 24 August 1969. This was prior to assuming my official position on 1 September 1969, as I needed to meet the people I was going to work with, and familiarise myself with the surroundings.

I also asked brother Graham if there was anyone available to meet me at the railway station. I travelled by train to this beautiful country town for the first time, and was met by a man who didn't know me and whom I didn't know. By some supernatural intervention our eyes connected and he asked me, "Are you the new Pastor for Aylesbury?" I said, "Yes." He smiled and introduced himself as brother Brown.

A little later, I learned that the Church which had only 4.5 members met at his home. The half member female who had as it were one foot in the Church and the other out. I had only a diploma in theology, but no ministerial credential. Nobody inducted me into the pastorate; I just went there and did as I was told – pastored the Church. As the numbers began to increase, we relocated to **St John Ambulance Scout Hall** on Walton Road. St John Ambulance is a leading first aid charity in the United Kingdom.

Being a young graduate without any employment, I had no money for my personal use. The National Office promised to give me an allowance of £30 a month, but did not send me any money for about six weeks, at which point the first payment came. By this time, I was employed in a printing company named *Hazel Watson and Viney*, on the Tring Road.

The dispatch for the firm was located straight across the road from my residence, and it was very convenient for me to get to and from work. The company's hooter sometimes woke me up at 7.30 am when the morning shift began. The company was a growing organisation with good prospects, and I could live a comfortable life on the wage. It was the highest pay I had ever earned.

I wrote to the National Office and thanked them for their generosity, but informed them that I had had to get myself a job in order to survive. They replied saying that I should return the money. I didn't, and all assistance from our headquarters ceased. They did not help financially with the purchasing or the maintenance of a minibus, which we bought for the Sunday school or with the rent for the scout hall. No one even said, "How are you getting on?" I was left to swim or drown, a sort of fight or flight situation. My wife named the minibus Lexie based on the first three letters of the registration number LXE 888E.

Aylesbury Church Minibus

I couldn't believe the treatment, and I felt a mixture of frustration, disappointment and indignation. Having no support from the Church's headquarters, I had to pay all this money from my pocket with the help of a couple more brethren, but as a good soldier of the cross I carried on faithfully. I didn't bargain on that; it was totally unexpected, and I dared not ask for anymore help from the powers that be.

What this experience taught me is that things will not always go your way. You cannot control the eventualities of life, but you can learn how not to react, and how to respond positively to them. I was doing the LORD'S work, and I trusted my superiors with the utmost confidence, but having faced disappointment at the highest level of the Church for the first time reality hit home: all men are fallible. Some things we enjoy, but other things we endure and keep on smiling. So: your success is not determined by how others treat you, but how you treat them, and how you respond to the circumstances of life. From time to time, you'll face setbacks. Welcome, you are not on your own; that's life. Take a look at yourself first, and then you'll look at others differently.

Happy is the man or woman who faces their own faults in the mirror and be willing to make changes, but pity that person who covers their mirror with a white sheet. Respond to your challenges holistically, and never descend to the level where you harbour ill-will or hold a grudge against anyone. Live above that!

My Marriage 1970

At some time or another, most young people ask questions like, "Who should I marry?" "What will marriage be like?" or "Am I ready for marriage?" Believing that this was God's plan and timing for my life, I was already besotted by the voluptuous, exquisite qualities of the charming Maxine Ann Janet Brown, a shining Star and National Queen from the NTCG in Leicester, and we were becoming keenly acquainted with each other.

She had recently won the *National Singing Contest*. Many doors were being opened to her, and it occurred to me that I might open another, ensuring at the same time that my profound attraction to her was unobtrusive. It did not become too obvious, too quickly and we gave no one any cause to be suspicious of us.

It was in the summer of 1969 that Maxine and I had met at the National Convention in the Grandby Halls – an exhibition and sports arena in Leicester. At that time, she was only seventeen years of age and was not thinking about marriage, and I had never had a girlfriend before. Providentially, my Bible school tutors Rev. and Mrs Parnel Coward had recently visited her local Church in Melbourne Road, Leicester. She was asked by her Pastor, Rev. Enos Gordon, to sing two songs during the Sunday morning and evening services – a divine setup.

After the morning service, sister Coward asked her if she knew a young British man at the Bible school in Switzerland called Barrington Burrell. Of course, she didn't know me so sister Coward promised to introduce us at the July National Convention: "I believe he would make you a wonderful husband and you would make him a wonderful wife," she said.

Maxine later confessed, "I was very anxious to meet brother Barry" as I was affectionately called by the Cowards, who were in the UK primarily to attend the National Youth Convention in April when providentially Maxine was crowned queen. Upon their return to Switzerland they reported to me about this charming young lady that they had met in the UK.

At the National Convention in July 1969, during the mission service on the Sunday afternoon, Maxine sang to the best of her ability, "It's Worth it all to be His Child", and everyone was tremendously blessed. There were over 7,000 delegates in the auditorium, but she couldn't miss one conspicuous young man sitting on the front row. I was immaculately dressed – wearing a black suit, bright white shirt, black bow tie, shiny shoes and had my hair well groomed. I showed no emotions and my facial expression appeared very serious. All that I needed to complete my attire was an ostentatious (or a fancy) robe and a wig on, but my searching eyes were animated as I looked at her intently. I saw what I wanted and she perceived love in my eyes. I do not think it would be boastful to say that "Maxine was somehow fascinated by my decorum and charm."

The afternoon session terminated and with her heart beating like a dove's she hurriedly left the stage and proceeded to make a quick exit out of the auditorium, but I was on the ball. I approached her and we started to converse as we walked along towards the exit. The interesting thing was that I knew who Maxine was but she had no idea who I was and she was too shy to ask my name.

This was quick thinking on my part and her mystery was soon to be unfolded. We had already exchanged particulars and agreed to start corresponding with each other when Rev. and Mrs Coward appeared and sister Coward, with the appropriate gesticulation said, "Oh you've met – brother Barry; sister Maxine: sister Maxine, brother Barry." I just gave a radiant smile, but Maxine exclaimed, "Oh no!" She had been pleasantly surprised. It all seemed unbelievable. "Cinderella" had actually met her real-life Prince Charming for the first time without realising.

She said, "For the rest of the convention I walked on air." Thereafter, I could spot Maxine wherever she sat throughout the convention, despite the large congregation. I also noted how she conducted herself and participated in worship during the sessions. The characteristics I observed indicated to me, to a great extent, the kind of wife she was likely to be in the future.

Having been working in her first employment as a Junior Clerk for *Steels and Busks Ltd., Engineering Services, Leicester*, Maxine was a paragon of beauty. She had always conducted herself circumspectly and in a lady-like manner. Within a short time, the relationship between us progressed rapidly into some kind of romantic courtship and we started dating, with a clear line of demarcation between fantasy and reality.

I was not looking for casual sex, that would have been too easy to come by; I needed a wife. The Bible says, "He who finds a wife finds a good thing, and obtains favor from the

Lord" (Proverbs 18:22, NJKV). A wife is for life, not just for Christmas. Women were plentiful, but wives were scanty, and finding the "right" person involved cooperation with God. Six months after our initial meeting, I proposed marriage. Once I had decided that Maxine was the chosen one, I followed the etiquette of the day and went to ask her father for her hand in marriage.

This tradition has rapidly faded away today, but it tells your father-in-law to be that you are a true gentleman with genuine intentions and that you respect your girlfriend's parents. I felt good that at least in my own mind I had done the right thing, and it was true that her family loved me, but nevertheless the bombshell finally dropped: her Pastor was unhappy that I did not seek his permission and this rocked the boat."

I was new to this and did not know that I had to obtain the Pastor's consent as well. Therefore, I asked my Pastor to intervene in the situation and, of course, he was the right person to sort it out. We had no formal engagement celebration and I did not give Maxine an engagement ring as this was against our Church tradition. Now that our parents and pastors knew our intentions and had given us their blessing, we could get on with the business of building our relationship towards the next level – matrimony.

For us, though, dating consisted of phoning each other every other day, sandwiching a letter in between and dreaming of the rest. I have kept all our love letters – they are stashed away for posterity in a secret location, and may be published later. But before you judge us for our innocence, let me point out that the lack of intimate engagements – going out for meals, holding hands, walking through the parks etc., and the distance between us did not lessen our closeness or the love we felt for each other.

It is true that "absence makes the heart grow fonder," particularly when it comes to romantic relationships, but "out of sight" is not always "out of mind." Of course, one would not have wished to compromise the high biblical standards established by the Church for many years, and to some extent, this kind of precaution was necessary because it helped to keep us from falling into the devil's snare trap and to live a life above reproach. From this perspective, "It's better safe than sorry." A risk may not only expose you to physical danger, but could jeopardise your integrity and godly reputation.

Unbeknown to me, a female pastor had planned for me to marry her daughter, but never told me until after my engagement was announced in my local Church. The news of my proposed marriage aroused a positive kind of excitement from those who were happy for us, but a negative kind from this disappointed pastor who said that I was "the only man she wanted to marry her daughter," and from other girls who were waiting with patient expectations. This was understandable because in those days, men usually chased women, but today the opposite is often the case.

Premarital counselling was almost unheard of. We were only told the basic things like "You must love each other deeply; love covers a multitude of sins." Well, of course I didn't know we were guilty of so many sins, but the impression given was that if you loved one another nothing would go wrong, or that love would solve all your problems. That is as far from the truth as the east is from the west. Love is one of the foundation stones for marriage, but not the be-all and end-all of marriage.

I was also advised that I should treat my wife to a restaurant dinner every so often, and always remember her birthdays and our wedding anniversaries, if I didn't want to sleep in the dog house. Historically, these things have been known to have a great deal of importance, especially to women. They are gestures that undoubtedly would have delighted one's wife, but you would have thought that every mature and wise man would be consciously aware of these obligations.

From my early teens, I dreamed of getting married to a special kind of a girl and having children. I even thought of some possible names for the children and how my son would look like me. This dream materialised and became a reality when I met and married Maxine. We knew that marriage was not a one-day event; that it is a journey of life and this was the beginning of our maiden voyage as husband and wife.

Getting married was one thing, but staying together was quite another matter. So it made sense preparing for marriage; it's like taking preventative medicine. There were many decisions that had to be made leading up to the wedding, but taking Christ on board was paramount. It was a matter of getting our priorities right. Too many young people put "the cart before the horse" and get their lives mixed up and "messed up." The Bible teaches that God should come first. God is the supreme priority, and if we give Him first place in our lives, we cannot go wrong.

From the outset, we wanted God to bless our marriage and to be an integral part of our lives, but we were conscious that God does not bless anything that conflicts with His Word. We were very God-fearing and would not dare do anything to reproach Christ or His Church. Our lives had to be pure and holy.

We never went out together on our own, and our first kiss was momentous and brief, at the marriage altar. As soon as the minister said, "I now pronounce you husband and wife," he added, "You may now kiss the bride." My throbbing heart missed a beat or two, and our trembling lips connected for a fleeting moment.

We know that the Bible condemns sex before marriage, but what about expressing other forms of physical affection before marriage? Some young people have challenged me that "there is nothing wrong with kissing before marriage, especially if you intend to marry the individual." Is that really correct?

There are over 150 different types of kisses, which have various meanings. It is beyond the scope of this book to attempt to describe the different kinds of kissing, but which of these kinds of kisses is okay before marriage? If you suck on an ice cube long enough, it will melt. More importantly, how far can you go before sinning?

In a romantic relationship, it all starts with a physical contact – touching, holding, hugging, cuddling, caressing and kissing. Nowadays, they call it petting. In this context, kissing is not an end in itself; it's a means to an end, and is therefore best avoided by Christians until marriage. We were very careful not to do anything that could damage our relationship with God.

On Saturday 4 July 1970, approximately nine months after we first met, Maxine and I married at the *NTCG Melbourne Road, Leicester*. Pastor Enos Gordon officiated, and because the Church was against men wearing rings I never received my wedding band until twenty-five years later when the ecclesiastical teachings were less rigid and we renewed our wedding vows at the NTCG Aldershot.

At the time of our marriage, I was only twenty-two years of age, my wife was nineteen and we were both innocent virgins, as the wedding photos indicate. Our wedding photos were captured in black and white (B&W). Photos were taken in B&W up until the 1930s and more often up into the 1960s. Thereafter, B&W photos were history and colour shoots are perceived contemporary, but people have had options and the pros and cons for one or the other became debatable. Colour photos seem more attractive, but it is believed that B&W images have more durability and can last hundreds of years. On 29 July 1981, some selected photos of Prince Charles and Lady Diana's wedding were taken in B&W and others in colour.

Choosing who to marry was one of my most important decisions, but perhaps the most memorable day of my life was my wedding day. It was such a wonderful, amazing and unforgettable day for both us – our big day indeed! Furthermore, it was the day when our dream of spending eternity together started budding.

The main wedding cake had four tiers and four side cakes, impressively designed and created to complement the occasion, with intricate detailed decoration and delicate royal icing, giving it an elegant appearance. Not only did it look amazing but the taste was finger-licking good and to the satisfaction of one and all.

The occasion of our marriage itself was spectacular with a dramatic wedding ceremonial entrance. We had 27 bridesmaids and escorts or groom's men. Maxine looked absolutely stunning, but more striking than any other feature of her wedding dress was the long magnificent fairy tale-like two-piece train (joined at the top), which extended ten feet long – and looked like a paradise Doctor Bird's tail, and of course, the Christian moderation in the way she dressed did not go unnoticed.

She knew that elegance or attractiveness was not determined by how much of her body she exposed (to give everyone a free show), but by being a true witness for Christ and maintaining the biblical standard of modesty. Furthermore, God intended that certain parts of a woman's body should remain a mystery to the world, and a revelation to her husband on the wedding night.

Someone aptly said, "Everything that God has made valuable in this world is deeply covered" and can hardly be seen, discovered or accessed. For example, gold, diamonds and precious stones are covered in the depths of the earth, and unearthed only by an intensive exploration; not located uncovered on the surface by a loiterer. So, the female's body is an irreplaceable gift from God, more valuable than all the fine minerals of the earth. It is right, therefore, that she should be well covered up and protected until her treasure is discovered by a well-balanced male explorer of God's choice, not by an arrogant exploiter with selfish motives, who brings nothing to the table.

We were very widely known and respected young people from two well-established churches. I was from Willesden and Maxine from Leicester. In those days we didn't use wedding invitations. We simply announced the occasion at church and anyone who wished to attend came along and some brought their friends too.

Over 500 guests attended our wedding, but there was more than enough food for everyone. They were there to celebrate the occasion with us, and everyone enjoyed themselves. After the informal wedding reception, we travelled 72.5 miles (or 116.6774 kilometres) to set up our matrimonial home in the Royal County of Buckinghamshire.

I was living in an immaculate and spacious one-bedroomed accommodation; no female could have kept it any better. I didn't have much money, but I grew up having pride in the way I dressed and how I kept my living quarters. I taught myself to wash, cook, and sew my clothes because I felt that a man should be able to look after himself as well as a woman can. On our first morning together as husband and wife, we tried to cook our traditional rice and peas for dinner, but that was a disaster, to say the least. The red kidney beans incinerated. Our love too was on fire – no wonder the beans burnt up. We nearly had to call the Hampshire Fire Brigade.

The lyrics of an English nursery rhyme, "Jack Sprat could eat no fat; his wife could eat no lean. And so, between them both, you see, they licked the platter clean," do not fully represent us. The problem Jack Sprat and his wife had was incompatibility, but they still complemented each other. My wife and I have some degree of compatibility, even though we are different. It is said that "variety is the spice of life," but it's not always true. Incompatibility can lead to marital conflicts if it is not managed.

We have had to do what many married couples have failed to do, make adjustments. Marriage is not so much about compatibility as it is about making adjustments to be the ideal spouse you anticipate in each other. So, we have spent over forty-six years together still learning to make adjustments. This is not a seven-year itch; it's a lifetime process. If you are experiencing marital struggles, please note: God isn't finished with us yet, and He isn't finished with you, either.

Our Honeymoon at Trafalgar Square, London, 1970

On 5 July, the day after we got married, I executed my normal Sunday duties, and we went on our honeymoon on Monday 6 July 1970. Since my wife did not know the City of London, I took her to Buckingham Palace and to see the pigeons at Trafalgar Square. I had promised to take her to Switzerland sometime in the future, but that trip never materialised. Mom cooked and took care of us during the honeymoon. We had ackee and salt fish, and ox liver with green bananas for breakfast. Maxine didn't like it at first, but it wasn't long before she got used to it.

My mother had always claimed to have had the two best sons in the world and the best daughter-in-law. Mom loved and respected Maxine so much that she always called her Sister Max and spoke favourably of her. To Mom, Maxine was the world's number one gospel singer and she was always delighted to hear her sing.

Right up until Mom's declining years, if she heard any great female singer on gospel cassettes (she never knew DVD's) she would have always been convinced that it was Sister Max and would have been very happy. So I recorded Maxine's singing on my mobile phone to play for Mom on my regular visits. Her first question would often have been, "Where is Sister Max?"

I was "daddy" to my wife and Church members before I became a daddy to my children. Three weeks after we got married, my wife and I went to a wedding and someone asked if her daddy had had anything to eat yet. I suppose this was due to the style of glasses I wore, which made me look much older. And if I may say so quite modestly, I was very mature for my age.

Subsequently, two other young people of my wife's age or thereabouts accompanied us by train to a church function in our district, and we had to take a taxi from the train station to the venue. When we arrived there, the taxi driver said to them, "Daddy will pay," and I paid. By the time our first child came, my wife too had started calling me daddy, which is what I was, "for real" this time.

Life in the 1970s was tough. Even though it was a time of technological advancements bringing significant improvements to home life and social enterprise, the economy was unstable.

Although the average house price was under £3,000, many people lived in rented accommodation either because they couldn't afford the mortgage or didn't know the potential value of their investment.

As a single man, I was renting a large, immaculate one bedroom accommodation at an **Edwardian**, bay fronted terraced house located in a popular area on Walton Road for £40 per month. The average weekly wage was around £32, and the average house price was £3,500 – £4,975. My mohair and tonic wedding suit cost £40, which was a gift from my mother. My wages were minimal, and I did not own a car.

Sometime after we got married we relocated to a nearby refurbished **Victorian** terrace **property** within easy reach of the town centre. This was our second rented accommodation in the neighbourhood. There was an unsaved young man living at the same house, and I felt that the LORD had positioned us to help him. We introduced ourselves informally and struck up a meaningful acquaintance.

One day while he was out, the police came looking for him. This was a matter of concern to us, and he had no idea what they wanted. He said that on his way from work the following day he would stop by the police station. I suggested that we go the same night, so I drove him to the police station and waited outside for him. After a long time waiting, he had not returned and I became perturbed. I went into the station and asked for him, but to my surprise the police said they had arrested him and that he would be going to Oxford prison in the morning for twenty-one days. They didn't even allow him a telephone call; his fate was sealed, and he was like a shocked bird in a cage.

I was a bit nervous, but I asked a few questions: why were they sending him to prison? An officer said that he had an outstanding fine of £21 for a motoring offence, and a warrant had been issued for his arrest. I said, what if I paid the fine? They advised that I would have to pay it the same night and in cash. I didn't have the money, so I drove to the Church secretary's home to borrow it from him or the Church. I went back and paid the fine. A police officer brought him from his cell with his head hanging down, and he was almost in tears. The officer said to him, "It pays to have a good friend."

This was a manifestation of God's love, grace and mercy, for he was engaged to be married in a couple of weeks. Had I not taken him to the police station that night, he would have gone there the following day and they might have sent him straight to prison, which meant that he would have been in prison on the date set for his wedding. The reality hit home and he was ready to listen to my message of salvation through Jesus Christ. He recognised the goodness of God and started going to Church with me.

He got married as previously planned, and I continued to witness to him and his wife. One day, he asked me a worldly-wise question and intimated that if I could answer it he would accept Christ. He said, "Adam and Eve had two sons, Cain and Abel, and Cain killed Abel. So, where did Cain's wife come from?" This question is probably older than all of us, and while the Bible does not state specifically who, when or where Cain married, it gives us a clear indication who his wife was.

According to Scripture, Adam and Eve's family consisted of three named sons, Cain, Abel and Seth, plus other sons and daughters. (See Genesis 4:25–26; 5:3–4.) At that time, there was no legal restriction against marrying one's biological brother or sister. Therefore, it seems logical to suggest that Cain's wife was his sister or his niece or a close relative. Whatever the case, in the beginning brothers would have had to marry sisters for the population to increase and to have succeeding generations. For instance, we know that Abraham married his half-sister Sarah. (See Genesis 20:12.)

This kind of marital relationship was strictly prohibited under the Law of Moses (Deuteronomy 27:22), which make Abraham's marriage seemed like a contradiction of God's Word, but God actually approved it. We need to bear in mind that the Mosaic Law was not given until around 1440 BC, some 2,500 years after the creation and more than 400 years after Abraham's marriage, and the Law couldn't have been enforced retrospectively.

In 1973, three years after our marriage, my wife and I were expecting our first child, Lorna Mae. The landlord decided to board up our only bedroom window, and turn off the gas so that we couldn't cook in his kitchen. We were unable to get much fresh air in the bedroom, and the light of day merely penetrated weakly through the Victorian sliding sash windows at the back. There was no problem with our rent and the landlord had not given us notice to quit. He felt the gas and electricity were costing too much money, and the tenants had to be blamed. He was a very miserable man, with an extremely grumpy personality.

The young couple were experiencing similar problems with the landlord, and faced the same predicament. We were the only tenants in the house. My wife and I invited them into our bedroom and cooked for them on our paraffin heater while playing gospel music on our **Blue Spot Radio Gramophone.**

I remember us playing one of the tracks on the Gospel Ayre's Album, "Life can be beautiful, if you live for Him." I taught the young man the whole Book of Revelation verse by verse, and it put the fear of God in him. He became very convicted, and both he and his wife received Jesus Christ and became active members in the Church. Later, the landlord too became a Christian, but attended another church.

Unfortunately, we had a devastating experience in 1975 when my wife sadly miscarried our second child (a son) at seven months. A part of us died, and this was an extremely painful time, but nevertheless something we had to pull through together. We were grateful for the amazing support from our families and friends, and the LORD strengthened us during the healing process. In November 1976, our second son Robert Charles came along and rekindled the spark in us.

Robert at 3 Weeks

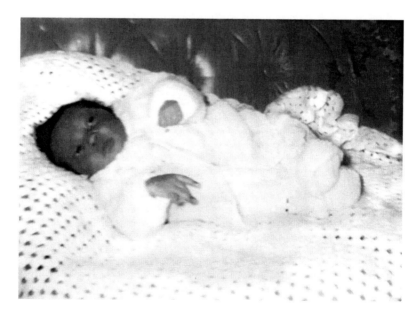

Our children were born at the **Royal Buckinghamshire Hospital,** Buckingham Road, Aylesbury, and so our new roles as parents and as conceptualised in western society were shaped for us. We had to learn fatherhood and motherhood and how to cope with some sleep-deprivation, but we enjoyed caring for our children. Fortunately, we didn't have the relationship problems that many new parents experience after a baby is born and the excitement wears off.

We welcomed each new baby and adjusted to the new roles of changing diapers and feeding, but did not feel overwhelmed by parenthood or our pastoral duties. We never took a baby bottle to Church for any of our children except when we were travelling out of town. We developed a routine whereby they were fed before we left home and when we returned after the service.

From about two weeks old, they started travelling on mission with us across the country in the cold, foggy and snowy winters and in the good summer weather. Yet, if there is such a thing as perfect health, they had it. I do not understand why parents blame their children for not doing what they should do. This model of behaviour is typical of many parents, and it is so unfair on the little ones. Scripture says, "Children are a heritage from the LORD" (Psalm 127: 3, NKJV), not a burden or hindrance to their parents.

When our children became toddlers at about 3 to 4 years of age, they had to sit on a chair in the front row at Church, and behave themselves throughout the service because their mother was playing the piano and dad was involved in either taking the service or preaching. We used our eyes and facial expressions to communicate with them, and make no mistake about it, they understood.

Robert was very afraid of people "getting in the Spirit." If he was sitting beside his mother, as soon as she raised her hand in praise to the LORD he pulled it down fast and started crying. He could always sense that move of the Spirit. Paradoxically, he has an apostolic calling on his life; and I just pray that he will walk in it and fulfil his purpose.

One Sunday, I took my family to a local Church of England church where I was invited to be their guest speaker. The service was being recorded. My wife was singing and playing the piano, with the Aylesbury Gospel Choir as her backing vocals. They sang and the atmosphere changed as the presence of God came into the place.

It didn't take long for Robert to sense that move of God, and he bolted from his seat straight across the platform to his mother and knocked over their recording equipment in the process. This was so embarrassing for us, but it didn't rob us of the wonderful service we had. The people were excited about inviting us back soon. Thank God!

As a family man, I have always been especially family-oriented, but I am a principled person. I taught my children to do what is right because I will not compromise with the truth to please anyone. For me, "wrong is wrong" and "right is right" regardless of who you are. I will always disapprove wrong doings and only rubber stamp what God has sanctioned.

I know how hard it is to communicate to your beloved wife that you cannot take her side simply because you are her husband, but only when she is in the right. Standing up for what is right is not always easy, but it's the right thing to do. Therefore, I have impressed upon my family the importance of staying on the side of what is right. We must cherish the values that have underpinned our civilised culture and human dignity, especially Christian virtues which have been and are fundamental to our faith in God.

I will not resort to violence, but if my family's rights are infringed then I will defend them fully, within a proper and biblical context. A man is the head of his family unit, and I believe it is not only natural, but right for him to protect his family and property. Self-preservation or the protection of a man's family is an instinctive tendency to preserve one's self or one's family from harm or danger. We must not relinquish the biblical roles of a husband as spiritual leader, provider and protector of his family for God is counting on us.

Furthermore, our children grew up in a normal way, but they had to follow the discipline of the home, not the influences or conventions of society. My principles and standards could not be wilfully compromised. They had to be selective in the kind of music to which they listened, the calibre of friends they had and what kind of Sunday activities they engaged in. Any deviation from this was usually without my knowledge or in my absence.

For me, disciplining meant educating or correcting. If the children did wrong, I would speak to them up to three or even four times about it before resorting to any sort of punishment, and if ever I flogged them I felt it was well deserved. My Mom used to tell me, "If you can't hear, you must feel."

When Robert was a teenager, one day he came home wearing clip-on earrings. I said to him, "No, not in this house, please go and take them off" and that settled the matter. Men must be real men, and vice versa. My daughter would not be allowed to come near our house at any time with her skirt 6–8 inches (15.24–20.32 centimetres) above her knees – a common practice nowadays, but one that would not be tolerated by me. As long as my children lived in my house, under my care, they had to follow my rules, and that was non-negotiable.

This level of discipline transcended my immediate family to include my extended family and beyond. Not even my father- in-law was allowed to smoke in my home, no unmarried couples were permitted to sleep together and no one could use foul or profane language. I was not trying to be a puritan, but I believe if we are chosen by God to do His work everything that we have jurisdiction over should be sanctified, including our home. The Bible teaches that the position (or office) of a bishop must be above reproach, and "he desires a good work" (1 Timothy 3:1, NKJV).

Hence, "A **bishop** then **must** be blameless, the **husband of one wife**, temperate, sober-minded, of good behaviour, hospitable, able to teach; not given to wine, not violent, not greedy for money, but gentle, not quarrelsome, not covetous; one who **rules his own house well**, having his children in submission with all reverence, for if a man does not know how to rule his own house, how will he take care of the Church of God?" (1 Timothy 3:2–5, NKJV.)

In one of the congregations I pastored, a teenage girl came to church one Sunday morning wearing a t-shirt with the words, "If you want it, you can get it," written across the front and back. I thought, "What is she advertising?" Maybe I am a little old fashioned, but I didn't consider that kind of dress appropriate and I spoke to her mother about it. Well, some guy did "get it" because not long after that she became pregnant and her studies curtailed. Juvenile delinquency is often the result of parental delinquency.

A "Christian mother" took her teenage son to me for counselling. I asked the boy why he was giving his mother so much trouble, but I was totally unprepared for the answer he gave me. To my amazement he said, "She won't stop swearing at me." In shock, I said to his mother, "You don't swear, do you?" She replied, "He makes me swear." I almost fell off my chair. She automatically disqualified herself from true motherhood, and it's no wonder her son was out of control.

Parents are responsible for the proper training and discipline of their children while they are still under their charge. God holds them accountable, but when the children are grown up and leave home they are responsible for their own actions – the consequences of which they must bear.

Hilarious Moments

My wife was very posh and I was merely a country boy. I think the Lord anointed me to humble her pride. Whenever we went to a restaurant she could hardly bring herself to open her mouth to eat the food and always had to speak in a whisper as if we were talking secrets. So I always finished eating my food first and had to sit there quite a while watching her chewing her food as if she would never finish. It's just as well we didn't have to take public transportation. In retrospect, I can see that it was simply the etiquette she had practiced.

On one occasion when we went to a very nice Greek restaurant to celebrate a wedding anniversary, and after having enjoyed a sumptuous meal, I looked at my wife searchingly. She was all set for some deep expression of love and may be a romantic gesture, but instead I asked her insensitively if she had seen my big screw-driver. She almost collapsed with a mystifying expression on her face and I erupted in laughter. I found it really humorous, but women are wired differently to men and what may be funny to us may be unamusing to them. Sometimes, knowledge comes through experience and maturity.

Another unforgettable moment was when I took her to the hospital for an appointment and we were in the waiting area speaking, but as usual she felt I was speaking too loudly and found it embarrassing. She wanted me to speak quietly so that no one could overhear what I was saying. That would have been very unlike me, so I stopped talking altogether and started singing, "There's wonder-working power in the blood," using my keys on my knees as a tambourine. She obviously was not amused, even though I was singing about Jesus.

If I ever started singing in the car when my family was present, our children would wind up the windows and maybe get down on the floor. On one occasion, I was walking through the shopping mall with my family when I felt inspired to sing. As I started singing, they momentarily dispersed and abandon me. I am glad Jesus never treated me like that. He still owned me despite my amateur and possibly unconventional singing habits.

We went to a bakery in Luton, Bedfordshire to buy some Jamaican patties. My wife was well-spoken and polished as per usual. I provocatively said to the lady serving at the counter, "How much fi de patty dem?" This means, "How much for the patties?" My wife's countenance fell and she immediately walked out of the shop and went home embarrassed. Her best husband had showed her up again. I don't believe the lady in the shop ever forgot us. I think we could have staged a good performance – featuring Maxine and Barrington Stand-up Comedy Show.

The Infant Church

106

The early Church work was quite strenuous and monotonous at times. Every Sunday morning, I swept up the cigarette butts, arranged the chairs, drove the Church's mini-bus to pick up people for the service, taught the Sunday school, preached, and then took the attendees back home. In the evening, I picked them up again, and preached the evening's sermon before taking them home. This is what life is often like when you have a small congregation, and there's no scope for delegation. You truly become "all things to all people," although I mean that in a different sense to the Apostle Paul.

Nevertheless, Aylesbury was the Genesis of our ministry – the place of new beginnings, and when one is starting anything, it is not always easy. "Uneasy lies the head that wears the crown." Shakespeare's King Henry IV used this idiom to express how tough his duty of kingship was and how difficult it was to take such a serious responsibility.[4]

As the Church continued to develop, we moved into *Walton Parish Hall*, Walton Street, where we stayed for the ensuing eight or nine years. Memories of the great things God did there will never be forgotten.

In 1973, my wife started a community choir among the young people as a means of evangelism and called it the *Aylesbury Gospel Choir*. They were invited to sing at a district convention convened locally. By the end of the convention most of them got saved, including three teenagers from the Derby family; Glenda, Diana and Leon, who became instrumental in what God was about to do.

(L to R) Dianna, Leon and Glenda

Glenda invited her mother to Church, but her mother declined saying that she did not "want to hear her Pastor Burrell preach or his wife sing because they are hypocrites." Bear in mind that she didn't know us! Furthermore, she said that Glenda would not be able to wear her jeans anymore and she would become an old bag. I said to Glenda, "We don't have old bags in the Church; look at my wife, does she look like an old bag to you?" She said, "No."

Leading up to their water baptism, I went to meet Mrs Derby for the first time. She was very courteous and cordial to me. She had no objection to her daughters' and son's baptism, and I invited her to the baptism which she gladly accepted. I preached and baptized the candidates myself. It was the first baptismal service that I conducted, but it was one never to be forgotten for more reasons than one. News of the service spread throughout the entire community, and many people were heavily convicted by the Holy Spirit.

This was good for the Church, but the baptism occurred at a historic period of political and financial unrest. Sir Edward Heath was Prime Minister in the 1970s when Britain plunged into the Three-Day Week crisis. This was one of several measures introduced by the Conservative Government to conserve electricity, the generation of which was severely restricted owing to industrial action by coal miners. (At times, it was difficult to know who govern Britain, the unions or the Government.)

The effect was that from 1 January until 7 March 1974 commercial users of electricity were limited to three specified consecutive days' consumption each week and prohibited from working longer hours on those days. The Government imposed a heating limit of 63°F (17C) in office and commercial premises and a reduction in street lighting, and speed to 50mph. The Prime Minister asked consumers on TV, "to cut down to the absolute minimum use of electricity in your homes." There were periodic power cuts and black-outs and television shutdown at 10.30pm except at Christmas. The only poem I have ever written was about "Britain's Three-Day Week."

On the eve of the baptism, the weather was bitterly cold with ice on the ground. The Baptist Church was cold and the electricity low. This meant that the chill was barely taken off the water and the baptism was the coldest I have ever experienced. As I went down into the pool I "froze" and became numb. "Can I go through with this?" I pondered. Shivering, I embraced myself and as the candidates prepared to enter the pool I whispered to them that the water was very cold.

I immersed the candidates quickly and got out of the water. A friend of mine by the name of John Kirby was very curious about the speed of the baptism and went to check the temperature of the water, which confirmed his suspicion. After I changed my clothes, I was informed that two or three more people wanted to be baptized. From a spiritual perspective, this was good news, but bad for me. I had to put on the cold, wet clothes and go back into the freezing pool, but it had no negative effect on me, thank God.

The next day, I went back to see Mrs Derby and she was overwhelmed by the baptismal service. She also liked my preaching. I invited her to the Sunday evening's service and offered to pick her up for Church. Again, she accepted my invitation, and that night she was wonderfully saved and filled with the Holy Spirit. She said excitedly, "What a shock! I never knew anything could go like this." She became an ardent member of the Church – on fire for God, and no one could say anything negative to her about her Pastor.

Race Relations Acts Amended

The Race Relations Act introduced by the Labour Government in 1976 when Roy Jenkins was Home Secretary was intended to replace and strengthen the Acts of 1965 and 1968. Further amendments have been made to the Act (1968). The police were specifically excluded from the provisions of the 1968 Act, on the grounds that they had their own disciplinary code. (Racism within the police force was not fully recognised until the 1990s after a black teenager Stephen Lawrence was murdered. The subsequent inquiry into the police's handling of the case found there was "institutional racism" within the Metropolitan Police.)

The shortcomings of the existing legislation were becoming increasingly evident by the early 1970s, and in 1976, a far tougher Race Relations Act was passed that made discrimination unlawful in employment, training, education, and the provision of goods and services. It extended discrimination to include victimisation, and replaced the Race Relations Board (R.R.B.) and the Community Relations Commission (C.R.C.) with the Commission for Racial Equality (C.R.E.), a stronger body with more powers to prosecute, with the intention of strengthening the Act.

Ministerial Certification Received

I pastored for approximately eight years without any ministerial credential, and in August 1977, after successfully passing the examination given by a duly constituted board of examiners, I received my Exhorter's Certificate, with the full rights and authority to preach and defend the gospel of Jesus Christ, to serve as evangelist and as pastor of a church, all of which I was already doing.

This is the first rank in the Church of God ministry. I do not mean to trivialise ministers' credentials, but it is important to note that they do not qualify you for ministry. They serve their purpose, but it's your ministry that makes room for you; not your certificates or academic qualifications. Scripture says, "Your gift will make room for you, it will bring you before great men" (Proverbs 18:16, NKJV). In other words, the gift you have for your vocation is the key to your success.

I was invited to teach on the "Second Coming of Jesus Christ" on a Friday evening at the NTCG in Aldershot, approximately sixty-five miles from my home in Aylesbury. At the time, I was working as a forklift truck driver for Hazel Watson and Viney printing company. One day, I had an accident at work; the big iron fork truck rammed my left foot against a wall, and I was taken to the local hospital. My ankle was severely sprained, swollen and painful. They wrapped a compressed bandage on my ankle, and advised me to avoid driving, and to rest the foot for a couple of weeks.

Knowing that the people in Aldershot were expecting me, as soon as I got home, I removed the bandage and forced my foot into a shoe. This was difficult and painful, but I took a couple of pain killers and started my journey to Aldershot. I had to use my right foot to press down the clutch of my car to change the gears. When I arrived near my destination the car broke down.

The Church was filled with people anxiously awaiting my arrival, and I was already late. The only consolation was that my wife had informed the Pastor that I was on my way. I started limping along and praying for healing because I was determined to make it. As I progressed in the right direction I began to gain strength in the leg, and by the time I reached the Church my ankle injury was completely healed. I spoke for about an hour and a half, and we had a great service. Again, Satan lost, and we had the victory.

The Great Aylesbury Revival 1979

The Church began to grow numerically and spiritually and I started to experience the power of God in a way I had not heard of before. The young people in particular were instrumental in this revival. They were very close to me, well-mannered and teachable, but most importantly they had a relationship with God.

The great revival started among the teenagers in March 1979. I always told them to call me whenever they needed me. At about 1.00am on a Saturday morning, one of the young people phoned and requested that I come to their prayer meeting at Sister Derby's home. I was very tired and had only just retired to bed, so I hesitated, but then I remembered that I had given them my word.

When I arrived at the house, the front door was opened wide; they were expecting me. Glenda, Dianna and Leon were in prayer, and the omnipotent hand of God was evidently upon them. I sat in their midst without saying anything, just observing what was happening. One of the girls spoke to the other and said, "Tell him." She then spoke in tongues and the other interpreted what she said. The instruction from the LORD was that I should get Sister Graham and a young man named Tony to the meeting.

Sister Graham was doing a night shift at the *Royal Buckingham Hospital*, and I went for her at work at about 2am. When she saw me, she thought something terrible had happened, but I assured her that everything was alright. I gave her the message from the LORD and she asked me, "What am I going to tell the *(night)* Sister?" I said, tell her that I have come for you. God worked in her favour and her boss consented.

We returned to the prayer meeting and I called and woke up Tony Brown to come along and join us. As he walked in, hands were laid on him and he was slain in the Spirit. There were more prophecies, including a word that Tony would receive the baptism with the Holy Spirit that same Saturday. The LORD also said that we should have a prayer meeting that evening and showed me how the chairs should be arranged under the platform at *Walton Parish Hall*, our usual place of worship.

Tony had already purchased his ticket for a concert in London the same day. We assured him that missing a concert and losing the cost of the ticket was nothing in comparison to what God was going to do for him. He obeyed the Word of the

LORD, and a few more people agreed to join us for the evening prayer meeting.

During the day, I went to London and the anointing was so strong I couldn't withhold my tears. Everywhere I went I was crying and God was speaking to me. My Aunt Ivy observed a difference in my countenance and asked, "Why are you so sad?" I replied, "I am not sad, God is going to do something great." She said, "If that's it, praise God!" That night we met for prayer as the LORD directed, and it was one of the most awesome prayer meetings I have ever attended. Indeed, God moved miraculously among the young people.

I noted some powerful things. A 13 to 14-year-old girl named Sandra was anointed to prophesy, but she resisted in fear. I observed that her jaws and teeth were virtually shaking and her physical frame vibrating, as with closed eyes she pointed to various individuals, named them and prophesied to them, even though some had come in late and she could not have been aware of their presence. Vivienne was very shy, but under the guidance of the Spirit she put her hand on Mark's stomach and prayed for him. That night, God miraculously healed him of a complaint of which none of us had prior knowledge.

Glenda was ministering to Tony, and he was slain by the Spirit. He was now on the floor and both Glenda and he had their eyes closed, travailing in the Spirit. Glenda said to Tony, "God is filling you with His Holy Spirit": then she said, "There's a cup in your hand, can you see it?" Tony nodded his head in the affirmative. She said, "Drink it, it's yours." Tony literally put his hand to his mouth as if he was drinking something.

Glenda put her right hand to her throat and said, "Yes, I can see it now, it's going down." She gently moved her hand gradually down to the bottom of her stomach as she repeated, "It's going down." Then she said, "It's coming up now, I can see it," and she slowly moved her hand upwards and as it reached her mouth, she said, "You've got it now, it's yours" and Tony began to speak in tongues. Glenda opened her eyes and checked her watch, and several of us also did the same; it was 11.58pm. God honoured His Word and there was a great time of rejoicing.

Bill was trembling as he exclaimed, "There's a man at the door watching us; he's dressed in white!" I calmly responded, "Be not afraid, He's the LORD." Amid all the glory and splendour, the Spirit said to me, "You can go home now, I will continue my work tomorrow." I related this to the group and spontaneously everyone was ready to go. I was due to preach in Reading the Sunday morning, but I phoned the Pastor and apologised. My presence was needed locally at that most crucial time.

We gathered at the usual time that morning for Church. The chairs were strategically arranged as directed by the LORD. Several people testified that as they came in and saw the seating arrangement they were blessed. The presence of God was so strong that the Sunday school teacher could not teach in the usual way.

The Holy Spirit took over the morning worship and there was no preaching – four people were baptized with the Holy Spirit. The service which was scheduled to finish at 1pm went on until after 4pm. The last person was saved and filled with the Spirit at about 3.55pm. She was in her early teens, and that morning she didn't want to attend Church, but her unsaved father insisted that she went.

The evening service was equally power-packed. Again God spoke through prophesies; more people received the baptism with the Holy Spirit and miraculous healings occurred, but there was no preaching, just praying. The service which was due to finish at 8pm continued until after midnight. God led us into a week of meetings. This meant booking the Walton Parish Hall for a week and although the young Church couldn't afford it, we obeyed God. The offering taken on one night was the exact amount we needed for the week's rent.

During the week of meetings, there was no preaching. After singing a few choruses, we read the Scripture which was taken from the same passage every night, and then I would lead the Church in prayer. As I prayed, it was just as if the heavens opened and showers of blessings fell. Miracles occurred every night and there was "noise abroad." Many who heard the good news said to me, "If we didn't know the kind of person you are, we would think you are all crazy."

We were not a very emotional Church, and I have never been a noisy person, except during my leisure time. What was taking place in the Church was a sovereign move of the amazing, indescribable and incomparable God. I'm not even sure that we understood it, but we submitted to the Holy Spirit, and God did the rest.

In one of the meetings, I had a vision of the LORD dressed in a purple robe with sandals on His feet walking gracefully down the aisle towards the altar. He carried something in His hand like a lit match with a glowing blue flame and He held it over the altar. The moment He did that, there was a sort of spiritual explosion and almost everyone at the altar was "slain" in the Spirit; some received miraculous healings.

One day while I was in my lounge at home, the LORD said to me, "You will be asked to preach at the district convention tonight." I subconsciously shouted "No!" A few hours later the telephone rang; it was my District Overseer who asked, "Can you please preach at the district convention?" Without thinking I said "No," then I remembered that the LORD had already forewarned me, so I agreed.

I prepared a three-point sermon to preach at the convention, but only reached the first point before the glory of God fell in the meeting. The District Overseer Rev. C. L. Hastings rushed to the altar and members of the congregation followed him. After the service, he shook my hand and said, "Brother, I believe now." Only then did I realise that he too had been having doubts about the great things God was doing in Aylesbury.

Most of the people who attended the prayer meetings were young people. One evening we were in a prayer meeting, and something spectacular happened. Sandra who was now about fifteen years of age began to manifest in the Spirit. I noted that with closed eyes she was tapping on a chair like someone using a typewriter.

I perceived in my spirit that she was trying to write something. I got some writing paper and put it on the chair and put a pen in her hand. She wrote awesome messages from the LORD to individuals in the meeting. When it was all done, I asked her to explain what had happened. She said that she had seen a screen with writing passing before her, and Jesus had told her to copy down what she was seeing.

A couple of the older folk couldn't flow with what God was doing and began to criticise the young people saying that they were not hearing from the LORD. The youngsters' enthusiasm abated and they began to sulk, and became withdrawn, refusing to prophesy again. I threatened to beat them if they didn't grow up and be more mature than that. I also counselled them not to take any notice of their critics, but to remain focused and always to obey God. The Holy Spirit continued to move mightily in the Church and Satan was all the more infuriated.

A Tragic Road Accident

This was the fifth deadly satanic attack on my life. My Datsun driven by Maxine, plunged horrifically into a ditch one Friday evening when I was giving her a driving lesson. As we negotiated a sharp bend, three times I said to her "Brake!" But nerves took over and her foot froze on the accelerator.

The vehicle collided with an oncoming van and leaped over the edge of the road. Fortunately, Maxine was unhurt apart from a couple of minor bruises, but my face was slightly injured, and I had a bad cut on my tongue and forehead. I felt as if my teeth had been knocked back into my head. While I was slowly drifting into another world as it were, I could hear the sirens of the ambulance and police from a distance, and I eventually saw the flashing blue lights emerging from concealment.

As my consciousness dwindled, I remember muttering to the devil, "You wait until my tongue gets better." In my semi-conscious state, I could vaguely hear the paramedics in the ambulance describing my condition to the hospital, but I still didn't know where I was or to which hospital I was going until I arrived there. Because everything happened locally, it wasn't long before members of the Church started rushing into the hospital one by one; then I remembered my prophecy to them about the accident.

Six days prior to the incident, I had prophesied it to the Church in a Sunday service, and had told them that they may hear of me being involved in an accident, but that they should not worry because I wouldn't die. After that I thought no more of it. Early in the morning on the day of the accident, God revealed it to me again in a vision, which I shared with my wife, but I still couldn't imagine it actually happening to me. I was like Peter and the other disciples, who saw Jesus walking towards them on the sea, but couldn't believe what they had seen. (See Matthew 14:22–33.)

I could hardly eat or drink for several days following the accident. When I tried to swallow, the food stuck in my throat, and I began to appreciate the real value of my tongue. One Sunday evening, I went to Church without being able to eat my dinner, and the District Overseer served Holy Communion. While worshipping, I remembered that I had not prayed for healing, so I did. The LORD healed my tongue, and that night I ate what Caribbean folk call 'hard food' and rice and peas. God came true for me yet another time and His mighty power prevailed, but to this day I still suffer a slight speech defect as a result of the accident and find it difficult to pronounce some words.

Bible Institute for Ministers

I am a people person; I love people. A vital part of my calling is to teach and mentor people for the ministry. My ministry is bigger than the confinement of a local church. Today, I am blessed with many sons and daughters globally, who are well-established in the ministry. It was during my tenure in Aylesbury that I started to recognise my mandate and make it real. I started teaching at local, district and national levels of the Church.

This gift led me to become involved in assisting Rev. Ben Cunningham to facilitate the *Bible Institute for Ministers and Lay Enrichment (BIME)* in Willesden, London. This meant that many of the NTCG ministers in the southern region were impacted by my teaching ministry.

One of my assignments in the BIME was to teach on Love, Sex and Marriage. Many men found the topic embarrassing and neither Ben nor I was particularly sympathetic towards them, but the women embraced it with open arms. They just wanted to hear more, and they requested that I should write a book on the subject. I knew this was a delicate and explosive topic, especially in the Church at that time, so I prayed and received God's approval.

I had never thought of writing a book before, so I decided to write a little booklet. The late Bishop Ira V. Brooks and Bishop Vernon Nelson discouraged that and advised me to write a proper book. Hence my book *Love, Sex and Marriage Volumes 1 & 2.* (The original version was typed by Vivienne Welsh, and published in July 1983 by Compeer Press Ltd., Birmingham.) All those whose lives have been enriched by these volumes can salute the BIME women, even those who have since passed away.

My Call into Full-time Ministry

The anointing of God was so strong on my life that it was difficult for me to even sleep at nights. Sometimes, I was up until the early hours of the morning travailing in the Spirit. I remember phoning a few ministers at unsociable hours – between 2 and 3am prophesying to them, but they all received the Word of the LORD gladly, and thanked me for being obedient to God.

At about 4am one morning when I was in a deep sleep, the LORD dwelt with me in the most unusual way. I heard Him speaking in my spirit and the words, "Get out of that factory, I need you in full-time ministry" came out of my mouth so loudly and forcibly that my wife heard them in her sleep. This was a shock to my system because I had never contemplated full- time ministry, and I was married with two children. I wondered where I would get money from to support them.

Nevertheless, I obeyed the LORD and stepped out in faith. At that time, I was working for an exhibition company, but I never resumed work. I called the foreman and apologised for any inconvenience that may be caused, but explained that I couldn't return to work because God had called me into full-time ministry. Owing to my constant witnessing at work, the unsaved foreman said, "You should have been doing that long time anyhow," and he gave me the name of a friend who was dying from cancer and asked me to pray for him.

Being fully persuaded about my decision, I phoned my National Overseer, the late Reverend Jeremiah McIntyre and told him that I was now in full-time ministry. After I explained the circumstances of my call, he said to me, "Only somebody as mad as you or I would do that." He further stated, "The local Church cannot pay you, partly because we didn't appoint you!"

That being said, God made the way for me when there was no way, and provided more money than I had had when I was working.

After I successfully passed the examination given by the duly constituted board of examiners for ministerial candidates, I was ordained (and consecrated) as a bishop in 1979. This is the third level and highest rank of the ministry in the Church of God. Pastors and others in spiritual oversight can appropriately be given the biblical designation of bishops, a title which implies hierarchy in the organisational structure. The ordained bishop has the full right and authority to:[5]

- Preach, publish, teach and defend the gospel of Jesus Christ.

- Serve as pastor and/or district overseer, or in other official capacities or appointments.

- Baptize converts.

- Receive believers into fellowship or church membership.

- Administer Holy Sacraments (ordinances).

- Solemnise rights of matrimony.

- Assist in ordination ceremonies of fellow ministers.

- Establish and organise churches

- Usethefollowingtitles whileholdingthesespecificpositions: State/Territorial Overseer (or international equivalent), Administrative Bishop, Executive Bishop, General Overseer or Presiding Bishop.

Miracles continued to follow my ministry everywhere, and news of this reached the National Office. Hence, my Overseer appointed me as the National Evangelist in 1980, and agreed to pay me a small salary. I was then the youngest ordained bishop in the NTCG (UK), and the youngest to occupy any national position in the Church.

The Liverpool "Nightmare" 1980–1981

I was posted to evangelise and pastor a small mission church in Liverpool, approximately 200 miles from my home and family in Aylesbury, while serving concurrently as National Evangelist, National Evangelism Board Member and on the National Youth and Christian Education Board.

We were meeting for worship in an ancient, derelict and haunted Anglican Church building near to the City of Liverpool. A light was left on permanently for the benefit of the falling angels that allegedly visited the Church from time to time. My colleague told me not to turn the light off, but I maintained that if the angels wanted light, they would have to provide their own. I was not prepared to waste electricity on any form of superstition, so I switched off the light and it never worked again.

I moved into the adjoining unfurnished two-bedroom parsonage, where I lived on my own in that desolate community. The National Evangelism Department gave me a bed, but I proactively used money raised in a special meeting at the Church to part-furnish the accommodation. One night I had a dream that demons came to my bedroom door and told me that they didn't like the colour of the paint I was using on the house.

I became righteously indignant and shouted "Get out!" so loudly that any passerby on the road could have heard. Another night, I woke up and my room stank of cigarette smoke. To convince myself that I was not still asleep I took up my pillow and smelt it and said, "If that's all you can do it's too bad" and went back to sleep. Sometimes God permits certain things to happen to us so that we may learn from our experiences. It is said that "Experience is a hard teacher, but a good one."

Corpse Found in the River Mersey

A young man in his early to mid-twenties approached me with a request for water baptism, which I declined on the grounds that he was not born again. He was very influential and had a number of young followers. They all met regularly to study the Bible and smoke marijuana (ganja). The leader told me that he wanted to be baptized, but I felt strongly that this was just a hallucination as a result of smoking ganja. Nevertheless, I tried to point him to Jesus Christ and gave him some spiritual guidance, which he did not follow."

One day, I observed that he was losing weight, and had a

fatherly talk with him. He explained to me that he often did not feel like eating. It seemed as though the marijuana was becoming a substitute for his food. He further stated that sometimes he "went out as a man and came back as a woman." I told him to put the brakes on because when this happens to any man he is too far gone. He said that he had heard the "voice of God" calling him to get baptized. That same weekend, he went and apparently "baptized" himself in the River Mersey, where his corpse was found immersed in the water. He had drowned.

Facing an Intruder

The parsonage was frequently visited by demons, and I repeatedly drove them away. There were 11 locks and bolts on 3 doors between the front door and my bedroom door. In addition, there were burglar bars on my bedroom window, and a hammer and a police type baton (or truncheon) under my bed. The hammer was to breakout the bars in case of an emergency, and the baton was my rod of correction for intruders.

One Sunday afternoon, whilst resting in bed with my Bible survey book beside me, and meditating on the evening's message, I heard quick footsteps coming up the stairs, closer and closer to my bedroom door. Then the door began to open very slowly as I watched quietly and anxiously. When it became slightly ajar, a man's head peeped in, and I virtually died.

As the man saw me, he froze and couldn't move; neither could I. We were both horrified and just kept staring at each other speechlessly. Then, suddenly, he yelled with a trembling, growling sound and ran off. I ran after him, but keeping a fair distance, and shouted with a loud tremulous voice, "Get ooout you demon!" When he heard that, his feet moved as though they had been powered by electricity.

I soon discovered that the man had kicked off the front door and broken in to the parsonage while I was asleep, and that the noise had woken me up. The trauma affected me psychologically for the ensuing few weeks. While I was preaching on that tragic Sunday night, I kept having visions of a man's head peeping at me. Subsequently, every time a door opened I jumped. For obvious reasons, I never told my family about the incident until I left Liverpool a year later.

Pauline and Dalton Bucknor, and my associate minister Reverend Basil Charlton and his wife were my loyal members and ardent supporters. I had only recently bought a used Rover 2.2, and while driving home from Liverpool one day, the engine spluttered and died on the M6 motorway. I was "broke, busted and disgusted" as they say, with no savings in the bank and very little cash in hand.

Dalton arranged for the car to be towed back to his home, and repaired the engine free of charge. I remember fasting and praying so long that one night, I momentarily lost my sight and had to feel my way around the room until I ended up in bed, but I could see again by the next morning.

Many of my pay cheques from the National Office had bounced owing to insufficient funds. My car tyres were frequently slashed by vandals and had to be replaced. On one occasion, the auto mechanic tyre specialist was so angry that he told me to put down the Bible and sort them out, using the most offensive language. He gave me the new tyre(s) free of charge. The flood light at the parsonage was maliciously broken one night; the fuse blew and left me in total darkness. Evangelistic advertisement posters on the exterior of the Church building were often taken down overnight and placed at the front door of the parsonage.

People used to excrete and plaster their stools over the

Church's main entrance door. One Sunday morning while the service was in progress, a neighbour excreted in his white handkerchief and plastered the excrement all over the windscreen of our minibus parked in front of the Church. I was never a violent person, but I became so frustrated and angry that I wanted to beat these people up – but first I had to catch them. I began to feel like an outraged vicar.

A meaningless sign saying, "**Trespassers will be prosecuted**" would undoubtedly not achieve our objective. Furthermore, the truth is that trespassers **won't** because one cannot be arrested or **prosecuted** for civil trespass – it's a civil wrong, not a criminal offence – but they can be asked to leave or be removed by "reasonable force" or in some cases they may be sued by the landowner in a civil court. This all seemed too complicated. Hence, I phoned the Merseyside Police and enquired whether it was illegal to stick up an intruder with a toy gun. They said "Yes, if it is done in public, but not in private."

British Law states that you may use "reasonable force" to restrain an intruder. This is the level or amount of power necessary to protect yourself, family members or property from a violent attack. In extremely dangerous situations, killing the attacker may be justifiable in law. It is not "reasonable excuse" but self-defense. However, "reasonable force" is not clearly defined, and one may easily apply a disproportionate use of force against an attacker. My cup of righteous indignation was full, and I had been relieved to hear that I could deal with the culprits within reason.

Nevertheless, the plan was not to injure anyone, but to capture the offender and give him a good beating. Whether this could be considered "reasonable force" was a different matter. I went through the main shopping areas in the City trying to find a good imitation gun to buy, but without any success.

A missionary evangelist was preaching in the City that same night, and I was invited to the meeting. The evangelist singled me out and delivered this message to me from the Lord: "My son, don't be afraid, I have sent you here for a purpose and no demon from hell can harm you." This was encouraging and by the same token deflating. So, I asked the LORD, "Why don't you want me to beat them?" I later realised that God was using this experience to prepare me for more difficult times ahead.

Dangerous Riots Broke Out

Michael Schawsmith had recently graduated from Bible school in Switzerland, and was placed in Liverpool to do his internship (or practicum) with me. I knew Michael to be a fine, astute and teachable young man with great ministerial potential, and we worked well together. Because there was no fridge at the parsonage, the chicken we had bought to prepare for our Sunday dinner went off and was spoiled.

I told Michael this was his opportunity to learn how to conduct a funeral. We took the chicken and the Church Hymnal to the back garden and conducted the burial. All this seemed hilarious, but it was a learning experience. As we had no dinner, after the morning service we had to dine at a Chinese restaurant in the City.

On returning from our meal, our way home was blocked by of the so-called "Toxteth Riots," which erupted on Catherine Street where we lived. It was 3 July 1981. The riots were sparked when police intercepted a motorcyclist in Selbourne Street. Some felt that the riots were the result of social problems, such as poverty and deprivation crowned by police injustice.

Whatever the cause, these were some of the most virulent

riots seen on the British mainland within living memory, and have been considered the most far-reaching. Scores of rioters travelling from Manchester, Birmingham and elsewhere converged on Liverpool causing a civil rampage and putting the inner-city on the front page.

Hospitals and other buildings were evacuated. Local pubs, furniture stores, and other shops were looted, and some 70 buildings incinerated. Many vehicles including buses and police cars were set on fire and some were turned over and ruthlessly vandalised. The police were in the spotlight again, but they were unprepared for this devastation, and were literally scared of the rioters. No police or emergency vehicles could enter some areas for fear of being destroyed so the rebels had free hand to do what they wanted without apprehension or reprisal.

The police were under heavy attack. At the height of the rioting in Toxteth, they sheltered themselves from missiles and petrol bombs as best they could, but not even their full–length riot shields afforded them enough protection. The rioters hijacked cranes to hoist themselves above the police shields, and I witnessed many police officers being knocked down mercilessly.

Several civilians lost their lives, over 470 police officers were injured, and 500 arrests were made.

Michael and I were on the streets until after mid-night and had first-hand experience of the whole atrocity. He held my hand and virtually pulled me along as we ran for our lives. Having seen the devastation on TV, our families were very concerned for our safety. They made several phone calls to the parsonage, but we were on the streets. It was not until the following day that we phoned home to account for ourselves, and everyone was relieved knowing we were still alive.

The day after the riots ended, many black and white mothers, faced with the severe and overwhelming shock and grief of the aftermath, wept on the streets of Liverpool, and pleaded with the young people not to do it again. These public expressions of outrage and sadness were like a mournful whistle. They coincided with a back lash of police retaliation, which led to the arrest of a significant number of innocent citizens. By this time most of the main perpetrators had already left the City.

Police Abuse

One night, I was driving in the City and unintentionally went down a one-way street. I was pulled up by a police officer who was very abusive. After shouting and swearing at me for my "careless driving," he asked me to produce my driving licence at the nearest police station within seven days. I had left my licence at home about 200 miles away, and so it would have been very difficult for me to do as he requested.

The next day, I went to the local police station and lodged a complaint against the officer for his inappropriate behaviour towards me. I apologised for breaking the law, but informed his superior that I was new to the City; the area was dark and poorly signposted. Furthermore, I explained that I was a minister of the gospel evangelising in the City. I told them that my work makes the job of the police easier and that they should be working with me instead of using their authority over me. As a result, the officer that booked me was severely reprimanded, and I had an apology from the police.

The mission continued its witness in face of all the riotous devastation and abuse. Despite having some help from the NTCG in Manchester intermittently, the Liverpool Church struggled from lack of financial support and human resources.

The growth was slow and the work stagnated. After my one-year tenure as evangelist, I returned to Aylesbury, and the Liverpool Church subsequently closed during the time of my successor.

Hitchin Church 1981–1982

In 1981, immediately upon my return from Liverpool, I was appointed to succeed Reverend Brian Robinson as pastor of the Hitchin NTCG and Overseer of the Luton District. As Hitchin was near to Aylesbury, my young family and I commuted to Church most of the time. The people were no less friendly and welcoming to us than elsewhere and our relationship was cordial.

One of the things about pastoring a small church is that you have to be almost everything to everyone, but this helps to consolidate the bonding and enriches the fellowship, and such was our experience in Hitchin. We will always remember the close connection we had with the young people, especially the Hitchin Gospel Choir which was my wife's initiative.

My tenure in Hitchin was mainly occupied during the winter months, and the winding roads were often quite icy and treacherous. One Sunday morning my car hit black ice and skidded into a lamp post causing over £2,000 worth of damage to both my vehicle and the post. Our children fell off the back seat and my son Robert sobbed, "Daddy, you are a bad driver!" Again, **I could have been killed** although that thought did not occur to me at the time.

We decided not to tell my mother about this, which would only give her more cause to worry. She was living in London, and we thought it would be unlikely she would hear any news regarding the accident. The next day, however, my Mom phoned and asked me, "Son, how is the car?" Strange! I was a bit taken aback, but kept calm and said, "Why Mom?" She replied, "I had a dream that you had an accident and smashed up the front of the car, but none of you were hurt." So, I had to confess what had happened.

During one of the superb district conventions held in Luton, I learned the importance of choosing and using my words carefully and appropriately. On the Sunday morning, I said to a sister, "Didn't we have a great time last night?" And she said, "Meet my husband!" (An unsaved visitor.) Then the penny dropped and I got the gist. We only spent a year in Hitchin and moved on to our next appointment at Clapham.

Clapham Church 1982–1987

At the beginning of the great Aylesbury revival, we were in a prayer meeting when God gave me a prophecy via Dianna – a young teenage girl, that He would be sending me to London because He had greater work for me to do there. Dianna was sobbing heavily saying, "Why LORD?" repeatedly, and I was unhappy about it because the Church in Aylesbury was going well and we had no problems.

Nevertheless, we were subject to the Master's will. Sometime later, I received a letter from Bishop Jeremiah McIntyre, the National Overseer, stating, "You will assume the pastorate at the Clapham Church" on a given date. I told Bishop McIntyre that I knew, and he asked, "How did you know?" I said that the Holy Spirit had already told me, and he looked a bit surprised. However, this had to be God's doing because no one could tell me, "You will assume anything" without first discussing it with me, and expect to get a favourable response.

In 1982, I succeeded the late Pastor Minnet Levy (affectionately known as Mother Levy) at Clapham NTCG, Ferndale Road, Brixton, London SW9. She and the Church gave a rousing welcome to me and my family. We settled down very easily, and the Church continued to grow numerically as my family relocated to the Brixton Hill area.

However, living in a flat at the top end of Lyham Road, inner-South London, situated near the C Wing at the back of Brixton Prison, was quite an unforgettable experience for me. HM P Brixton is a men's prison tucked away in Jebb Avenue off Brixton Hill in the London Borough of Lambeth, one mile South of Brixton on the A23. It was very rare for any inmates to break-out of the Prison, but it has been known to happen, and this was a potential risk to the community as the Prison sometimes incarcerated dangerous high profiled prisoners.

Nevertheless, I was moved by the familiar sight of prisoners being driven to the Prison, and I felt like John Bunyan an English writer and Baptist preacher who, on seeing the condemned prisoners being taken to Bedford Prison, wrote in his Christian allegory The Pilgrim's Progress published in 1678, "There but for the grace of God go I." (The original saying seems to be about 200 years old, though its authorship is uncertain.) Bunyan himself was arrested and spent twelve consecutive years in jail for refusing to give up preaching.

Prisoners are often transported in a specially designed police vehicle, usually a van or a bus with small dark windows. These transportations usually carry new prisoners along with existing prisoners returning to prison after court appearances, and only have police bike riders or armed squad cars escorting them if the incarcerated persons are very high risk profile prisoners. Otherwise to the uninitiated, prison vehicles look similar to security vans.

The Brixton Hill area, including Lyham Road was linked not only in people's minds, but in criminal statistical reports with urban decay and crime. A man was shot dead near to my address and police found the gun hidden under our house. One evening at dusk while the police were searching the area for the fatal bullet, I was watching the operation. Suddenly, I had a Word of Knowledge and the Holy Spirit told me where the bullet was. Without any premeditation, I informed a police officer where to look and as he shone his torch under the bushes he found the bullet. I nearly fainted because I thought they were going to arrest me, but one of the officers simply remarked, "You are in the wrong job."

On another occasion, our flat was broken into one Sunday while we were at church. It seemed as though our place was being watched, if not targeted. We have never been a victim of burglary before. So, this was a new and frightening experience, which left us not knowing how long it would take before we could feel safe in that house, if ever again. The realisation that our private space had been invaded or violated by intruders made us feel shocked, robbed, disgusted and demoralised with a sense of loss.

The thieves who raided our flat, presumptuously left my Bible saturated in the fish tank. They stole my chequebook and used it to buy a few items locally. I did my own detective work and found out who broke into the flat, where they spent my money and what they bought with it, then turned the matter over to the police, but they did not do anything about it. That was typical of a lot of inflammatory things which occurred in prejudiced Brixton, but we were just unfortunate to get caught up in "the spider web."

A Regular Sunday Morning Service

Our mission was of a different nature, and the Church stood-out as a beacon in the darkness of its community. Following prayer, each Sunday morning service commenced with a procession of the choir led by the Pastor. Mother Levy was very supportive to me and we got on extremely well, but she did not tolerate any nonsense from anybody.

One Sunday morning, a man was disturbing the service from the back. I looked straight at him and pointed directly to him. I don't know how he interpreted my gesture, but perhaps he thought I was sticking him up with a gun. He walked down to the altar and deposited some money in the offering receptacle, then went back to his seat still causing some trouble.

The male stewards appeared afraid of him, but Mother Levy went over and slapped him with a few licks, saying, "Get out!" after each blow. Now it must be said that she made more noise than the man had done. I told the stewards not to let it happen again because they should have taken control of the situation and not allowed Mother Levy's temper to boil over, and caused her blood pressure to rise.

One Sunday night, my wife sang a solo entitled "I am free", which was a tremendous blessing to everyone. Sister Z. Miller went home after the service and was praying, still consumed by the song, and received the baptism of the Holy Spirit. We had just retired to bed when the phone rang; it was Sister Miller on the line. She said, "Pastor I just phoned to tell you that I got filled," and that's all she could utter in English. For about the next twenty minutes she spoke in unknown tongues. My wife and I were delighted and shared her joy.

As with all other churches, you get the good, the bad and the in-between or the complicated. God raised up three successful pastors out of that Church, and the Church was blessed with many excellent workers. However, aside from the wonderful experiences, we also had some unpleasant situations of which I'll mention a few instances:

- A man who imitated another brother's hallelujahs out of jealousy became very offended and rebellious when I addressed his behaviour. Amazingly, he started doing unprecedented and bizarre things at Church.

  One Sunday morning, I saw him reading a sex magazine during the message. He appeared to be mentally challenged and his condition deteriorated rapidly. Another Sunday, he drowpped a stink bomb in the service, which was very gross and repugnant. On another occasion, the congregants looked through the Church window only to be greeted by his naked posterior up against the glass, but that was not the end of it.

Things deteriorated badly, and we were unprepared for his next move. During one Sunday morning service, he entered the sanctuary from the back entrance and appeared on the platform totally naked in front of the congregation, which included his wife and children. He was apprehended by one of the sisters and a couple of the brothers, who covered him with a jacket and escorted him out, leaving everyone appalled and shocked.

- One Sunday evening, sister Adora Nelson, a faithful child of God, died in the pew during her testimony. She gave one of the most beautiful testimonies; sharing her love for God and the Church. In the midst of it, she had a massive brain haemorrhage and collapsed and died.

  The paramedics were called, but it seemed as if the whole Church had died with her. As the pastor, I still had to preach, and it was difficult, but before my message concluded the believers were rejoicing and praising God. That was one of the occasions when God dried the tears of His people and comforted their hearts.

  At the funeral, her daughter Carol stood over the open coffin, and with tears flowing down her cheeks she raised her hands toward heaven and glorified God. Not even death was strong enough to shake her faith in God. This was one of the most beautiful things I have seen in church.

The following incident did not occur within the Church building, but it was indirectly associated with us:

- A young man, who was the son of one of the sisters phoned me about 5am one morning and requested a meeting with me. He sounded very anxious and said he had an urgent message for me. He turned up at my home about 6am and told me that they said to tell me, "Right is wrong and wrong is right." Ironically, there can be a paradoxical truth in this, depending on the context and interpretation. An effective lie must have a high content of truth.

Nevertheless, I must have seemed a bit puzzled by his rationale so he attempted to justify it: "God is dog spelt backwards, in the same way rats spelt backwards is star, and love spelt backwards is evol (another way of spelling evil." Then I understood. The "they" who had sent him were in the marijuana (ganja or weed) he was smoking. Is a dog God? It is said that a man's two best friends in life are a dog and God. They place a dog on a par with the unique incomparable God. (See Isaiah 40:18: 46:5; Psalm 113: 5–7.)

The devil is a liar! There can be no similarity between "dog" and "God." The first place Satan launches his attack is in the mind. Why? Your mind is Satan's battlefield, and the strategic control centre of your entire being. Satan knows that if he can dominate your mind, he can determine your thoughts and control you. But why did this young man come to me with his problem? I think it was because his life was in a mess. He realised that he needed deliverance and the only answer to his dilemma was in Christ.

The Scenario at Ocho Rios

Incidentally, I once went on a trip to Jamaica with the National Executive Council (NEC). We stayed at the beautiful all-inclusive *Jamaica Grand Hotel* in Ocho Rios, where we had a fantastic time. The name Ocho Rios means "eight rivers" in Spanish, and has many waterfalls and sporting activities on the northern coastline, which makes its geographical location an ideal site for a retreat.

I have known Professor Clinton Ryan, who was then a member of NEC, since I was seventeen years of age, and I always seized the opportunity to tease him. One hot sunny day, he and I took a stroll with others to the Straw Market so that we could stretch our legs, but primarily to buy some souvenirs before our return journey home.

He was speaking as if he had just graduated from Oxford or Cambridge university, with a plum in his mouth. I said to him, "Man you can't talk like that in this market; forget the professor twang and let me do the negotiating." I spoke in elegant Patois (with a tinge of Britishness of course), and secured some good deals for us.

I left the market feeling proud of my achievement and to my amazement, the thanks I got from Dr Ryan was this: he phoned over 4.6 thousand miles back to England and told his wife Yvonne, my former Sunday school mate, how I had showed him up in the market. I said amusingly, "Showed you up? "You should be glad I got you some good prices." This story teaches us that some people are never grateful to those who help them! On the other hand, I suppose that I was being tested.

Another day, things got worse when Dr Ryan caused me to "sin." I ordered a virgin pina colada at the hotel. Dr Ryan provocatively told the bar attendant to "put a little something in it," so the barmaid added a tip of rum, and the instigator watched my response, thinking that I would throw away the drink. I never said a word; I just consumed it without any misgiving.

Dr Ryan was unamused and professed shocked at my "unchristian behaviour." He said, I "shouldn't have drank it." I said, "Hold on a moment, how can you rebuke me for indulging? I didn't order it, you did. You are forgetting that the upholder is as bad as the rogue." My other colleagues laughed, and this incident became a standing joke for the rest of our trip and beyond.

This reminds me of a song we used to sing in Jamaica about the Great Judgment Day. The songwriter expressed a vision of the Day of reckoning, and one of the verses says that "the drunkards were there at the judgment with those who had sold them the drink and the people who gave the vendors the license, and together in hell they did sink." The only ones that the writer forgot to mention were the ones who had ordered the drink, although they had not even the remotest intention of drinking it.

Men Are Boys Grown Tall

My friend and colleague Rev. Brian Robinson and I have known each other from our early teens. I am the older of the two, but we both developed together in the ministry during the same era, and served simultaneously on the National Youth and Christian Education Board for several years. After my tenure of eight years (1977–1985) expired, I had to leave the Youth Department owing to time constraints.

To be honest, both Brian and I were very mischievous (in a harmless, playful way), and we enjoyed playing pranks on each other, one of which I will mention here. In 1986, during the National Youth Convention at De Montfort Hall, Granville Road, Leicester, on the platform before some 2, 200 delegates, Brian decided to pull one of his pranks on me, but unfortunately, things went badly wrong.

The National Youth Director, Rev. R. H. Parkinson was presenting me with an appreciation plaque. I suddenly felt something like a bee sting me on my posterior. Without any effort or premeditation – and not thinking what it might be, not even dreaming for a moment that it was Brian who had stuck a pin in me, I whacked him to the ground reflexively with a spontaneous vertical elbow strike backward.

Brian got up quicker than he hit the floor as if he hadn't done anything, and just as if nothing had happened to him while I stood there looking on in shock and dismay. This provoked much laughter from those who saw what had occurred, and we both had to live with it. I was not Henry Cooper with a dangerous left hook, but I am prone to take instinctive action towards anything or anyone who agitates me from behind.

Now, I am not a black belt karate expert, but my wife has been cautiously warned not to make any approach from behind, not even to kiss the back of my neck unexpectedly because I cannot be held responsible for my natural, unpredictable and unconstrained reflexes. Please observe my disclaimer: I am innocent, although my undesired and guilty impulses may need to be sanctified. Beware!

My First Adult Funeral

Up until then, I had a chronic fear of doing funerals. They are so sad, and I always dreaded what might happen, especially at the burial. My first adult funeral occurred at Clapham Church and I had two funerals in the same week. That was very difficult for me, having to go from one bereaved home to the next, but I had no option. I did fairly well at the first funeral service until I reached the graveside and nerves took over.

Half way through the interment, I realised that I was reading the committal for a cremation instead a burial. However, I managed to keep my usually cool composure and continued from memory, and I supposed nobody noticed. As is customary, some family members took up the shovels and started filling the grave with earth, and then they passed on the shovels to others who did likewise.

Unexpectedly, a man jumped into the grave and started trampling the earth down. One of the deceased's sons became very angry and began cursing and using offensive language. I was left shocked and speechless by such profanity and not knowing what to do I just left them to sort it out.

My First Wedding

The first couple I married were from the Clapham Church. Unbeknown to me, Colin and Hilda had been admiring each other, but Colin was hesitant to make the first move for fear of rejection. They were two of our finest young people in the Church. One day, I saw them both together in the Church hall discussing some matters pertaining to their Sunday school duties. I walked up to them (as I was led of the Spirit) and said simply, "You two are going to be married to each other," and they laughed heartily.

Later, they became engaged on 22 June 1986, and I guided them through the process of premarital counselling. I warned Colin to pay attention to the wedding vows and to listen carefully to what I was saying before attempting to repeat it.

I conducted their wedding on 27 June 1987 at the Parish Church, St. Andrew with St. Bartholomew in Bristol. On the occasion of his marriage, the moment Colin set his eyes on Hilda at the altar, he must have thought, "The Lord is my

Shepherd, I see what I want." He was besotted with her and apparently forgot everything else. He did not even remember to repeat a significant part of the wedding vows, which are at the centre of any marriage ceremony, because here the couple faithfully express to each other both an intent and a promise before God and His people.

When Colin realised what had happened, he got confused and started to mumble gibberish. Forgetting that I had a clip-on microphone, I said "shush," and it echoed across the congregation like a rushing mighty wind. I had to wait for everyone to laugh themselves out and simmer down before proceeding with the vows. Apart from that little hiccup, the wedding went smoothly, and they had a splendid day.

Hilda and Colin Miller's Wedding

In addition to my pastorate at Clapham, I was a homiletics and evangelism teacher at the *Ebenezer Bible Institute (EBI)* in Hackney, London. My former Sunday school mate and colleague Rev. Dr Joel Edwards was the Principal. Although the journey to EBI was quite tedious at times, I was doing what I enjoyed and God blessed my efforts.

Simultaneously, my wife Maxine began to emerge on the gospel scene with her unique style of singing, and participated in many powerful gospel concerts, including her UK tour with the famous heavyweight Clark Sisters from the USA. She won the *UK Gospel Music Award* for Best Newcomer in 1986. She also started to write gospel songs and recorded her first single EP, which became very popular, "Do You Know My Jesus?"

My Trip to the Holy Land

I went on a Christian pilgrimage to the Holy Land for fourteen action-packed days to see the land, meet the people and savour the experience. This gave me the opportunity to explore some of those historical places where Jesus Christ walked, worked miracles, and preached the Sermon on the Mount, and where He was crucified, was buried and rose again, an opportunity which brought the Bible to life.

This exciting and enriching insight was a life-changing experience. Some of the modern and historic places of interest which I visited included Jerusalem, Galilee, Palestine, Jericho, Capernaum, Bethlehem's Church of Nativity, the Dead Sea, the River Jordan and the natural hot springs. I also went on a boat trip across the Sea of Galilee.

I walked along the Via Dolorosa, a street within the Old City of Jerusalem, traditionally held to be the path that Jesus walked on the way to his crucifixion (Matthew 27:2–26). It is now marked with fourteen "stations of the cross" commemorating fourteen incidents that took place along the Via Dolorosa, which means in Latin, "Way of Grief," "Way of Sorrows," "Way of Suffering" or simply "Painful Way."

Following this momentous experience, I went down into the (Christian's) sepulchre of Jesus Christ, served Holy Communion with Bishop Trevor Smith in the Garden of Eden (or Gethsemane), baptized candidates in the River Jordan and spoke briefly in the "Upper Room" (also called Cenacle) – a room in Jerusalem traditionally held to be the site of the Last Supper; it was here that the disciples received the baptism with the Holy Spirit. (See Acts 2:1–4.) I even went to Egypt; visited the pyramids and rode on a camel, but for me one of the highlights of the tour was floating in the Dead Sea – an unforgettable experience.

The Dead Sea is popular with tourists from all over the world for its reputed therapeutic effects and other benefits. Unlike the oceans that have about 4% salt in the water, the Dead Sea water has a salt content of 29%, which makes impossible for anyone to sink, and allows them to float because of its greater density. Salt can also be seen along the shore of the Dead Sea. The Dead Sea produces minerals such as magnesium, sodium and potassium which enhance your skins' ability to retain moisture, making it healthy and silky smooth.

My Visit to the Great Pyramids in Egypt

On our excursion to the Holy Land, we went to Egypt for a few days during a very volatile time, but we had police escort up ahead and behind our coaches. One of the highlights of the trip was our visit to some of the pyramids. There are 138 Egyptian pyramids that have been discovered as of 2008. It is believed that most of these were built as tombs for the country's Pharaohs and their consorts (queens).

The most famous Egyptian pyramids are those found at Giza, on the outskirts of Cairo. They are generally considered the largest man-made structures. Egyptologists believe they were built by 20,000, to 30,000 or even as many as 100,000 labourers over a period of 10 to 20 years.

The oldest and largest of the three pyramids in the Giza pyramid complex on the outskirts of Cairo is called the **Great Pyramid of Giza** (also known as the Pyramid of Khufu or the Pyramid of Cheops). It was the tallest structure in the world (146.5 metres or 481 feet) for over 3,800 years, and is the only one of the **Seven Wonders of the Ancient World** still in existence. Today, it stands as a monumental symbol of greatness, but how it was built and by whom remains a mystery to the entire world.

Camel Ride in Egypt with Pyramids in the Background

Miracles at National Convention

I was privileged to conduct the only planned miracle service ever held at a NTCG National Convention UK. This was under the leadership of Bishop S. E. Arnold, National Overseer. The agreement was that I would hold a seminar during the day on the healing and miracle-working power of God and a subsequent healing session in the main auditorium. I had asked Rev. John Grey to assist me with this, and he was more than happy to participate.

When I arrived at the convention on the Saturday morning, no emphasis was put on the miracle-service. As a matter of fact, it wasn't even announced, and those in charge seemed to be "of little faith." They merely used a common expression of the day, "The sick will be prayed for." This statement covered them just in case no miracles occurred, and I certainly was not amused.

For me, it was not about praying for the sick; there's no such mandate in Scripture. I am not saying that it is wrong to pray for the sick, but I am advocating that it is not a biblical mandate. A mandate is an official order (commission or authority) to perform an action. Our mandate from the LORD Jesus Christ includes preaching the gospel, healing the sick and casting out demons. Today, many Christians pray over the demon possessed and speak in tongues. That's not how Jesus did it!

I told John Grey that I was not going to share the revelation I had had, and that I wouldn't even pray for the sick because they didn't expect anything to happen. I recalled that Jesus couldn't work any great miracles in His hometown because of the unbelief of the people. (See Mark 6:5–6.) However, not long after I started teaching, people did begin to receive their healing and I had to go with the flow. Many healings and miracles took place. During the miracle-session in the main auditorium, the deaf heard and other outstanding miracles were evident. Bishop Arnold was so excited, he told me that he had to share what he had seen with the European Superintendent.

The difficulty many Christians face is knowing where to draw the line between traditional church practices and biblical mandates. I grew up among all the old traditions; some I never followed and others it took me a while to drop. Nevertheless, this was a church era in which discipline was the order of the day. I still respect that, and do not wish to depart from it, but I have learned that sometimes we can overstep the mark. That is why we need always to allow the Holy Spirit to lead and guide us.

At one of my local churches, I was leading a prayer meeting, and a young lady came late. She was wearing a fashionable one-piece garment with sleeves and legs called a jumpsuit, and she looked like a model. I watched her as she walked straight down the aisle and sat on the front row. After a while she made herself comfortable by putting both her feet up on the chair. To me, this was not lady-like and undeniably inappropriate.

In line with my customary strict attitude, I attempted to tell her to sit properly, but the Holy Spirit said, "No, leave her." I didn't understand why because I felt I was doing the right thing, but I obeyed. A few minutes later, the young lady got off the chair and knelt on the floor with both hands raised in worshipping the LORD. Then I noticed she was filled with the Holy Spirit and speaking in tongues beautifully. I rejoiced with her for what the LORD had done. This led me to reappraise how I was delivering the ministry.

Sometimes, God works in ways contrary to our cherished traditions or beliefs. Jehovah is bigger than our denominations and cultures. Therefore, we cannot confine Him to our little traditional boxes or narrow religious structures. He cannot be limited to our likes and dislikes, because He is God and will not relinquish His sovereignty to anyone.

Aldershot Church, 1987–2003

On 1 February 1987, I succeeded my friend Bishop U. L Simpson as Senior Pastor of the Aldershot NTCG and concurrently as Overseer for the Aldershot District. He was transferred to Lee in London. Aldershot is traditionally known as the home of the British Army, but it has a lot more to offer than simply its military base. Located in the Royal County of Buckinghamshire, it has a lot of magnificent features, many social activities and beautiful country scenes, and it's not as cold as London. I loved it there.

I received a warm welcome from the Aldershot Church, and the honeymoon period was the perfect example of any normal pastorate. Also, I saw Aldershot as the "wedding church." This is the place where most of my early weddings occurred, and I probably conducted more weddings here during my first three years than in any other church which I pastored, and thank God most of the marriages have been successful.

Bernadette and Trevor Heron were married on 12 September 1987, and later they became the successful pastors of a church called *The Way Fellowship*. They are blessed with three children and one grandson. Beverly and Wayne Perkins got married on 28 July 1990, and they are blessed with four children. Today, Wayne is the Bishop and Senior Pastor of the NTCG, Slough, and he has a dynamic ministry. These are just four of my many spiritual sons and daughters that I am proud to have nurtured. There are others but I specifically mention these because they excelled in the ministry.

Bernadette and Trever Heron

12th September 1987

Beverley and Wayne Perkins

I was living in my predecessor's three-bedroom house in at 1 Fry's Acre College Road, Ash Vale, Aldershot, which was again rented accommodation. Very early one morning I was prompted by the Holy Spirit to pray on the floor of the dining room, and an intolerable situation in the Church was revealed to me. This was borne out in one of my sermons and problems started. The Church was accused of "taking the individuals' business to me," the novelty of the honeymoon period waned and my popularity diminished.

Eventually, God sorted the situation out and the Church moved on, but other minor problems subsequently emerged. Secret prayer meetings were held against the leadership. I turned up unexpectedly to a home where one such meeting was just about to commence. Of course, I was politely asked to join them, but I knew that this was only a sham so I declined.

Apostle Dr Renny McLean

Apostle Renny McLean has been a long-standing friend of mine. He is a true brother in Christ, a man of integrity and a source of inspiration to me, but most importantly, he is a man of God, who I love and respect very highly. I invited him to preach at our Church, but I knew that this servant of God was "dangerous" and that God would use him to stir up the "ants' nests" in the congregation.

After he arrived at my home and we were at the dinner table eating, he said to me, "Barry, I am going to move in Word of Knowledge tonight, is your Church ready for this?" I said, "Yes Renny, move in whatever you want," still a bit mystified – because coming from a traditional church background, I had never heard anybody talk like this before.

When Renny got up to minister, he preached under a heavy prophetic anointing and started to move accurately in Word of Knowledge. He talked about their secret "prayer meetings" and revealed some things that he couldn't have otherwise known. The guilty parties got upset and accused me of telling Renny these things and bringing him there to curse them. Of course, he did no such thing. He merely spoke what God told him.

A sister was holding her own fasting services and selective members were invited to join her in "binding up the pastor." When it was brought to my attention, I called her and another sister who had been brainwashed into this, and investigated the matter. They both admitted it, and the instigator explained: "I had a dream that I saw a man coming into the Church wearing a black robe, and the description matched you wearing your black minister's garb." That was possible, except that I never wore my garb to Church, I robed in my office.

Her interpretation of the dream had led her to believe that I was Satan disguised in ministerial attire. As a result, she started to convene fasting services at her home to bind up the Pastor. I asked them, "Where in the Bible have you read this?" Their eyes were opened and they could see that they were misled. One of them swiftly exited the office crying, and later apologised for her action. The other expressed gratitude for the way I handled the situation and thanked me for not exposing her to the Church. This did not affect our relationship and God was glorified in the solution.

One of my spiritual sons from Fiji got saved and baptized in Aldershot. He had come to the UK to join the British Army, but failed the required standard for entry on medical grounds. He had three testicles and it would have cost him £1,000.00 for a surgeon to remove one testicle.

This is a very rare congenital disorder called polyorchidism (or triorchidism, or tri-testes.) One evening, he came to my office crying because he didn't have the money for the operation and would have to return home. I prayed for him and God miraculously performed the surgery, without any residual scarring. He passed the medical examination and joined the Army.

I invited him to join me at the Church about 10am one day for prayer. He came and I taught him about the baptism with the Holy Spirit for about fifteen minutes and asked him if he wanted it. He said, "Yes." I prayed for him and he was filled with the Holy Spirit in about five minutes. I gave him personalised ministerial tutoring and some appropriate books to read. He was the kind of person who listened attentively to me and practiced what I taught him. Later he married a pastor's daughter and became the Senior Pastor of a powerful Church with signs and wonders following his ministry.

One Sunday morning I preached a salvation message and a young lady from abroad was overwhelmed. She responded to the altar call and accepted Jesus Christ in her life. After the service she said to me, "Wow! How come nobody told me this before?" By this time, my wife and I had sold our residential property in Stockport Road, Streatham Vale, London, and bought a lovely three-bedroom family home located in a private cul de sac at 60 Highclere Road, Aldershot, Hampshire, within easy reach of the town centre.

I invited her to our home the following day in consultation with my wife, and she came. I gave her my Bible opened at Acts 1:1–4 and asked her to read it. She gasped, "Wow!" I asked her, do you want it? She said, "Yes." I prayed for her and she was sweetly filled with the Holy Spirit.

She went home and told her husband. He said, "I want that as well." The next week they both came to our home. I explained that this was not something he could intellectualise or analyse: he had to receive it by faith. I prayed for him and he appeared to have received a greater dose of the Holy Spirit than his wife. He had taken drugs before, but the Spirit took him to a new height. He was drunk and fell at the bottom of our stairs. Fearing that he might lose what he had received, he said, "Can I sleep at the bottom of your stairs?"

On another occasion, just outside our Church, I saw a Church of England man who I had met previously. He thought very highly of his Priest because he explained, the Priest took some of them for a drink after the service. We talked at length about salvation, prayer and fasting and then we went into the Church and sat on the front pew.

As we continued talking about the baptism with the Holy Spirit, he said to me, "Please pray for me," but I perceived that he wanted me to pray for him to receive the Spirit. As I prayed, he was filled with the Holy Spirit in a couple of minutes and began to speak in tongues. I said, "What are you going to tell the Father now?" We were both very happy and I told him to pray for his wife when he got home that she too might receive this gift.

The LORD continued to bless us, and many people got saved and filled with the Holy Spirit and some were miraculously healed. God led me to start conducting miracle crusades with phenomenal results, and the Church adopted the suffix *"Miracle Deliverance Centre"* as a part of its title, although it was widely known in the community as Pastor Barrington's Church.

My first miracle crusade was held at the Aldershot Church. God gave me the words of the crusade banner, and an unsaved art teacher wrote it on white PVC canvas at minimal cost to me because he said, "I believe in the work that you are doing. I wouldn't do this for anybody else." Again, this was the favour of the LORD.

Aldershot Church Platform

A lady who attended a healing crusade read the banner before the service began, and as she came to the word "now," she was miraculously healed by the power of God. The meeting was well advertised and the response was great. People who came for their healing from near and far were queueing up outside the building before the Church opened. When I stood up to minister the devil said to me, "There won't be any miracles tonight because you are not anointed."

The truth is that I didn't feel anointed, but I became indignant and said to the devil, "You mind your own business. This has nothing to do with you. It is between God and His covenant people, and you are outside of the covenant. Let's see if there won't be any miracles!"

God honoured His Word and outstanding miracles occurred. Apart from the obvious miracles witnessed in the meeting, I had many testimonies of healings by phone. Women would physically grab me and hug me on the road, and as I was wondering what was going on, they would say something like, "You don't know who I am, but I received healing at your crusade." Following this event, my miracle, healing ministry began to spread like wild fire even more than before across the country and over foreign fields.

It was during this time that my wife made her debut on national TV on the *"People Get Ready" UK Gospel Show (1986)*, and the Southampton Studio erupted in exuberant praises to God as she sang, "Jesus is Lord of the Way I Feel". She has written over one hundred songs, and recorded five CDs and a few cassettes. She has sung across the United Kingdom and abroad with tremendous success, and is a sought-after psalmist.

For many years, literally thousands of people, both Christians and non-Christians have been challenged and blessed by her singing ministry, which has taken her to places she would otherwise never have been. She gives God all the praise and glory. There's something about being a Christian songwriter and an anointed gospel singer that generates a lot of energy and sparks an unquenchable fire in Maxine. Once she starts singing, it's difficult to stop her. She would sing all night if one allows her.

Maxine declined all offers to sing secular songs. Her lyrics, to which she is unpretentiously committed, has remained absolutely gospel. She was always very clear about what she wanted and what she was doing, and she knew why. The range of her music has expanded to reach many peoples and nations globally, but the unadulterated message of her songs was consistent.

In all the churches that God has led me to pastor my wife has occupied a major role in the music, the worship and the women's ministries. Despite the various challenges, each differing from one church to the next, she has remained unreservedly committed to the cause of Christ, and has maintained her faithfulness in the good times and the bad. I cherish these commendable qualities in her. Often, we minister together, she sings and I preach – God ordained it this way.

A Powerful Vision

Every time my ministry was about to change, the LORD appeared to me in a vision. One night I dreamt that I was at Church ministering. The altar was filled with sick people; lame, crippled and with many other complaints. I prayed for them, but nothing happened. I was frustrated and angry with the devil. I looked ahead and saw Jesus looking at me gracefully.

Simultaneously, a big hand came down from heaven and stopped in mid-air within my reach. I knew in my spirit that this was the hand of Christ. I reached up and held His hand, and Jesus said to me, "As long as your hand is in mine, there's nothing you can't do." With my right hand firmly in His, I looked at a young lad in a wheelchair and said, "It's alright now, you can walk." He got up and started walking, and I continued speaking healing words to the others and most if not all of them were set free from their ailments.

Clearly, this experience changed my life forever. I stopped praying for the sick in the traditional way, and started speaking to sicknesses and diseases in the authority of Jesus and commanding them to leave. Numerous people were miraculously healed and delivered by the grace and power of God.

After that, I was praying in the Church Office and a revelation broke in my spirit: "You and Christ are one." I thought, "Wow! Hallelujah! That means I can do what Jesus did." So I started to study the life of Christ, and particularly noted how He ministered healing and deliverance to people and I imitated Him.

Jesus truly became my pattern and partner for ministry over the ensuing years, and my healing ministry expanded.

However, one of my greatest passions is to mentor ministers. Four pastors evolved from the Aldershot Church under my leadership, although they did not all remain with the NTCG. I am blessed with many more spiritual sons and daughters in the UK and abroad, who occupy strategic positions in the ministry.

A Jamaican proverb says, "De higher monkey climb, de more him expose to de wind," which means "The higher the monkey climbs, the more he exposes himself, or the more he is exposed to danger." Instead of thriving, Satan wants to make our lives retrograde, but God's purpose is to upgrade us. The more God elevates us, the more Satan attacks us, but our victory is guaranteed, so keep climbing higher in God.

More Problems with the Police

In those days, a black person in the UK lived at the mercy of the police, rather than under their protection. In July 1988, I was accosted outside a public convenience in Oxford Street, by two plain clothes police officers, who alleged that they had been into the toilets and seen me behaving inappropriately. They asked me to accompany them to the Police Station, and I did. After giving me the third-degree treatment, they trumped up a charge of indecent exposure, which didn't make any sense to me, but at least I was then allowed to continue my journey home.

Following this, I was summoned to the local Magistrates Court. Owing to the nature of the charge, I engaged legal representation and explained my position unequivocally. I won the case and was completely exonerated. Even though the whole demoralising drama was a shock to my system, I had the full support of my wife and the general Church, enhanced by the prayers of the believers. God will not allow the devil to destroy your reputation; He will stand by you and protect you.

On another occasion, I took brother Cecil Campbell from Aldershot to the Home Office in London to sort out his immigration status. As I drove into a side road to park for lunch, I was pulled over by a senior police officer who asked me, "Is this your car?" I said, "Yes." Then He asked, "What is the registration number?" I told him that I didn't remember it. After a sarcastic comment, he took a few steps back and wrote down the details of my vehicle. Then he continued by explaining that I had almost hit a woman on the pedestrian crossing. I became angry and asked him, "Was she a ghost or something?" He officially recorded my response in his notebook (or PNB).

I stated explicitly that there was no one at the pedestrian crossing when I passed by, and the police car was several metres away – approaching from the opposite direction. Nevertheless, I was later charged and summonsed to court. Many police officers were notorious liars, and knowing how difficult it was to beat them in court, I decided to "plead guilty with explanation."

I wrote a lengthy typewritten letter to the Courts pleading guilty, but pronouncing the judgment of God on the unjust legal system. They replied and said, "Mr Burrell, we are not sure how you intend pleading, so we would suggest that you attend court."

I represented myself at the Court, and changed my plea to not guilty. During the cross examination, I spoke slowly and deliberately while staring into the eyes of the prosecutor. I deliberately asked the policeman, "Officer, were you the driver of the panda car at such and such a place on such and such a date and time?" He replied "Yes." I then asked him, "Officer, would you agree that it was a very busy time of the day, and based on the dimensions of the road, for you to turn your car around and pursue mine, you would have had to travel a fair distance in the opposite direction?" He agreed.

It was intriguing to see the magistrates out of the corner of my left eye nodding in agreement. This edged me on to pursue my line of questioning. I said, "Officer, at that very busy time of the day, would you also agree that there were many blue cars on the road?" Again he said, "Yes." "Well, how can you be certain that my blue car was the one you saw at the pedestrian crossing?" I think he froze.

Needless to say I won the case. The magistrates concluded, "Mr Burrell, there is no case for you to answer." I claimed £200 expenses, and the presiding magistrate asked me, "Mr Burrell, are you claiming expenses just for yourself or for you and your friends?" I told him that I was claiming my own expenses. I was previously advised that the Court would normally award only 50% of the costs, but they awarded me the full amount. Again, this was the favour of God.

I had the opportunity to become a magistrate, but after weighing up the pros and cons, I declined because it would have been too demanding on my ministry. But if I could choose a second profession, it would be a litigation solicitor (lawyer) to defend the less privileged. I believe we must use the gifts that God has given us to bless and edify people, not to abuse or destroy them. Don't waste your energy fighting your wife, your husband or others. Instead, fight sin, sickness, demons and injustice.

Mission to Alberta Canada 1988

On 4 August 1988, I went to Calgary, Alberta, Canada to minister at a week of meetings hosted by Rev. Errold Hamilton. Calgary – a very westernised city, had an estimated population of 1.16 million (residents and metropolitan area (CMA) in 2014, which made it the largest city in Alberta and the third largest city in Canada, with a metropolitan demographic. The weather has an annual average temperature of 17°C (62°F) and the coldest average monthly temperature is in January at 7°C (19°F). The weather is so unpredictable; one would not be surprised to have virtually all four seasons of the year in one day.

My fellowship with the Hamilton family was great as per usual, the revival meetings were successful, and I have a few lasting memories of Calgary. I remember the mountain goats and polar bears, which are aggressive and extremely dangerous to human beings. I also recall how during the cold weather they had to plug the car engine into the electric socket overnight so that the vehicle would start in the morning. However, the incident that stood out most in my mind was one evening when I had to take Bible study and it turned out to be a drama.

Travelling to the worship centre, the cloud became dark-grey as if a storm was brewing up. When we arrived, I said to the driver, let's get in quickly before it rains, so we rushed into the building as it started drizzling. Immediately, the rain poured down so heavily that water began flowing into the Bible study area and the class was cancelled. Within half an hour everywhere was flooded, inside and outside and we couldn't return home by road.

Rev. Hamilton got some wellington boots for me, and we had to walk up a hill and gradually make our way through the grass and mud to a neighbour's home. The road had about six feet of water flowing like a river, covering the parked cars and police boats sailed up and down, rescuing people from their flooded homes. Fortunately, because of the steep location of those who assisted me, we were not too badly affected by the water. It was about mid-night when the treacherous waters subsided and the Pastor sent a little pickup truck for me.

Mission to Ghana 1989

My ministry expanded beyond the confines of the local Church and I started preaching in different parts of the country and in foreign fields. On 24 November 1989, I went to Ghana, West Africa. When I got out of the Airport in Accra at about 8.30pm, the weather was so hot, it felt as though fire had descended on me from heaven. To survive in Ghana, I had to take three cold showers daily.

The people were very friendly, hospitable, respectable and welcoming. Ghana is a country with many major languages, and a population numbering 20 million people as of 2013, but one word that I cannot forget is "akwaaba," which in the Akan language means "welcome." As a matter of fact, all visitors to the country will see it in large letters on the building at *Kotoka International Airport.* Everywhere I went the people bowed and greeted me with akwaaba!

The Ghanaians are very religious and God-fearing people. Many are professed Christians, and a number of banks have thirty minutes' devotion before opening time. I heard them singing familiar songs from our Church Hymnal at one of the banks. Children and businesses are frequently named from the Bible, and the man or woman of God is highly respected.

During my mission to Ghana, I spoke at the Church of God Bible School and conducted productive miracle crusades for approximately three weeks in Kumasi, Sunyani, Accra and Obuasi, which has one of the top-9 largest gold mines in the world, originally known as the Ashanti Mine. I was accompanied by the late Bishop Isaac Carter, a faithful man of God (and the founding Pastor of the Wood Green Church), who the people called Daddy.

Bishop Carter fell several times and I had to pick him up each time, but we got on very well, and it was a blessing to have had his company. He certainly made me laugh as we travelled together. Our various experiences made the trip worthwhile, and we blessed many people financially.

We had the opportunity to visit Cape Coast and Elmina Castle, a large fifteenth century commercial fort and trading post, which was eventually used to imprison slaves, who were reduced virtually to the status of cargo. In other words, this and other castles were slave dungeons. Cape Coast Castle – one of about forty "slave castles" built on the Gold Coast, is the oldest European structure in Ghana.

These castles provided the last experience the slaves had of the "freedom" of their homeland prior to them making their final journey to foreign lands, never to return. Once the slaves were captured, they were held in barbaric confinement for about three months before the survivors were shipped to other countries. Elmina Castle was the first European Castle erected by Portuguese in 1482.

At Elmina Castle, I was shown two average size late Medieval dungeons where captive slaves were imprisoned in former times. They had no toilets or lights, not even bunk beds, and a limited supply of food. Both males and females were kept in the larger of the two prison cells, in which they had to urinate and defecate, and which had only one small window at the top about 10 inches (25.4 centemetres) square as their only means of illumination and ventilation.

Therefore, it was not surprising that the confined air and noxious body odour combined with the smell of their excreta, together with the malnourishment and persistent emotional, mental and physical exhaustion they suffered caused many of them to faint, and even to die before they were exported. As part of the complex, there was also an underground passage leading to the slave ships where they were chained together in small rows above each other with little room to move, even for toilet convenience.

Captives from different nations were usually mixed together, so it was more difficult for them to communicate and plan rebellions. The second dark prison cell was even more heart-breaking; it had no means of ventilation. This was reserved for "stubborn or rebellious" slaves who were abandoned in it until they died, either from starvation or suffocation. These death dungeons were a warning message to others to not get out of line.

There were huge heavy cannon balls in the courtyard, which I could not move or shake, with big chains attached. Periodically, female slaves were taken from their cells and chained to these iron ankle balls. The British governor would inspect them from his balcony and pointed out who he wanted to have sex with.

The chosen women were forcefully ushered up the staircase that led directly to his boudoir (a small private room) where he would rape them. If they became pregnant they were released from the prison, otherwise it was business as usual. This meant that one woman could have been subject to brutal rape several times. Women who refused to comply with the governor's sexual demands were severely beaten and chained to the cast-iron balls in the blazing hot sun as a punishment.

Bishop Carter and I visited the "Christian" church (next door to the governor's chambers) that would have had Sunday services for the governor and his staff directly over the male dungeons. I witnessed many African Americans losing their temper and swearing vehemently as they relived these historical moments and shared the torture, anguish and dehumanisation.

Some people have asked to be locked in the cells so that they could contemplate these experiences as momentary prisoners themselves.

During the period of the transatlantic slave trade, over six million slaves were shipped, but about 10–15% perished at sea and never reached their destination. It is one thing reading about such atrocities – but being there to witness in person the dungeons and chains, one can empathise with the people who had been enslaved and were encountering such inhumane brutality.

The Aldershot Church sponsored Rev. Stephen Awuah, a native pastor in the Volta Region of Ghana. Stephen later visited me in the UK, and I cooked for him my version of fufu made from pounded yam. He said, "This taste like the real fufu." I said, "What do you mean taste like, it's the real thing!" He said, "Only the soup is missing." Soup in Ghana is not the same as our soup; it's really grease, so I made Stephen some chicken gravy and he was happy.

Mission to India 2001

On 10 March 2001, my colleague Bishop Norman Gooden and I went to Mumbai (formerly known as Bombay), a densely-populated city on the west coast of India – a financial centre, and India's largest city. From there, we travelled ten hours by train to Malakapalli, West Godavart District, South India for three weeks' mission. I had forgotten my anti-malaria tablets on the train, which invoked fear in some. India is a high-risk country for yellow fever and malaria – two major killer diseases usually caused from the bite of an infected mosquito, but by the grace of God I returned to the UK in good health. Norman had been to India before, but this was my maiden trip. My local Church had blessed me liberally to support the missionary work, and what a trip that was!

We were met at the place of disembarkation late in the night, and I was formally introduced to our host Pastor Babu. Beautiful garlands were hung around our necks as a sign of honour and respect, but they have many other traditional purposes. When we arrived at the hotel, a porter took our luggage to the bedroom, and the tip we gave him was more than his monthly wages, so he was extremely grateful. But having just arrived and still struggling with jet lag, my tiredness was exaggerated by the nightmare of being in a strange country far remote from home and western civilisation.

I had a culture shock when I sat on the bed and almost broke my bottom. I wanted to rest my weary body and exhausted eyelids, but there was no mattress as we know it, only a thick sponge on bare board. I asked my colleague Norman for the toilet but there was none, just a hole in the floor which I could hardly find. He laughed at me. It was a good thing that we had carried our own toilet rolls from the UK, as none were provided. Nevertheless, I quickly adapted and we had a successful mission.

The people were most welcoming and accommodated us in every way. They had "guards" to protect us and to watch our every move, ensuring that we were not kidnapped or harmed by anyone. It is reported that Christian Missionaries have been burned alive in India in some States; to some extent this may depend on whether you get involved in the politics of religion. It is always safer to preach the gospel and avoid insulting the religions of Hinduism or Islam.

We preached in different meetings and wonderful things happened, but my heart was moved with compassion when I saw people devastated by persistent poverty, especially the children with a look of despair in their eyes, for whom hope was almost gone. I was able to bless the mission from the monies provided by the Aldershot Church: purchasing clothes, sandals, bath towels, and rice among other things.

One night we attended a meeting out in the jungle. I preached and then we went for dinner with our host, Pastor Babu. What happened next was hilarious. While everybody else ate their curried lamb and rice with bare hands, Norman and I had difficulty eating ours with teaspoons (the only utensils available to us).

On another occasion, we were somewhere else having an evangelistic meeting in the jungle. They ran an electric wire with a light bulb to a nearby tree. The place was semi-dark, and the meeting was in progress. Something fell out the tree on my face, and I slapped my face so hard that I almost demolished my nose, and my glasses went flying into the dark.

Norman panicked, "What is it, what is it?" I thought it was a lizard, but it was actually a little insect called a cricket. I started to search frantically for my glasses, which I needed to read my sermon notes. The Indian boys laughed hilariously as their brilliant white teeth shone conspicuously through the darkness.

One of the highlights of the trip was the children's prayer meeting. Each night before retiring to bed, they assembled for prayer without any supervision. It was amazing to watch those young children, many of them under ten years of age organise themselves and conduct their own prayer meetings. They prayed with such fervency, enthusiasm and maturity that the glory of God just filled the place and it was a delight to watch. I had never seen anything like it!

Gold Dust/Flakes Fell from Heaven

In a vision one night, I saw gold like snowflakes falling out of the sky on me and I collected them like a child making a snow-man. In the morning, I told this to my colleague Norman. During the day, I went shopping with two American women and an Indian lady, our interpreter. The standing joke for the day was that everywhere we went the Indian men thought I was a rich African with my three wives.

On my way back in the mission's minibus, I began to share my vision with the three women and my Hindu driver. Suddenly the women started getting excited, and one said, "It's all over you!" Another said, "Has it ever happened to you before?" I was wearing black trousers (or pants to our American friends) and a dark blue shirt, and gold was sparkling in my hair and all over my clothes. I became speechless, and just kept staring at it in awe. As soon as I got back, I rushed to tell Norman what had happened. His response was, "Well, you'd better look in the mirror because it's still on you." I had a shower, but the gold was still on me.

Upon my return to the UK, I shared my testimony and many people were sceptical about it. Some asked whether this gold dust had any significance. I replied that it was an end- time manifestation of the glory of God. One Sunday after I preached in Aldershot, gold appeared on Trevor – our youth director. Some of the young people tried to retrieve some of it, but they couldn't. At one of our fasting services, gold appeared in the palm of the leader's hand. A sister said to me, jokingly I supposed, "I wanted to get some in my hand bag."

Gold Dust Spread to Wolverhampton

On one occasion, when I was ministering in Wolverhampton for Bishop Winston Willis, gold appeared on his wife and the glory of God was upon her. I said to my colleague, "Look at your wife's face." He said, "I have heard about this but was sceptical. Now my eyes have seen the salvation." That same night I had a vision that Mrs Willis was covered in gold dust.

The next day when Bishop Willis came to see me, and I told him to tell his wife that more gold was coming upon her. He said to me, "You tell her yourself." "Ok," I said. So I phoned Mrs Willis and told her what I had seen. Soon after that she received a lot more of the gold dust. Some of the older folk, thinking that she was becoming worldly, asked her, "What is that you've put on your face?"

The NTCG recorded one of our Sunday morning services in Aldershot for Songs of Praise, which was aired live on BBC 1. This was a specially arranged event with a few other churches joining; the National Youth Choir sang and the late National Overseer, Bishop Dr S. E. Arnold preached. Many people were tremendously blessed around the country, and we received several letters of commendation and monetary gifts.

The Aldershot Church Secretary and CPC proposed in conference that the Church buy me a car as a personal gift. This was unanimously passed and the Holy Spirit took over the conference. Many began to speak in tongues and praise God in exuberant celebration. It was the best atmosphere I had ever seen in a Church conference.

They bought the car for me as agreed, but I told them I couldn't accept it as a gift because of legal ramifications. They kept it as a company vehicle and I used it for that purpose. My wife and I became so close to the people in Aldershot that it was extremely painful on both sides for us to leave.

Over the past four decades, I have seen how Christian principles have been substantially and dangerously eroded to an unprecedented level in the corporate church, but moving to Wood Green was another major culture shock and a big eye opener for me.

Wood Green Church 2003–2017

Initially, the Wood Green congregation was very traditional and lacked the standard of discipline to which I was accustomed. As a result, I was hesitant to accept the appointment to the pastorate, and refused the Administrative Bishop's offer. He then asked me to pray about it, and I did but was still dubious about the whole idea. God showed me the Church in a vision and revealed many licentious practices that were going on there, which I was assigned to address. So, my job was already cut out for me. He told me that my predecessor did not know these things – and prepared me for what was ahead.

On Sunday 3 January 2003, I assumed the position as Senior Pastor of the *New Testament Church of God Cathedral of Praise (NTCGCOP)*, Wood Green, and concurrently served as District Overseer of the Wood Green District for the ensuing fourteen years. My predecessor had recently been promoted, and I supported his vision fully. We loved and respected each other. He was a close friend of mine. We had a good relationship like the Bible characters Jonathan and David.

The Honeymoon Period

Like most other black-led churches, the congregation was predominantly female, with probably an 80–20 ratio. Furthermore, many of these women had had problems with men, who were already in a disadvantaged position, and to add fuel to the fire, they got another man as their pastor. (In all honesty, some women prefer being among men than with other women, but they are in the minority.) Therefore, one of my first priorities was to protect the women of our Church from the abuse of men in any way, shape or form. Obviously, one wanted to build a cordial relationship with them.

However, for the first three months after my induction, I was inundated with a spate of funerals. During this period, I conducted more funerals than I did in the sixteen years of my previous pastorate. In order that I might have adequate time for the ministry, I had to pray against the spirit of death which apparently hovered over the community. Providentially, scarcely anyone from the Church died.

On Wednesday 6 January 2003, I attended a Bible study session at the Church, conducted by sister Earla Green. The Church had a recorded membership of 424 and only 11 or 12 people attended the Bible study; this set off an alarm bell in my mind. Nevertheless, everyone seemed to have enjoyed the class, and Earla asked me to pray the closing prayer. I began to pray as the Spirit led me, and a sister was baptized with the Holy Spirit and spoke in tongues for almost half an hour.

This was like a breath of fresh air to the Church and, indeed, an answer to prayer. It marked the beginning of scores of believers who received the in-filling of the Spirit. Most Sundays, between four and eight believers were filled with the Holy Spirit, and many souls were converted. I started to conduct baptismal classes and pray for the candidates to receive the Holy Spirit.

Many got filled with the Holy Spirit in the classes, and by the time of the baptism most of the candidates were already endued with power from on high. This became the norm rather than the exception. We did not have a single baptism where some of the candidates were not filled during the baptismal classes. We have had one or two baptisms a year, baptizing twelve to thirty-two candidates each time, and added approximately ninety percent of them to the membership of the Church.

A Miraculous Restoration

My mother visited me here at Wood Green during her declining years, and spent some time at the parsonage. She got up early one morning and was going downstairs in the dark to the kitchen. She said she didn't want to cause any disturbance to wake us up. Mom either missed her step or had a blackout and fell head first down the flight of ten steps and hit her head badly on a cross bar at the bottom.

She was not certified dead, but had been knocked unconscious. I had to pray life back into her and she regained consciousness before the ambulance came, but even then, she was still disorientated. I still believe she had actually died, but I have no proof. Thank God for the resurrection power of Jesus Christ!

Mission to Nevis 4–9 February 2007

On Saturday 3 February 2007, Evangelist Glenford Reid, a member of the Wood Green Church and I set off for our maiden voyage to Nevis, eastern Caribbean, accompanied by one of my spiritual sons, Trevor Heron from Slough. We boarded a Virgin Atlantic flight from London Gatwick (LGW) to Antigua, and a small connecting flight for about half an hour to Nevis. Trevor was very ill at the airport in Nevis, but after a time of rest he recuperated and our mission went on as planned.

We were met by Andrew Richardson, Trevor's brother-in-law, who worked in conjunction with Pastor Morton to organise and host the crusade in Nevis. Andrew was originally one of my computer technicians from the UK. The same evening that we landed, we went to the TV studio and I had a live interview about the miracle crusade, which commenced the following day.

Generally, the people there were sceptical about miracles, but I was privileged and honoured to be the first preacher to proclaim and demonstrate God's miracle-working power in Nevis. It was fascinating to watch the faces of so many people as miracles occurred before their eyes for the first time. Following the healing of a lame man, a brother went to work the next day and shared excitedly, "I saw a miracle last night!"

We had a great time in Nevis. Nevis is the smaller of the two Caribbean islands which made up the nation of Saint Kitts and Nevis – a very peaceful, beautiful and relaxing island with white cloud-capped mountains and gorgeous weather. In 2007, Nevis had a population of about 12, 200, with one round-about and no traffic lights.

Our daily routine in Nevis included: morning prayer, light breakfast, swimming in the Caribbean Sea, back for lunch, afternoon rest, corporate prayer at home, miracle service in the evening, a late dinner at the Church and then retiring to bed.

One morning, we decided to do something different and went to the Atlantic Ocean to bathe. Unlike the more peaceful Caribbean Sea, the Atlantic impressed us with the majestic beauty of its mountainous waves 6–8 feet high or higher. This was quite challenging to say the least, but we braved the powerful energy of the ocean and went into the water.

Andrew, Trevor and I enjoyed riding some of the waves and ducking or diving under others while Glen stood in the shallow area watching the waves and us. A boisterous wave passed over us and knocked Glen straight to the shore, baptizing him in the sand. I think this experience was enough for him, and he wouldn't allow it to be repeated.

Those ocean waves certainly taught us lessons that we won't ever easily forget. Once a wave of this magnitude picks you up, you have no control over what happens next. That was great fun, but a very dangerous adventure since some of the waves do create seaward undercurrents. But of course, we didn't know which ones, and could have been swept away but for the grace of God.

After the crusade terminated, Glen and I went to chill out in St Kitts for a week's break, approximately eleven miles by sea from Nevis. Rarely is earth's natural beauty more evident than when one is making a journey by road, in day-light. This reality was vividly brought home to me when Glen and I visited St Kitts – a beautiful country located in the eastern Caribbean, strategically positioned between two oceans, offering a bird's-eye view of smaller neighbouring islands within close proximity across the Caribbean Sea, or the Atlantic Ocean, depending on the angle from which you are viewing them.

A traveller on the short breathtaking journey around the guitar-shaped island is mesmerised by the spectacular coastal scenes so skilfully and marvellously portrayed by the divine Artist on the vast canvas of nature; high, white-cloud-capped mountains with a blue-sky background overlooking the coasts, highlighting the rendezvous of the Caribbean Sea and Atlantic Ocean, converging in calm and fascinating serenity below the cliffs of the "Black Rocks" (so-called because of their colour and embodying the remaining fragments of a historic volcano) and characterised by the sparkling crystal reflection of the bright dazzling sun on the glossy seas, with brown, black, and gold sandy-beaches decoratively bordering the magnificent island, giving the visitor a great feeling of extreme pleasure and utter relaxation.

Driving or walking along the narrow winding road that goes around this unique country, so marvellously endowed by nature, one is captivated by the stupendous panorama of this enchanting landscape, enriched by the atmosphere of timeless tranquillity that pervades these idyllic scenes, and by the grandeur of the green hillsides sloping down into the blue transparent waters of the warm seas, all animated by exotic birds, animals, plants, and multi-coloured psychedelic flowers of various descriptions.

Each day concludes with a spectacular sunset over the western horizon, too beautiful for words to describe, with the sun appearing to descend into the Atlantic Ocean, overshadowed by darkness, and kissing the salty waters, as it were, bidding "good night" to nature and the inhabitants of the region. Glen and I spent a whole day by the beach, swimming, eating fish and ice cream and sleeping in between. We returned to the UK naturally tanned and marvellously refreshed and blessed, ready to resume ministry in our local Church.

The Shaking Began

One of the sisters from our Church came to my office and shared with me some shocking examples of misconduct, which had been going on for years, and said that they had been covered up. The LORD had already pre-armed me for this, so I stopped her in her tracts and said, "That is not true! If you hear it again from anyone, correct them.

That was not to say that bad things were not happening. For instance, used condoms were found in the Church hall and in one of the side rooms. Some members had major issues with pornography and other forms of sexual immorality, and a few had acute drug addiction problems. There were also less complicated issues, which were nonetheless detrimental to the health of the Church, but there was no evidence of a cover-up.

As a spiritual leader, I dealt with these sensitive issues calmly, professionally and with discretion, without involving the corporate Church. My purpose was not to embarrass or condemn the erring ones, but to restore them to a right standing with God. Some of them had to be suspended from their activities during the process as a means of discipline, but they were all offered counselling and support.

It is tempting to react to events like these emotionally without looking beyond the surface in a discerning way. Hence, interfering members of the Church criticised and verbally abused me because they had no idea what I was dealing with. I never divulged any of these issues to my critics because it really had nothing to do with them. I could see "the storm clouds" gathering, and feel the contrary winds blowing, but I remained resolute because I knew God would be with me in the centre of the storm.

The behaviour of many Cathedral of Praise (COP) members were simply unbecoming, unscriptural, and unspiritual. Some congregants had their selected seats, and if these were taken by anyone else, the occupants were asked to move. Others who were not quite that presumptuous often failed to cooperate with the stewards, and sat where they wanted. Time after time, members had to change their seats, to avoid the grumbling and unsavoury behaviour of certain individuals.

My predecessors had experienced major problems with certain factions, which I inherited. A couple of the trouble makers had resigned from their positions, and some stopped attending the Church, even though their names remained on the membership record for some considerable time after they defected.

Oftentimes unruly and disruptive members occupy key positions in the corporate church – most churches do have them. They are strategically placed by Satan to achieve his objectives. If you leave them in their office it can damage the health of the church, and if you move them it may be double trouble, so what do you do with them? Do you just ignore them? No, you pray that God may shape them up or ship them out!

I had a member like that in the Church, and I honestly couldn't wait to see the back of him. One day, on my way to the office, I began to ask God when this brother was going to leave. Upon my arrival I saw a letter from him in my office. I picked it up hesitantly and began to read. To my amazement, it was his letter of resignation. I shouted the biggest "hallelujah" ever. Not only did he resign, but he left the Church shortly after. Some people are not a blessing to the church; they are a liability.

For about three consecutive years prior to my induction, no report from the local Church was sent to the National Office, and the Church owed the National Headquarters over £40,000.00, which I made an agreement to settle by instalments. The Church's total indebtedness was over £60,000.00, which by the help of God and faithful members was paid off in a short time.

Furthermore, it appeared that a lot of the Church's funds were treated in an offhand way, and often wasted, so I put a moratorium on the spending. This did not go down well with some members who said I was stingy. The congregation had strong cliques, so if you were not a part of them, you were alienated. I was uncomfortable with this behaviour and decided to address the situation promptly.

Consequently, I began to dismantle the cliques, and affirmed the equity and rights of all members. I realised that for the principles of equality and discipline to prevail, they had to be embedded in policy. So, I proceeded to make fundamental changes, creating the infra-structure for discipline and order in the Church, which undoubtedly went against the grain of the factious groups that later concocted complaints against me to have me ostracised.

When some people couldn't manipulate the leadership, and get their own way, they became withdrawn and instigated trouble. Some were unteachable and rebellious, feeling that they'd been around too long to be taught certain principles by me or my wife. They were not always right, and they were not the best at everything, but they were just too arrogant. You should understand that every person you meet can teach you something, even a child and you should be willing to learn.

Some criticised my wife and accused her of using the Church's money to buy her clothes. An outsider asked some grumblers if they were aware that my wife had a full-time job? Evidently, they did not guess that she was dressing like a queen before they met her. Others resorted to bullying tactics to frustrate and intimidate the leadership.

Some made derogatory phone calls, circulated text messages, and sent emails to each other criticising the Church and Pastor's Council (CPC), and undermining, scandalising and vilifying me, but this time they had no idea who they were dealing with. I am a calm, cool and collected person, but I am not anyone's doormat, and most importantly, I am a defender of the faith. In my theology, meekness is not weakness, and humility is not humiliation; sin can make you stupid, but Christianity is not stupidity.

Amazingly, some of the members did not speak to me unless I first spoke to them. They often walked past me as if I was not there. One Sunday morning, I was at the Church door greeting the congregants in my usual way as they exited the building. One of the brothers passed by as if I was non-existent. Sister Pat rushed after him and shouted, "You ought to be ashamed of yourself." I called her and asked her not to do that again, but just to leave him.

Later, I decided to do a teaser. I went to the Church Hall one Wednesday at the close of the fasting service and positioned myself at the exit where everyone would have to pass by me.

I watched the "holy saints" who had just finished praying, shouting hallelujahs and speaking in tongues, walk by me as if I was nowhere in sight. I guess they thought they were insulting me, but they were only manifesting their hypocrisy.

That was bad, but unfortunately, not all the CPC members were loyal. A few had their own hidden agenda and this compounded my problems. Confidential information was often leaked from the CPC meetings to the factions to forearm them against me. One CPC member was caught red-handed recording a (private) council meeting on his mobile phone or relaying it to outside contacts.

This behaviour constituted gross misconduct for which he was openly reprimanded and could have been instantly dismissed from the CPC, but he was unrepentant and continued to be disloyal until a new council had been elected. Judas was a traitor and although Jesus knew it, He still allowed him to remain on His council of twelve. Sometimes the wheat and the tares must grow together until the day of harvest. (See Matthew 13:30.)

Those God-appointed members of the CPC, who gave me

100 percent support, came under fire frequently both from disgruntled members of the Church and those CPC members who felt they were representing the aggrieved ones. The devoted CPC members were often accused by the dissatisfied or discontented church members of supporting the Pastor and not representing or defending their cause. One senior council member would usually respond by saying, "Tell me what wrong he has done."

The church conferences sometimes came to resemble a fish market or a war zone. Some people seemed to have had the notion that "conference" meant "contention;" so they seized the occasion to let off steam. The hateful character of the accusers and their profuse corruption exhausted many loyal members of the Church, who became wearied, disgusted and irritated.

Following one such event, a brother told me that he had left the conference thinking, "Bishop is dead now; he can't survive this." The following Sunday I preached as if nothing had happened and he was "blown away," but very encouraged and strengthened. From then on he began to see me in a new light.

The faithful members sometimes left the meetings in tears and had sleepless nights over the affairs. Some genuine believers refused to attend anymore conferences for fear of another insurrection. A few of them said to me, "Bishop, I just can't take it." While it was their constitutional duty to attend the Church conferences, I understood and sympathised with their position.

Vivian is one of those who has always given me wholehearted support, and he couldn't understand the grievance of the unhappy group. He was so disgusted and angered by those who had an acrimonious dispute in one of our Church conferences that he ended up in hospital for three days. One day as a brother looked at the culprits, he said to me, "Bishop, I feel like hitting them." I said, "No, don't hit anybody."

The situation was so sensitive and volatile, we could have had an altercation, but by the grace of God we didn't.

Having heard and seeing the provocation and atrocities, a beloved senior member of the Church, Mother Imogene Robinson, consoled me: "Bishop, don't cry you know, don't shed a tear; I am praying for you." She had no idea how much these few words meant to me.

You don't have to fear if you know that God is with you. When people thought they were hurting me, they did not know that God was preparing me for greater things, and that they were providing me with material for my book. The only way to keep a good man down is to stay down with him, and only a foolish person would want to do that. "What then shall we say to these things? If God is for us, who can be against us?" (Romans 8: 31, NKJV.)

I can endorse the words of David, "Yea, though I walk through the valley of the shadow of death I will fear no evil; For You are with me; Your rod and Your staff, they comfort me" (Psalm 23: 4, NKJV). The Psalmist was talking about going through the darkest valley or experiencing circumstances that are as dark as a valley and as painful as death, but he says, "I will fear no evil as long as God is with me." The presence of God in one's life makes all the difference.

The Burgeon Church – Revival in The Valley

Despite all the misgivings and misdemeanours, God continued to bless our ministry tremendously, and the Church began to experience phenomenal growth. As a matter of fact, the national and local records show that the Church grew more during this period than at any other time in its entire history. The Church then had a net membership of over 556, with an average Sunday morning attendance of 400 – 450 on a normal week, and the Sunday evening attendance escalated by over 400 percent.

Many more souls were converted, baptized in water, and added to the membership. Over 150 believers received the baptism of the Holy Spirit within the first two years, and outstanding miracles occurred regularly. The gifts of the Spirit operated strongly in the Church, and many individuals experienced breakthroughs in various areas of their lives. The Administrative Bishop acknowledge or commend us for the work, not that we needed it, but instead made innuendos in private about how we were going to sustain such a rapid growth, and generally gave off negative vibes.

The Devil Got Mad

Satan doesn't like progress. There followed hot on the heels of the rapid growth of the Church a spirit of jealousy and severe onslaught on the Pastor. This unprecedented attack got out of hand. False brethren rose up against me with devious intentions. Someone reported me to the *Copyright Licensing Agency (CLA)* for infringement, but I only heard about it when the CLA contacted me.

My critics complained that I was showing sermon videos to the women in their Tuesday meetings. That was untrue! I didn't attend women's meetings. Their intention was to prove to the Administrative Bishop that he had appointed the wrong person, and to make him appear ignorant and incompetent. A large element of the onslaught was an indirect attack on the Administrative Bishop, but he didn't know it.

Subsequently, I was reported to the National Secretary/ Treasurer (NST) for the alleged misappropriation or embezzlement of £16,000, with a threat to inform the Charity Commission. So, obviously the NST had to investigate this before it got out of hand. He later reported to the Church in conference that he "found nothing untoward."

Some individuals who held strategic positions in the Church, and should have known better, accused me behind my back of overspending the Church's money, which would have been impossible. Furthermore, I only found out about this allegation when I read the investigation committee's report. I am sure the Church knew nothing about it.

In our Church system, the Pastor does not handle Church-money. The people who made the allegation were privy to the decision; they simply lied about it. Furthermore, the CPC (not the Pastor) is authorised to spend a maximum of £5,000 at any given time without prior consent from the Church. All major disbursements must be approved by the majority of the Church members in conference. Not only this, but my accusers were actually a part of this decision-making process because we do things by the book at our Church.

The same individuals complained to the investigation committee that I was not having any *Family Training Hour (FTH)*. I know that some folk in the Church had talked about "going back to the FTH," but to the best of my knowledge, most of our churches had discontinued this activity, which had been superseded by something else, but they thought it was their place to tell me what to do. They were always wanting to "go back to something" whereas I was moving forward to something more advanced and beneficial for the Church.

A further complaint was made in writing to Barclays Bank that I had no authority to sign the Church's cheques. This led to an investigation by the bank, which invited me to a meeting with them. I went to the bank and demanded to see the complainant's letter, and verified that it was from a long-standing member of our Church – shock, shock, shock! It was the same person who had previously alleged that I had stolen the Church's money, still fabricating stories. I advised the bank that I was the new Bishop, with full rights and authority to sign cheques on behalf of the Church. I also informed them that any further inquiry should be directed to the National Office for them to pursue, and the bank agreed to do so. Well, I heard no more about that.

The complainants decided to take another course of action: they reported me to the **Enfield Borough Council** about Health and Safety issues, which I knew nothing about at that time. Without any prior warning, the Council sent inspectors to carry out an inspection of the property and subsequently made legitimate recommendations for us to pursue. This backfired on the complainants because it restricted the freedom they had to use the main kitchen at their leisure.

Basically, they "shot themselves in the foot." They were no longer allowed to use the kitchen facilities without the supervision of someone with a food hygiene certificate. Private users with the above qualification had to provide their own liability insurance. We the built a smaller kitchen fully kitted out for the use of our members, on the condition that they leave it clean, but this was not enough to satisfy some disgruntled people.

Many of them began to grumble and complain about how they had raised money to build the kitchen and now were locked out of it. Additionally, owing to certain security challenges that we faced, all locks to the main doors of the building were upgraded and coded locks fitted in the private areas. Only a few authorised key-holders had access to the premises outside of the designated service times. In-house critics said that we turned the Church into "Fort Knox." They might well have called it "John Knox" or "Silver Fox." However, this led to more dissatisfaction, more complaints, and eventually further investigation of the Pastor, who became one of the most investigated ministers in the organisation.

More criticisms and controversies ensued, along with secret pastor-bashing synods held in a couple of the members' homes under the guise of prayer meetings. At one of the gatherings, an outside visitor was so disgusted with the complainants that she rebuked them sharply and said, "You ought to be ashamed of yourselves to be talking about your Pastor like that!" She had thought that she was attending a genuine prayer meeting.

Other discussion groups assembled with their agenda to overthrow the Pastor at any cost, and various anonymous letters against me were sent to the National Office. There were also a few signed letters from contemptuous members. When all these attempts had failed to achieve their objective, they resorted to a more deceitful measure, which escalated the problem and basically made an unpleasant situation volatile.

Severe Persecution 2008–2010

This was a difficult period – the most severe adversity and victimisation in my entire life – and an ordeal which lasted for two years. "Religious affliction" is one of the most heinous or abominable types of persecution, and it usually occurs without any logically valid reason. The illogical fallacies which precipitated the problems that escalated in our Church led the perpetrators to write an outrageous letter to the Administrative Bishop, and for reasons known only to themselves, they copied it to some prominent ministers of other church organisations. This marked the beginning of a series of grave trials and tribulations.

The deadly "complaint letter" was not only abusive, but libellous and scandalous, with defamatory criticisms and accusations about me. It contained thirteen allegations, including misuse of the Church's funds, neglect of the elderly, and mistreatment of individual members, and a request for my removal as pastor from the Church. It also gave an ultimatum that they would contact the Presiding Bishop in America if their demand was not met. This was unprecedented! I had never heard of church members threatening the Administrative Bishop like this before. Oftentimes such cantankerous behaviour is a sign that individuals are unhappy in themselves or feel threatened or deprived of something.

In addition, the letter stated that there was going to be a protest outside the Church. This sounded like scaremongering, but regardless of how frivolous it appeared to have been, these people were serious about their intentions. I could easily have taken legal action against the guilty parties, but I didn't want them or their families to suffer any repercussions. Even more importantly, I was still their pastor.

(A few of the most significant qualities of a credible pastor are integrity, character, foresight and good judgment, and the earlier we learn them, the better our chance of succeeding. These lessons are as important as brushing your teeth twice a day.)

Their "letter of complaint" dated 21 May 2008 was widely circulated. Between 80 and 100 transcripts of the letter were made, and members, non-members, and even unsaved folk were canvassed or coerced to endorse their complaints. Two copies were signed by minors under the age of sixteen; this was a disgraceful and inappropriate act. While I was preaching one Sunday morning, inconspicuous duplicates were discreetly circulated to individuals within the congregation for their signatures.

As a matter of fact, many who signed the letters never knew what they were signing. The perpetrators' behaviour would have been inappropriate and unacceptable in the world at large, and much more so in the Church. They preyed on some senior folk, and forged over 50 signatures. A few of the signatories apologised to me, and wept bitterly when they discovered the deception and trickery practiced on them by some of their Church brothers and sisters whom previously they had trusted.

One elderly lady told me that she was given a blank sheet of paper by a senior sister (who she named) who asked her to put her signature on it. She was also told to ask her children and grandchildren to do likewise. She did it in good faith (thinking it was for a genuine petition) and all these signatures were copied to letters they knew nothing about.

Most of those family members were not Christians or people who attended the Church. I have reason to believe that some of them didn't even know me, and I didn't know them. The lady wept sorrowfully when I made her aware of what had transpired, and she apologised to me profusely. She also wrote to the Administrative Bishop, explaining the deception and apologising to him, but to no effect. Despite significant counter-evidence, he continued to take action against me.

One of the main instigators of this appalling misconduct – a senior female member of the Church threatened to fight me because I had spoken to her about her inappropriate and unacceptable behaviour. And when I say "fight," I mean she actually said, "I will fight you..." She was one of those involved in forging the signatures of innocent people. She left the Church with others who have not returned because of shame.

A few members made it their duty to meet with the new-comers to try to poison their minds against me, and to speak derogatorily about the Church. One such individual was being driven home by Garnet, one of my spiritual sons. A conversation started like this: "Have you heard what's happening in the Church?" Garnet replied, "No, what's happening in the Church?" He said, "The Pastor is mashing up the Church." Garnet stopped the car immediately and told him to "Get out!"

On another occasion, while I was preaching one Sunday morning, the same individual, who had previously handed out petition letters in the Church and had accused me of "mashing up the Church," started to criticise me again. An unsaved man, who was visiting the Church for the first time became very angry and told him to "Shut up!"

The visitor's wife told me that her husband wanted to deal with this person right there; she had to calm him down, but he never came back to our Church. This brother later apologised to me for his behaviour. He said that he was wrong for what he had done, and asked for my forgiveness, which I wholeheartedly gave.

God blessed my wife with the courage, tenacity and strength to face what was coming. Through it all she held her peace and watched the palaver coolly without getting angry or excited. I was graced with the propensity to remain resolute and absolutely calm with unwavering confidence in my position, knowing that if God hires you, no man can fire you, and what God allows, no one can disallow.

The Administrative Bishop's approach to the whole matter was not conducive to my position as a pastor or to the solution of the problem. Furthermore, it was potentially detrimental, not only to the local Church, but the entire Organisation. I became the subject of a number of investigations based on unfounded allegations over a short period, all of which amounted to nothing.

In the first place, the Administrative Bishop wrote to me on 13 June 2008, and summoned me by Recorded Delivery to an *"informal investigation"* meeting *on* the 10 July 2008. He advised that he had received over 80 letters from parishioners of the Wood Green Church with sensitive complaints regarding my care for the spiritual well-being, financial management and accountability of the Church.

He further suggested that the matter would need to be handled according to the Church's own regulations, but in line with UK Employment Law, and that the meeting would form part of an informative investigation, which may or may not result in disciplinary proceedings, although he was careful to also state that no formal action would be taken until he had a response from me regarding the allegations. This letter was fundamental and crucial to everything that subsequently developed.

Again, in his letter of 13 June 2008, the Administrative Bishop wrongly assumed that all the letters he had received came from parishioners of the Wood Green Church, and on that basis, he wrote to all the unidentified complainants simultaneously stating, *"As you are no doubt aware, I have received many similar letters from a number of other members of the Wood Green Church."*

How could they be "aware" of this unless it was a conspiracy to overthrow the Pastor, especially since many of them were not a part of the Church? One should bear in mind that the Administrative Bishop had not yet spoken with me, and an investigation is usually a legal or formal process. He further stated that he had *"a particular connection with the Wood Green Church."*

This statement, in my opinion, not only demonstrated a potential conflict of interest, and possibly raised questions of integrity and fairness, but also prejudicially incriminated the Pastor. Therefore, it potentially rendered any further investigation null and void.

Furthermore, the administrative Bishop did not furnish me with a copy of this letter until I requested it in my letter dated 20 June 2008. In his letter of 13 June 2008, he further state his intention to write to the complainants and to explain that he would be holding a meeting with me to investigate the issues.

No one had previously contacted me about the allegations, and I was extremely surprised to have been invited to an "investigation meeting." Before any allegations of this nature are examined, it is pertinent to have the integrity of the complainants investigated as petitions can be falsified, and it is the normal practice to check and verify the signatures before any action is taken. This is important because the letters could have come from mentally challenged people or from disgruntled church members who had a personality conflict or just a personal vendetta, as was later proven to be the case.

The "Informal Investigation" Meeting

The "informal investigation" meeting was held on 10 July 2008 at the National Office in Northampton in the presence of Bishop E. George Beason and Bishop Louis McLeod. At the beginning of the meeting, to my surprise, the Administrative Bishop raised a personal issue between both of us which had already been resolved and disposed of, but he mentioned how offended he had been by it. This was alarming and unprofessional to say the least, and from that moment I could have seen that the investigation would have been flawed. This is one of those hearings where the verdict was apparently determined before the case began – a meaningless action without any value.

One of the first questions I asked the Administrative Bishop was, "Who were those people who made the allegations against me?" Surprisingly, he said that he did not know, despite having stated in his letter of 13 June 2008 that they were *"parishioners of the Wood Green Church."* I refuted his assumption, and felt it necessary to draw that blunder to the attention of the meeting because it seemed absurd to discipline anyone on the basis of a petition or unfounded allegations from people, many of whom were unknown.

I further pointed out to the Administrative Bishop that the allegation concerning my treatment of a certain sister was untrue, and the subsequent allegation relating to my removal of a particular clock from the wall was also false, for the clock was still in place. I did not highlight these factors because I wanted to challenge trivial points, but simply to give the Administrative Bishop a flavour of how unfounded the allegations were, as a whole. However, by the comments which emanated from our discussion, I felt that he had no interest in what I had to say, and the outcome would potentially have been negative.

It is important to note that at this "investigation meeting" I initiated the discussion and raised all the pertinent points above. To the best of my recollection, the Administrative Bishop did not question me about any of the 13 allegations made against me, and he had not enquired into *"the spiritual, financial or social well-being"* of the Wood Green Church, as mentioned in his letter dated 13 June 2008. So, without any due diligence or properly conducted inquiry, The Administrative Bishop informed me at this initial meeting on 10 July 2008 of his decision to transfer me following the allegations which he had received about my performance as a pastor.

In addition, the transfer was intended as a punishment or "disciplinary action" for the perceived (un-quantified) division in the Wood Green Church. Further, my contention is this: if he had already predetermined the consequence of the meeting based on unfounded allegations made by unknown people, his flawed investigation apparently was deceptive, and his precarious decision seemed to have been a revengeful or vindictive exercise, not a leadership strategy.

Furthermore, where was he moving me to? He had not made me any offer of another placement, and did not give me the opportunity to appeal. Subsequently, I noted that the National Secretary/Treasurer had recorded in the minutes of the said meeting that, "... *confirmed that this was a formal meeting (with) BB as a Minister/Employee.*" This implied that UK Employment Legislation and Standards should have been followed, but the Administrative Bishop potentially breached the law by his failure to observe due process.

The greatest danger to the survival of our Church comes from inside, not outside and this threat is increasing. As ministers and members of the body of Christ, we must unite under God to stop the proliferation of nepotism and anarchy in the Church. We deserve better than a "survival of the fittest," which puts our success in the Church on a par with the natural world and would leave us governed by the struggle for existence despite our ordeal or difficult circumstances.

We need to strive to tangibly demonstrate true Christianity, in which the equity of all is promoted and validated. Only then can we restore the faith of our people in the organisation, especially in the credibility of its leadership. There has been a need for more professionalism and a caring servant-hearted leadership – a shift from self-serving "leaders" to leadership that serves others.

It should be noted also that the vital principle of "training the trainers" is lacking in the hierarchy of the corporate Church, and this is detrimental to our progress. An employment solicitor who examined the facts asked me, "How did the Administrative Bishop get his position? Who appointed him?" I answered, "He was elected by the duly constituted body of our Church, in a national ministers' conference." Perhaps we need to re-evaluate the process of selecting our national leaders.

Approximately fifteen months into the "investigation," The Administrative Bishop seemingly changed his stance, and stated contradictorily in his letter dated 29 October 2009 that the decision to move me was *"not a disciplinary sanction but was required given there had been a breakdown between you and an element of your congregation."* This was incredible. How did he come to that conclusion? The allegations were not properly or completely investigated in accordance with his letter dated 10 September 2008. The committee appointed did not interview the complainants, and the Administrative Bishop had not visited the Wood Green Church in this regard.

The main instigator of the conspiracy alleged that it was the National Office that advised them to write the "complaint letter." When I inquired about it, both the Administrative Bishop and the National Secretary/Treasurer denied this allegation, and inferred that no news of the potential transfer had been leaked by them or anyone else in the office.

To the best of my knowledge, there has never been a precedent in our denomination for moving a minister based on this premise. Naturally, in every church setting, there is always likely to be "a breakdown" between the minister and an "element of his or her congregation." Why would an experienced Christian leader be surprised to hear that seditious or factious groups exist in any large church? Even the little group of disciples that Jesus pastored had a division among them.

Historically, the Wood Green Church started in a divided context – being the amalgamation of three churches. Tottenham and Hornsey branches came together and formed the Wood Green Church on 6 December 1977; the Haringey branch merged with them on 31 March 1991. Ever since its inception, there have always been factions within the Church. Some were of "Paul," and others of "Apollos." My predecessors were obviously aware of this situation which I inherited. Yet, no previous minister has been disciplined for it, obviously because they were not at fault.

As news of the proposed transfer f iltered down into the local Church, allegedly from the National Administration Department, a brother appointed himself to stand at the Church door each Sunday morning, announcing to arriving congregants that "the Burrells are leaving at the end of the month." Some people were pleased about it, but others were evidently very upset; so now the Church had become more fragmented, and I was blamed for that too.

The situation continued to escalate as incorrect and misleading information about me was communicated to the National Executive Council (NEC), emanating from both local and national levels. By this time, everyone involved had been grossly misled and it was broadcast that the Wood Green Church was "mashed up."

A senior colleague and father figure who visited our Church was so impressed by what he saw and heard that he remarked: "If this is a mashed-up Church, I think every pastor would want their Church mashed-up." He further stated that the order and discipline in the Church service exceeded all that he had seen in his many years of ministry. However, neither the Administrative Bishop nor the NEC was cognizant with the calibre of Church we had at Wood Green because the disgruntled complainants had painted a totally negative picture.

The Administrative Bishop (and CEO) erred terribly, and was in violation of his own policy:

- The policies and procedures of an organisation can indicate to its managers, members, employees and other stakeholders the rules and byelaws they must observe. The policies, rules and byelaws stipulate how the company regulates itself, and the Church operates in just the same way. If a manager or CEO of an organisation violates certain aspects of their policy, they may also break the law, and this may incur legal consequences.

- The Church's Rule Book, more commonly known as the Minutes Book states: *"Loyal, tithing members of a local church (who) have a legitimate concern as it relates to the welfare of their church..., have the right and privilege to contact their state overseer, after they have contacted their pastor and district pastor... These concerns should be preferably in writing, not as part of a petition."*[6]

- The allegation letters seemed to have been copies of the said complaint, but bore different signatures. They all had the same date, but appeared to have been circulated over a period of five weeks from the 21 May to 25 June 2008, which rendered them tantamount to a petition. Constitutionally, our Church does not deal with petitions, so the letters should have been discarded.

- There was a gap between July and September 2008 when no obvious action was taken, so I thought the matter was discarded. From the very outset, I had advised the Administrative Bishop in my letter of 14 July 2008 that his investigation process was procedurally flawed, and from my perspective the matter was deemed to have been closed.

Surprisingly, in September 2008, the Administrative Bishop appointed a committee of three to conduct an "investigation conference" at the Wood Green Church. His letter dated 10 September 2008 to the Chair of the committee stated that following a recommendation from the NEC, a committee had been appointed and that a complete investigation would have been undertaken " *with a view of bringing an end to the persistent complaints emanating from the ministry.*" This statement seemed undermining, prejudicial, and unreasonable. Furthermore, there could not have been any independent and objective investigation, for the Chair was apparently pointed in a particular direction, with a predetermined conclusion.

I was concerned as to why the Administrative Bishop (and CEO) of the Organisation, should get involved personally, and then after investigating the matter over a period of four to five months, turn it over to his subordinates for further investigation. This fallacious procedure was like "putting the horse before the cart." If I was dissatisfied with the investigation committee's report, to whom would I have the right of appeal? By this time, I was extremely frustrated, and very stressed over what seemed to have been escalating towards a major disaster.

Therefore, in an attempt to avert this catastrophe, I wrote to the Administrative Bishop on 6 November 2008, stating:

I have noted carefully the contents of your letter of 31 October 2008, and I note that the purpose of the visit from Bishop LAB (the Chair) is to "enquire into the spiritual, financial and social well-being" of the Church. It does seem to me that this is too broad and potentially wide-ranging a remit for enquiry, which as currently framed is unlikely to assist in establishing clear terms of reference for enquiry by reference to the specific issues raised in the "complaint letter" of 21 May 2008.

If it be the case that you intend to continue with the enquiries by Bishop LAB (the Chair), I trust you will appreciate it is essential that the enquiries must be focused, proportionate and relevant. I am also deeply concerned that the "enquiry" should not descend into a general casting around for expressions of discontent to further undermine my work as the Senior Pastor of the Church Community and that of the hard working members of the CPC, or to demoralise the membership, and I assume that you will be anxious to ensure that the enquiry process is carefully managed to avoid creating a humiliating, degrading or hostile working environment such as to undermine my position and create an impression that I have lost the confidence of the Administrative Bishop.

I note that it is proposed that the visit by Bishop LAB (the Chair) comprises three elements: a meeting with myself and with the CPC and a general meeting with members of the Church in conference. As for the third element, i.e. a meeting with the Church members, I am firmly of the view that to hold a general meeting with members in conference on the basis of vague and unsubstantiated allegations will be divisive, demeaning to my leadership and to that of the CPC, and in any event of no value.

Having reviewed the content of the "complaint letter" and noting the lack of particularity, it is clear that a members' meeting would not be an appropriate means to address the issues identified. I am concerned that if such a meeting is proposed, the purpose of it must be clear, and furthermore it is essential to set out in advance the topics for discussion on the agenda. Therefore, please advise what is the purpose of the members' meeting? What are the topics for discussion on the agenda? How is it envisaged that such a meeting is probative, relevant, appropriate (as in a fair process) and/or proportionate to address the issues set out in the "complaint letter."

I would therefore request sight of written and clear terms of reference and guidance as to how it is intended that each matter in the "complaint letter" will be investigated in advance of the proposed meetings to ensure that the purpose and scope of the enquiry are carefully and fairly managed and to ensure I am in a position to make representations."

Again, I wrote to the Administrative Bishop on 8 November 2008:

I am writing further to your letter of 31 October 2008 and the email from your PA… this afternoon confirming the meeting with Bishop LAB on 26 November 2008. I also wish to refer to your letter of 13 June 2008, in which you have referred to UK Employment Law and its application to my situation. I confirm that I am mindful of the relevant statutory provisions and case law related to harassment, unfair/wrongful dismissal and constructive dismissal. However, I acknowledge that allegations have been raised and that it is your intention that these matters should be looked into. Accordingly, I wish to assist the enquiry process by making the following proposals to ensure that the objectives of the enquiry and the process are focused, proportionate and relevant.

Addressing each issue in turn with a view to identifying what enquiry is merited and/or possible, and if so, to propose an appropriate method of investigation, I propose as follows:

Re. allegation 1 – I am very concerned that given the unusual provenance (to say the least) of the "complaint letter" it simply cannot be asserted and or assumed that any actual signatory to the letter was in fact present at a meeting on 25 January 2007. Even if I had said that "I am not your shepherd" (which is not true) this is an entirely uncontroversial statement and in the absence of any

199

context in particular or any detail as to what the matter was that had been raised, or by whom and to which I am alleged to have given this response, this allegation is simply unsuited to any proportionate investigation and in any event, does not merit any further enquiry.

Re. allegation 2 – there is no detail as to who the elderly members are that are said to have complained to which members of the CPC and when any such "complaint" was made. It is entirely inappropriate to seek to deal with this issue by asking broad and bland questions of CPC members to the effect of whether they have received any such complaints. It is a matter of basic fairness that those seeking to advance these matters must particularise the complaints they bring with sufficient detail to enable these matters to be investigated and for my part such that I am able to make representations on my own behalf.

Re. allegation 3 – Similarly as set out above this is an allegation which it is impossible to investigate. In particular, I have no idea who is said to have been intimidated or summonsed to meetings etc., on the basis of things they said in a conference. It is entirely inappropriate to conduct an enquiry on the basis of unspecified allegations.

All 13 allegations were identified and addressed separately in the above letter – a kind of template of how a proper investigation should be carried out, but I did not receive a reply to any of the letters.

On 7 October 2008, I wrote a grievance complaint to Dr Larry Hess – the Field Director for Western Europe/Medit/ Mid.East (copied to the Administrative Bishop) explaining my predicament and requesting his intervention. He was attending a meeting in Germany at the time, so he asked me to email the relevant documents to his wife in the USA for his attention when he returned home.

I did as he requested, and also pointed out that the unreasonable action to which I was subjected by the Administrative Bishop was procedurally flawed, and if allowed to escalate could have very serious implications for the Organisation. A copy of this letter was sent to the Administrative Bishop. Dr Hess said that he had discussed the matter with the Attorney General of the Church of God in America.

The Head Attorney of the Church immediately saw the legal implications, and advised Dr Hess that the matter should be referred back to the Administrative Bishop and NEC for the United Kingdom, who were still in their twilight dream. My complaints were not addressed at any level of the Church. I knew my rights as an employee, and that there was no fear of losing the case, but I did not want to pursue any legal action against my Church.

On 17 November 2008, I wrote a grievance complaint letter to the NEC (copied to the Administrative Bishop) relating the facts, and requesting their intervention. I was just pleading for help. I wanted them to put an end to the situation before it escalated and damaged the wider Church, but I did not receive any reply. The letter was not dealt with and the grievance not disposed of. Basically, I was again ignored.

I fully understand what David experienced when he said, "... It is not my enemy who reproaches me; then I could bear it. Nor is it one who hates me who has exalted himself against me; then I could hide from him, but it was you, a man of my equal, my companion and my acquaintance..." (Psalm 55:11–14, NKJV.) My confidence in the leadership of our Church waned, and I became disillusioned with the National Organisation. But for the bountiful supply of God's grace, I would have been defunct (finished) as far as the denomination was concerned.

The Investigation Conference 26 November 2008

The "investigation conference" was chaired by Bishop Levi Bailey. The other two committee members were Rev. Lloyd Henry and Rev. Donovan Allen. The former was recently appointed to the bishopric and the latter was a junior minister, both of whom were occupying their first pastorates and had not had experience investigating allegations of such magnitude. In keeping with proper procedure, a bishop or more senior ministers should have been appointed to a committee, whose disciplinary investigation relates to the conduct of a bishop.

Regarding the contention that the committee had been appointed to advise on what changes were necessary to address the concerns of the membership, this was clearly a statement confirming that the remit of the committee was limited to investigating and reporting upon the issues that form the subject matter of the complaint against the accused and inevitably predetermined or predicated the decision to transfer me. I must say – with all due respect – that any attempt to divorce the remit of the committee's terms of reference from the complaint was pure sophistry (the use of clever but false arguments, especially with the intention of deceiving).

Furthermore, as I mentioned previously, there is no provision for an investigation conference in the *Church's Book of Discipline, Church Order and Governance (2008), or in UK Employment Legislation,* and in over six decades of my life, I have never heard of anything like it. This was the most undermining and humiliating experience I have ever had to tolerate. Quite apart from that, it was shocking to watch the well-orchestrated performance of some of the complainants, who manipulated the conference and maneuvered deceitfully in order to ostracise me.

At the beginning of the conference, the chairman explained that the reason for the conference was that "several allegations had been received by the Administrative Bishop from members of the Wood Green Church." He did not state what the allegations were, and most of the attendees had no idea what he was talking about.

The Chair failed to check and ensure that all the attendees were members of the Wood Green Church. He did, however, inform the conference that the meeting had nothing to do with the Pastor's ministry – an apparent contradiction. "Bishop Burrell's ministry," he said, "was not in question." He then added that their (the committee's) *objective is to determine the health of the church, and to report back to the Administrative Bishop and the National Executive Council.* He also said that no one was on trial, and that he and the other members of the committee were sent by the Administrative Bishop to investigate:

1. The spiritual well-being of the Church

2. The financial well-being of the Church and

3. The social well-being of the Church.

The agenda in the above order, was projected on the overhead screen, with the following footnote: *"This meeting will be minuted only by the Committee."* The conference was also informed that the proceedings would be recorded for accuracy. They had a small desk recorder for that purpose. The Chair asked the meeting the following questions:

Question 1

How do you view your Church right here in Wood Green?

A few people began to speak favourably about their Church and how the ministry had changed their lives, but it was not long before the disgruntled members and non-members seized the moment to launch a personal and acrimonious attack on the Pastor.

Some of them began by saying, "There is nothing wrong with the Church at Wood Green, but Bishop Burrell," and then proceeded to hurl vicious allegations at me. They sounded irrational like people with a delusion of persecution, transitioning between malicious intent and hostile harassment, appearing somewhat like a melodramatic TV show. Worse yet, throughout the exaggerated drama, I was denied the right to respond in my own defence or to give any clarification.

A very large percentage of the Church members did not attend the "investigation conference" (by this time they had had enough), and most of the faithful ones who attended were not given the opportunity to speak. As a matter of fact, many were appalled and shocked at what they saw and heard, and others were equally bemused.

In British Law, a man is innocent until he is proved guilty, but evidently it was not so on this occasion. The above statement, "There is nothing wrong with the Church at Wood Green, but Bishop Burrell," indicates the direction the conference took. The focus was taken off the Church which was "perfect" and redirected to "Bishop Burrell" the accused who became the subject of the debate. I tried to use my parliamentary privilege to raise a point of order, but the Chair told me to "wait until the end of the meeting to make my response." These unparliamentary procedures went unnoticed by the conference, but I remained magnanimous in spite of the unfairness and hostility directed at me.

Since I was forbidden to speak, I listened intently and made my observations, while meticulously noting all that occurred. One's blood runs cold to think that in the twenty-first century, one could be treated so despicably within the Church under the guise of Christianity. Such a contemptible and taunting behaviour makes a mockery of spiritual leadership and divine justice. It was not only a poor performance, but a deplorable representation of the sacred cause which we profess to acclaim.

My "ministry was not in question," no charges were levied against me, and I am the Pastor of the Church with constitutional rights, responsibilities and authority, but this was not acknowledged or respected. The law of the land gives the worst criminals the right to speak in their defence, but the committee denied me that right in the face of public abuse, insults, harassment, and grave victimisation, but I forgave them. I don't think the committee meant me any evil; they were just misguided. These men regarded themselves as my friends.

Question 2

Are there any other issues that members would like to raise?

This seemed like a diversion from the remit set by the Administrative Bishop and simply amounted to throwing the fishing net out. As a result, the conference descended into a series of insults, and a public humiliation of myself by the disgruntled members and others such as I had never experienced in my forty years of ministry, and the chairman did not once call for order.

In a pre-conference session, I had informed the committee that if a certain brother turned up he should not be allowed to speak in the conference because he was no longer worshipping at our Church and for other legitimate reasons which I related to them.

This "gentleman" attended the conference, as one had suspected he would, and indicated that he wished to speak. The Chair tried to stop him, but he insisted on expressing himself. The committee was apparently intimidated by his eloquence and recognised him. He attacked me outrageously, and moved down the aisle towards the front, as though he was going to assault me physically, but still I had no protection from the Chair.

Question 3

How is the pastoral care administered?

This ambiguous question opened up a "can of worms," and gave my accusers the chance to have a field day. They made many derogatory remarks about me, and indulged in one of the worst kinds of character assassination; but again, the chairman permitted the onslaught. Not once was I given any protection from the Chair, who seemed intimidated by the aggressor's eloquence and ferocity.

The people were given free range to say whatever they wanted because the committee indicated that they were there for just that reason – fact finding. By this time, I was mentally and physically exhausted and ready to leave, but I held my peace. My wife felt just the same, though she never said a word, but exhibited a great deal of strength and character throughout.

Question 4

How is the social care of the Church addressed?

This question did nothing to change the attitude of the

disgruntled attendees or the mood of the meeting; again, I was taken aback by the intensity of their outburst. Apparently, everything was done to justify creating an atmosphere of hostility towards me to enable the committee to see the Church at its worst, and they did. I could not and still do not understand why the chairman did not protect me, since I was "not under investigation or trial." It seemed like I was being invaded by aliens, but was stuck in a dead-end road perplexed and horrified.

The conference was poorly conducted, and the proper procedures, as outlined in **Roberts Rules of Order** (recognised by our International Church) were not followed. Some of the people there behaved more like a mob, and the meeting was out of control. This was shocking for me, because we had and still have a great Church, and this faction did not by any means represent the Church as a whole.

The disgruntled, delinquent members and non-members had free speech. Clearly most of these people, were not loyal tithing members of the Church, and did not attend Church regularly. Many were co-opted just for the purpose of the conference. I understand that the main proponents of the allegations contacted them by email and text message, among other means.

When a certain woman was recognised by the Chair, I told him that she was not a member of the Church. Rev. Lloyd Henry audibly called for two volunteers from the Church and Pastor's Council (CPC) to approach them at the table, and asked if this individual was a member of the Church. They looked at each other (with some hesitancy or uncertainty) and dubiously confirmed that she was a member, so the committee permitted her to take the floor. I was flabbergasted.

This action discredited me, and undermined my position as the Pastor. I felt disappointed, cheated and betrayed by those CPC members, but their unreliable behaviour was not surprising. The individual was not a member of the Church. As a matter of fact, she was baptized two months later and was received into the Church in January 2009.

The usher who took the roaming mike around to individuals on the floor who wished to speak, was among the main proponents of the allegation letters. Normal procedure is that members only speak in a conference when they are recognised by the Chair. I was disheartened and appalled at what I saw: the microphone was carried around by the usher to his friends, also proponents of the allegations, and they were allowed to speak freely without any recognition or control from the Chair.

According to the Church's constitution,[7] only members of the Church have the right to attend church conferences; this was violated during the "investigation conference" as one or two non-members who attended were allowed to speak on the floor. I watched some of these eloquent individuals being given the chance to air their views two, three and four times before some loyal members who wished to speak were recognised even once.

This was inconsistent with **Roberts Rules of Order**, which states that no individual should be given the opportunity to speak twice before others who wish to speak have had the opportunity to do so. I pointed this out to the investigating committee when it became clear that some people were dominating the conference, but Rev. Donovan Allen said to me, *"Don't say anything."* In other words, my presence was ignored by the committee. I was put at a disadvantage – apparently there to be seen, but not to be heard. It was not clear to me whether this was a part of their remit.

In retrospect, I feel that the conference was convened in deception, in that the Chair told us, *"No one was on trial; the meeting was designed to check the health of the Church."* On the contrary, it turned out to be an outrageous quasi trial of the Pastor, which in itself was procedurally flawed and detrimental to the health of the Church. The fabrications of those who assassinated my character went unchallenged and unproved as justice virtually disintegrated, but righteousness prevailed.

The Chair recognised a member from the floor, who held up a letter in his hand, which he claimed I had written threatening to take him to court. That was not true, but I was forbidden to speak, and neither the Chair nor any member of the investigation committee requested to see the letter. They just listened and made their notes, while I looked on in dismay.

I was denied natural justice and fairness because of the investigation committee's failure to interview all the complainants, or a representative (i.e., a spokesperson) of the complainants, or even a fraction of the congregation selected at random. Their omission rendered the investigation incomplete, and procedurally flawed. It was all like a horrible nightmare, and no doubt we wished it was, but neither my wife Maxine nor I shed any tears. We demonstrated absolute strength throughout.

At the end of the "discussions" and before the conference concluded, I asked the committee for the opportunity to respond and the chairman told me "No!" When the meeting terminated, many of the boastful complainants unashamedly celebrated ostentatiously with laughter and high-fives, while some loyal members had headaches, and others were in tears as they exited the building frustrated, disappointed and disgusted by such a palaver.

I discreetly expressed my disappointment to the committee about how they had conducted the conference. They were saddened by this because they were genuine men, with good intentions, but just didn't have the experience or expertise to deal with that situation. Wood Green was not a church that just anyone could pastor and still retain their sanity, and these ministers simply lost their equilibrium and could not deal with what had occurred. I had been acquainted with them before the investigation. One has died since, but the other two and I continue to have an amicable relationship.

To my displeasure, a few days after the conference, I found out that the PA men who had operated the mixing desk and controlled the public-address system had secretly recorded the meeting on CDs, and duplicated copies which they took away for their own devices. To me, this action was like putting bombs in the hands of terrorists. The unauthorised recording was a breach of copyright law, and a violation of the conference policy.

Summary of The Case

Although I was strongly persuaded that the method adopted for the investigation was flawed, of course I had no objection to the Administrative Bishop instigating a formal inquiry into the allegations; that was his prerogative. My only concern was that the inquiry should be conducted in an equitable manner and have regard to the relevant Employment Law. I gave full co-operation to both the Administrative Bishop and his committee in order to aid the investigation process. This is confirmed in the Complaint Investigation Report.

In the first place, the Administrative Bishop replied inappropriately to the allegation letters before any consultation with me, and breached the constitution of the *General Assembly of the Church of God* and *ACAS Code of Practice 2009,* in several ways. ACAS is a legally binding Code of Practice on disciplinary and grievance procedures. It gives practical guidelines for handling these issues in the workplace.

- In his letter dated 21 November 2008, the Administrative Bishop stated that the minutes of the "conference with the membership" would be available to me. Yet, upon my written request for copies of the minutes, the committee's report, and other relevant data which were germane to the investigation, he adamantly refused to furnish me with them, without any clear rationale, until he eventually did several months later in October 2009. This seemed very unreasonable, and was a breach of the *Data Protection Act(DPA) 1998 Section 7*, which requires an employer to provide the requested data within 40 days.

- After I made several written requests to the Administrative Bishop, he reluctantly sent most of the data, over one year and seven months after my initial request. I was professionally advised to take legal action against him, without any cost to myself, but I didn't. That's not what I wanted to do.

- On 24 December 2008, the Administrative Bishop wrote to one of the complainants and advised him that he was waiting for the report from the investigation committee before any further action would have been undertaken. However, he added that in the meantime, *"please remain encouraged and encourage those under your charge."* I felt that this letter was inappropriate and potentially divisive; not only that but it was not copied to me voluntarily either.

- The procedure adopted throughout the investigation process was fundamentally flawed, and as a result, was in breach of natural justice, and moreover Employment Law. Therefore, the investigation committee's report to the NEC was unreliable and unacceptable. It undoubtedly clouded the judgement of the NEC; hence their misconceived perception of the Wood Green Church, and wrongful recommendation to the Administrative Bishop.

- In essence, the Administrative Bishop said that he would be transferring me on the recommendation of the investigation committee and the National Executive Council (NEC) because the Church was divided, and also was *"beyond redemption under my leadership."* This implied that he had succumbed to the demands of the petitioners and his proposed transfer was as a consequence of their allegations. However, his decision was not in accordance with the Church of God Rule Book, otherwise called the Minutes Book.

- Furthermore, this so-called " divided Church" was not congruent (in agreement or harmony) with the allegations; neither was it proved that the division occurred under my administration, and there was certainly no evidence offered that I was at fault for the division. Furthermore, the division had not been adequately qualified or quantified, and there was no rationality to the assertion.

- In their letter dated 15 April 2009, the Church's legal representatives made comments about the Church being "seriously divided," but again this perceived division was not quantified. If the allegations were made by 78 members of the Church, as they said, then this represented only 14.5% of the then membership of 537.

- Some of those "members" who appeared to have complained had actually left the Church between 3 and 7 years earlier. According to my calculations, the disgruntled faction constituted only about 8% of the Church's membership at the time, and would constitute an even smaller percentage later considering the significant increase in membership at the time.

- As everyone of us knows, in any grouping of individuals, there will always be an element of disagreement. In this case, to proceed with a pastoral change on this basis seemed totally unreasonable, and would have set a dangerous precedent that any church with a division or faction constituting at least 14.5% of the total congregation must have a change of pastor.

  Furthermore, the perceived "division" should have been viewed against a backdrop of an ever-increasing membership, which coincided with my leadership. We should be mindful that the bona fides of some of the 78 complaints were questionable, given the Church's definition of membership. Membership is *"evidenced by consistent attendance, financial support and service to and through the congregation,"*[8] not just a list of names on the record.

- When a church has serious problems with its membership, this is reflected in a fall in attendance and in its ability to raise money, but in this case, the opposite was the reality

– the Church grew and its finances increased – in marked contrast to the alleged breakdown.

- If I was deemed to be responsible for the division and sent to create the same problem in another church, that would be like spreading a malignant disease somewhere else. On the other hand, if I was not at fault for the division the stigma would still have percolated into all my future pastorates and spread through the community like wild fire. Also, I would have had to leave the Wood Green Church like a lame duck since the Administrative Bishop had moved me from there to "rescue the Church from the alleged disaster."

- This would stigmatise me, potentially compromising 40 years' irreproachable reputation and tarnishing my ministry. Furthermore, as I have said, if I had divided the Wood Green Church, why would any other church want me to be their pastor? Might history not repeat itself?

- Perhaps I could have managed elsewhere with further training or closer supervision, if that was necessary, but this was not considered an option. The intended transfer was potentially an unlawful victimisation, and under those circumstances, I believe the process of the potential transfer and the entire investigation were not only wrong, but unjustifiable, unreasonable and could have brought the Church into disrepute.

- In his letter of 6 April 2009, my solicitor comments, "…we do not consider that the complaints whether individually or collectively (insofar as they have been sufficiently particularised) amount to an allegation of misconduct that warrants any disciplinary action more so the invocation of disciplinary procedures and ultimately the sanction of a transfer. It is clear, based on the evidence to hand, that NTCG has adopted a procedure that contravenes the 2009 Code of Practice (and its predecessor)."

- Also, in the same letter dated 6 April 2009, my solicitor rightly pointed out to the Administrative Bishop that he "ought to be aware, as a matter of Law, NTCG in the course of investigating any complaint that could give rise to a disciplinary penalty (e.g., a transfer), is required to adhere to ACAS Code of Practice with effect from the above date. The principles of fairness, amongst other things, require employers to deal with issues promptly and ensure that they do not unreasonably delay meetings, decisions or confirmation of those decisions."

- "Further, employers should carry out a full investigation, in order to establish the facts of the case and ensure that employees are made aware of the basis of the concerns and provide the employees with an opportunity to answer the case before a final decision is made." I was horrendously deprived of this opportunity, and denied my contractual entitlement as outlined in the ACAS Code of Practice.

The Church's legal representatives further confirmed in their letter of 15 April 2009 that the investigation committee *"spoke to Bishop Burrell, the Church and Pastor's Council and the membership of the Church in a conference."* They certainly did, but failed to interview the complainants specifically. In my opinion, this was a serious breach of the recognised procedure for dealing with grievances or complaints in the workplace.

The nature of the allegations could have had a serious impact legally, practically and spiritually on the organisation, affecting the morale of the congregation and the minister's productivity. How then can anyone rationally respond or realistically investigate such complaints without speaking to the complainants?

In their letter dated 15 April 2009, the Church's Solicitors had previously asserted that *"the transfer was being undertaken under the Administrative Bishop's authority as State Overseer to appoint pastors to congregations."*[9] I was aware of the guidelines for State Overseers.

I did not challenge the Administrative Bishop's authority to "appoint district overseers, pastors, and make changes or fill vacancies in pastorates when necessary." Notwithstanding, it was apparent that the decision to transfer me was not a normal change of the pastorate. Therefore, this stipulation was not applicable.

However, I contended that the various responses from the Administrative Bishop and his solicitor's letter of 15 April 2009 seemed to confirm that the decision to transfer me was a direct result of the complaints letter to which they referred. I also took issue with the casual connection of the proposed transfer with the said complaints, and the consequent unreasonable treatment. It is inconceivable that the procedure adopted by the Administrative Bishop could reasonably have been said to be "preliminary" or "informal" given the sanction proposed.

Furthermore, I had no reason to believe that the transfer was genuine. Hence, I refused to move from my job under those conditions and be misrepresented and falsely accused. Throughout the entire episode, the loyal members of the Church stood by me, and were unerringly faithful in their support and encouragement, although they were not fully aware of what was taking place.

There were many occasions when loyal members got angry because of the situation, but they maintained their integrity and held their peace. Some of them wrote supportive letters to the Administrative Bishop, but they were simply ignored. He replied to one sister and told her to "stay out of this!"

I have never belittled my position by quarrelling with any church members or behaving vindictively or maliciously towards them. I pastored them despite their failings or bad behaviours. There were times when I 'threatened' to use the rod of correction, but hardly ever did. My "bark was worse than my bite."

However, there have been critical matters that needed to be dealt with expeditiously. Regrettably, I have had to take drastic measures against a couple of individuals to protect the wider interests of the Church, and in particular the more vulnerable amongst its members, but this too is a part of successful leadership. As the saying goes, "If we don't stand for something, we'll fall for anything"[10] or the other version "When you stand for nothing, you fall for everything." There must be a standard!

What annoyed me the most was this: at a *National Key Workers' Conference*, the Administrative Bishop called me to the platform along with other minsters to recognise us for special achievements. He named each minister and commended them for the number of people in their local Church who had received the baptism with the Holy Spirit in a given period of time. A significantly higher number of people had received the Holy Spirit baptism in the Wood Green Church than in any other NTCG branch in the UK.

Yet, when my turn came, the Administrative Bishop publicly announced to the audience of about 1,800 people that "Bishop Burrell built two toilets in the Wood Green Church."

The sense of being mistreated and insulted filled me with righteous indignation. **Righteous** anger is justly expressed when we are confronted with sin or injustice.

I was so angry that I contemplated walking out of the meeting and going home, but I recollected that this behaviour would have been inappropriate, and would have set a bad example for my Church members who sat there empathising with me. I wouldn't have minded if he had not mentioned my name or the Wood Green Church; that would have been like "water off a duck's back."

Following this incident, I made an appointment and went to see the Administrative Bishop at the National Office. I told him exactly how I felt about the situation and he listened. I also said to him that we should not allow church members to come between us, for when his tenure as Administrative Bishop expired he would need me and I would need him. He thanked me for coming to speak with him and expressed his appreciation for it. I left his office feeling good and hopeful for better things, but amazingly nothing changed.

Although I had told the Administrative Bishop from the outset that his procedures were flawed, even though his legal representative and the NEC had also told him the same thing and despite the fact that he himself knew it, nevertheless, as a Christian leader, he never had it in his heart even to say, "In retrospect things could have been done differently." That would have been sufficient for our reconciliation, and it would have restored his credibility which had probably been damaged in the investigation process.

This prompted a number of pertinent questions: does God know our limits? Will He give us more than we can bear? Was there no alternative? Why did I stick this out to the end? There were days when I felt like I'd had enough. I could easily have given up, "washed my nets" and walked away; but quite apart from my own personal awareness and integrity, I did it for the sake of my younger colleagues in the ministry. I considered that if the Church had treated me so badly, what hope would there be for the younger ministers? I was willing to sacrifice self in order to set a president for fairness and justice in the Church from which both the young and the old could benefit.

Quite frankly I don't care much about the religious rhetoric and church politics, which simply gloss over the surface of complex and detrimental issues, but fail to address our endemic problems. Religiosity is not Christianity. The challenge of the church is to be relevant and remain Christ-like in words and deeds.

If we only treat the obvious symptoms of the rampant epidemic and not the root cause of being where we have always been and doing what we've always done, we are rapidly becoming an endangered species, seriously at the risk of extinction.

There is nothing wrong with our divine mandate, it's as up-to-date as today's newspapers, but we need a new paradigm, a new vision and a new approach to ministry in our contemporary generation. We must lay aside the sin that so easily beset us and get hold of eternal values as we run this race with patience.

What the church needs is not more programmes or modern sophisticated buildings, but a new ethos and God-fearing leadership that will say "Thus says the LORD, not thus says my pride." "Pride goes before destruction, and a haughty spirit before a fall" (Proverbs 16:18-19). The word haughtiness originally comes from the Old French adjective haut meaning "high" and later developed to mean having a high estimation of oneself. It is a proud, snobbish and scornfully arrogant spirit that permeates many contemporary leaders.

The twenty-first century Christianity demands that we as leaders should be humble servants of God proactively building healthy churches and getting things done the right way for the right reason. This was not a "Deal or No Deal" power game, or an antisocial personality issue, but about building the Kingdom of God. It is better to be radical and honest than popular but insincere. Young ministers, in particular, should be aware that the stronger the anointing on your lives, the greater your trials and persecutions, and the more you'll be misunderstood. Between the beginning of your journey and your destination, potentially deadly storms may arise to impede your progress or to curtail your success, but your victory is predetermined by the Master of all circumstances.

Luke states that a great storm arose while the disciples of Christ were at sea (Luke 8::22–25). The storms of life will always blow; that's natural. All of us have to deal with them. Without any forewarning, you may find yourself in the middle of a devastating crisis. Some of you may spend a night in the storm, others a day, some a week or even a longer period of time, but you can be assured that if Christ is in your boat, you can overcome your troubles. The big question is this: "Is Christ in your boat?" While other boats are sinking in the stormy weather, the Christian's boat will stay afloat.

Even the very elements of nature that sometimes work against us for our destruction, will work for our protection, if we recognise the voice of Christ and obey Him. Satan brings trials and difficult circumstances to destabilise us and mess up our equilibrium, but God uses the same elements of life to bring us to stability, maturity and responsibility.

Jesus and His disciples were in a similar situation, at the same place and the same time, but Jesus was calmly asleep while the disciples panicked. Why? Because Jesus was never controlled by difficult circumstances. He controlled circumstances, but the disciples were circumstance-controlled.

Scientifically, a storm erupts when "extreme air pressure is created at an atmospheric level as warm wet air rushes, causing cold air to move towards the area where air pressure is lower, eventually creating a rotation."[11] Metaphorically, a storm is the natural result of the circumstances of life, but we should learn from our master teacher how to speak to our storms and say to them, "Peace be still."

Even though I had spent over two years on my stormy sea at Wood Green, I never panicked or allowed myself to be driven to despair because I knew that Jesus was with me and my victory was guarantee. Waves are not permanent; it's just a matter of time and they'll subside. After every storm, there'll come a calm.

The Inevitable Conclusion

The NEC eventually accepted that the process of the investigation was procedurally flawed and incongruent with Church of God Policy and brought it to a conclusion. All my legal costs were paid by the National Office. Evidently, God was with me throughout the whole episode, and He vindicated His son.

God's timing is different to yours, but it's always perfect, and if you trust Him, He will surely deliver you! Sometimes, when God is about to move you into your destiny, He uses an adverse circumstance as the escalator to elevate you to the next level. Your journey may be rocky at times, but if God is with you, you can move up the King's High-Way, trusting in amazing grace, and pursuing your spiritual journey with confidence and a great sense of achievement. We have the assurance that no man hired God, and no one can fire Him. He will always reign supremely as God! So our position in Hi is secure.

From the very beginning, the LORD had shown me in a vision my impending conflict with the Administrative Bishop (a conflict which occurred because of the firm stance I took in the local Church), and the potential outcome. I then shared this with a couple of my close colleagues in the ministry. So, the attacks themselves were not surprising; it was the ferocity of them that shocked me. I was not even accustomed to being dragged into church politics much more before a religious firing squad.

One night in my sleep, I heard through the Spirit the NEC discussing me in negative terms. In the morning, I said to my wife, "They are at it again; another Recorded Delivery letter is imminent;" it came a few days later. I had become accustomed to this sort of letter, either demanding that I stop the building renovation work or just threatening me with some uncalled-for and unjustifiable action, but I persevered and succeeded.

In Bible days, spiritual dreams and visions were commonplace. An angel of the Lord appeared to Joseph in a dream (Matthew 1:20); Paul saw a man from Macedonia in a vision (Acts 16: 9), and God still speaks to us through these means today (Job 33:14–15). Prior to the "investigation conference" of 26 November 2008, I had another vision in which I saw many reindeer with huge antlers chasing me around the Church hall. I beat them back and they ran out of the hall deflated. There was a man standing at the entrance (their exit) and they complained to him that they couldn't get me. He was very angry and said, "Go and get him; you have to get him now!"

As I pondered the meaning of the latter vision, I perceived that the reindeer were demon spirits working in individuals assigned to attack me. The angry man at the door was Satan himself who had sent them to "get him now!" This implied a sense of urgency – time was short. The devil knew that if they failed to get me at that conference they would never succeed again.

My next vision was more direct. I dreamed that I saw the Administrative Bishop in a park. He was coming towards me with two guns in his hands – a long rifle and a small pistol or revolver. I thought, "If I run he'll shoot me," so I went at him and knocked the guns out of his hands. He frustratedly looked at me with baleful eyes and said, "You have won this time, but it's not over yet." This led me to believe that he had a plan "B" up his sleeve. So, I was always ahead of him and kept him "under surveillance."

Following my grievance complaint in which I challenged the flawed investigation process that was adopted, the Administrative Bishop appointed an independent law specialist to facilitate the grievance hearing held at the Wood Green Church on 4 February 2010. In attendance were: Ms Theresa Bewes MCIPD, HR Consultant of First Assist Services Ltd., Bishop T. E. Caine, representing New Testament Church of God and Bishop I. Lewinson, who accompanied me to offer support.

The purpose of a grievance meeting is to consider the various complaints, and "to provide the employee with an opportunity to explain their grievance and how they think it should be resolved," not as the Administrated Bishop stated in his email dated 2 February 2010, to determine whether "...*the correct procedures have been followed in accordance with employment law...*"

It was determined by the committee that the way in which the investigations were carried out was procedurally flawed, and was not in accordance with current employment legislation or the Church's own constitution and procedures. This required urgent action on the part of the NEC to bring about a speedy and satisfactory conclusion.

As there was a "potential" conflict of interest, it was further recommended that the Administrative Bishop should be withdrawn from the process, and the NEC should appoint a capable, independent person to report to the Church in conference, and arrange an urgent closure to the matter. However, this was a part of the outcome of the meeting with Theresa Bewes that led to the appointment of a closure committee. The closure statement was prepared with my agreement. The committee appointed to conduct the closure conference consisted of:

- Bishop D. Webley (Chairman)

- Bishop I. Lewinson (Member)

- Bishop H. R. Parkinson (Member)

The Closure Conference 4 May 2010

The committee planned a closure conference in consultation with the Administrative Bishop and myself for 4 May 2010. The Chair, Bishop Derek Webley welcomed all members and thanked them for attending the conference. He informed the conference that they were not there to entertain any questions or discussions, but to bring closure to the investigation. He also made positive comments about the phenomenal growth of the Church and read the actual closure statement which included:

- *The integrity of the complaints was questionable, and the allegations were unsubstantiated.*

- *We confirm that we take the view that Bishop Burrell's integrity as the Senior Pastor of Wood Green Church was not tarnished in any way, or called into question as a result of the allegations and subsequent investigations.*

- *Furthermore, it was noted that in the interim, the Wood Green Church continued to show significant growth. (An apology was also made to me and my family.)*

- *The National Executive Council (NEC), the Administrative Bishop and Bishop Burrell now consider the matter to be closed, and we the national Executives encourage the leaders and members of this Church to give Bishop Burrell your full support as you work together to advance the Kingdom of God.*

[End of statement]

This period of persecution turned out to be a minor setback for a major comeback. I walked by faith, not sight. What we see can be very discouraging, disheartening and off-putting, but I endorse the words of Jesus: "To this end was I born, and for this cause came I into the world, that I should bear witness unto the truth" (John 18:37). I am a witness of God's saving grace and a conduit of His miracle-working power. If we don't know the reason for which we are manifested, Satan will try to blur our vision and distort our purpose.

Maintain a level-headed and positive attitude in times of success, difficulty or failure. You can't fight fire with fire; you have to use water or fire extinguishers. Some people wondered how I made it. Some have said, "I know God is with you or you couldn't have survived." A senior deacon said to me, "You must be sent by God," for no normal man could go through what you experienced and still stand."

There are godly principles that govern our stability. A strong determination, hard-work, resilience, perseverance, prayer and supreme confidence in God's Word are the tools that help us overcome the most difficult phases of life. We are sustained by God's grace which prohibits us from rendering evil for evil, and are compelled by His Spirit to love even those who hate us without a cause." We must not just do the right things, but with the right motives. For example, individuals may avoid committing fornication for the fear of catching aids rather than because they love the righteousness of God.

It should also be understood that I was not so naive nor ignorant as to miss the fact that there were hypocrites in the Church, and I am not so smart as to understand all the ways of God, but I can tell you how appalled I was that some professing Christians and members of the Church were so malicious, unscrupulous, and evil. A lot of the dissent and controversy were precipitated by unfounded jealousy, vindictiveness and a lack of discipline from people who saw my glory, but didn't know my story.

Immediately following the closure, things changed significantly. All the fiery darts of unjust men, and the overzealous expectation of moving me unjustifiably were finally extinguished, and once again I was at liberty to pastor the Church. The bright grins on the faces of some of the complainants faded into tears and their celebrations turned into sorrow when it became clear that they had failed to achieve their objectives, and a few of them lost their positions in the Church.

For many of these poor souls, life was hell at home, and they expressed their frustrations in the Church environment. This was understandable, but it was only a matter of time before their deeper problems surfaced and the undercurrent of despair pulled some of them out into the depths of the ocean with devastating consequences, and it was a privilege to have availed myself to help rescue them. I had forgiven them! This is what our LORD would have done.

In His historic Sermon on the Mount, Jesus declared emphatically "…Love your enemies, bless those who curse **you,** do good to those who hate **you,** and pray for those who **spitefully use you,** and persecute **you**"(Matthew 5:44, NKJV). Now this is hard, but the grace of God makes it possible. At His crucifixion, Jesus looked down from the cross upon those who persecuted Him and prayed, "Father forgive them for they do not know what they do"(Luke 23:34, NKJV). Here, He demonstrated what He preached: grace, mercy, forgiveness, victory and deliverance. As Christians, we can find ourselves dealing with conflicts of varying degrees, and sometimes we may even feel as though we are being crucified by many who we serve, but we must always forgive.

Dealing with people, even some professing Christians can be extremely difficult, and if you try to please everyone you'll only fuel your ego but lose sight of your goals. Don't always use your rights (or pull ranks, being officiously arrogant), but humble yourself and do what is right.

Someone has said to me, "Why did they treat you so badly in the church?" What they did to me, they did to Christ because we are one. Some may say, "What's wrong with the church?" The problem is not so much with the church; it's with us fallen creatures. The church is not a perfect institution because it is a composition of imperfect human beings, who are subject to limitations and failures. There's an old joke that says, "If you find a perfect church don't go there; you'll mess it up." I can concur with that.

Most of the trouble makers involved have left our Church, and this has been a blessing in disguise. I believe that God has orchestrated these events as a means of cleaning up His Church. Most of those who remain have repented and changed their attitude, although a few are simply conforming or who have piped down and become less vocal. Malicious rumours are circulated at times, but they are often met with the contempt they deserved. These contemptuous people are not any threat to the Church; it's the dawn of a new day and a fresh wind of change is in the atmosphere. This offers us the opportunity to make a new start, with a new hope and aspiration.

New Era, New Church

What "the powers that be" conceived as "investigation," I perceived as persecution, but after the winter comes the spring; after the shower, the rainbow; after the night, the morning – bidding all darkness good bye; and the hotter the battle, the sweeter the victory. We have come a long way, and the Church still moves on. New believers are constantly being added to its membership, righteousness prevails and God be praised.

We are committed to ensure that all our guests feel comfortable and have a great worship experience with us. We endeavour to be welcoming and friendly, practical and relevant, and we are constantly making progress by our cohesive efforts to create the kind of environment where all our presentations and facilities are worthy of their presence. We wanted all our people to have a sense of belonging, a home away from home and I believe we have achieved that objective.

Our newly renovated Church building is meticulously furnished and kept in a remarkable condition for its age, which has pleased everyone, especially those regular passers-by who have commended us, and also the civil dignitaries who have made positive and encouraging comments. We have also received accolades from the Administrative Bishop and his wife.

New Testament Church of God, Wood Green, London

We have spent over £1.5 million on modernising and refurbishing the Church building, which has included putting a new roof on for £150,000; building a new kitchen and upgrading the former to a Four Star standard; providing two new toilet facilities and disabled access, buying new carpets and upholstered red and blue cushioned seats for the benches; fitting an intruder alarm system and fire alarms; creating a new administration office, a furnished reception area, and an executive board room; and installing state of the art equipment, including a sophisticated heating and air conditioning system costing over £65,000. In addition to this we have recruited another full-time member of staff, Earla Green, increasing the number of staff to three.

Earla was and is the Church's administrator, my P. A. and right hand person. She wears many hats, but she is comfortable with all of them. She is a tremendous asset to the Church. Having successfully passed the exhorter's examination, she has become very active as an anointed minister of the gospel. She epitomises humility, reliability, dependability and accountability. May God continue to bless and reward her faithfulness.

Going forward, we foster programmes, which help train and develop dynamic men and women of God, who are now a blessing to the body of Christ. Today, we have an excellent Church, with a fantastic ministry team, a great atmosphere of fellowship and friendship – and some of the most wonderful people one could ever meet.

They love their pastor, and I feel privileged and proud to be their leader. They are faithful, supportive, and dependable. While we are still limited in some aspects of the ministry, we are thriving in other areas. Our worship is exuberant and each service is enriched with the presence, power and glory of God. The gifts of the Holy Spirit manifest frequently and the miraculous is ongoing.

The Ordination of Joan Gamra 2010

Sister Joan Gamra is an ardent member of the New Testament Church of God Cathedral of Praise, where she has proved herself to be a loyal and faithful child of God. I have had the great privilege of mentoring and training her for the ministry, which is very close to her heart.

Sunday morning 15 August 2010, history was made at Cathedral of Praise (COP). In response to the call of God on her life, I ordained Joan a minister of the gospel and released her for Mission to Nigeria. The power of God was in the sanctuary, and as I prayed for her there was a supernatural impartation – the same awesome anointing on me came upon her.

Pastor Gamra writes, "The day I was ordained, a sister in the Church came up to me and said, 'Sister Joan, how do you feel now that you are ordained, do you feel different?' I replied to her and said, 'I don't feel anyway different,' but I spoke too soon because at midnight or there-about, I woke up under a heavy anointing. I couldn't sleep because I felt the weight of the anointing of the Lord so heavily on me. When I got up, I couldn't even stand straight. I thought I could not carry it, so I went into the bathroom (to avoid disturbing my husband) and prayed to the Lord to remove some of it, which He did."

On 10 November 2010, she returned to her homeland and started a mission in Ilorin, Nigeria – a strong Muslim community. Despite major opposition and the adverse challenges that she faced, the Church emerged and prevailed with signs and wonders following her ministry.

Pastor Gamra later invited me to officiate at the inauguration of the Church. The name *Living Power of God Church* was adopted. God has blessed her ministry enormously, and the Church is on fire with signs of significant growth. She has trained two other pastors, and is in process of starting another mission station. To God be the glory!

Today, Pastor Gamra is one of God's end-time prophetesses with an apostolic mandate. She is absolutely and unreservedly committed to Christ, with a profound passion for the work of God, and her preaching/teaching ministry is in great demand. She still regards my wife and I as her spiritual parents and we are proud of her and what God is doing in her life.

Whilst visiting Nigeria, I made about three and a half hour's journey with Pastor Gamra and her brother Steven to a village called Ada. There, I stayed with Oluwatoni and his parents at MicCom Golf Resort. It was a very hot night and the air conditioning was not working. Toni's dad, brother Olatunde Araoye, an engineer, decided that he was not going to allow me to stay in those conditions. He is a man of God with great faith. Brother Tunde (Olatunde) asked the Holy Spirit if it was safe for us to travel somewhere else at that time of the night and the Spirit gave him the okay.

Without any hesitation, we checked out of the hotel after mid-night en route for the City of Osogbo, about one hour away. We drove along the dangerous lonely country roads, and through the bush without any form of road lighting system. This is something the average person in Nigeria would not normally do, and we never met a second vehicle on the road. As a matter of fact, the Nigerian Travel Guide advises people to " limit road travel at night as far as possible," for their own safety and security. We knew that we could have been ambushed and killed by robbers, but we went because the Holy Spirit said we could go.

As we pursued our journey that night, we were stopped twice: once by security and then by the police. On both occasions, they shone bright lights into our car and checked us out. After they were given some money, they allowed us to continue on our way. At no time did I fear for my life, but thank God for His journeying mercies; things could have been otherwise.

When we arrived at the Atlantis Hotel in Osogbo just after 1am, they had only one available room. Toni and I were left at this hotel and his mum and dad continued travelling after 2am in search of other accommodation, but the LORD protected them. The next day, I was on my own at the hotel relaxing. I was sitting on the bed reading and meditating.

The Holy Spirit told me to move to the other side of the room, and as I did, an electrical plug on a double socket extension lead right where I was sitting exploded with a loud bang and blew up in a shower of dangerous sparks which caught fire. This was a disaster had been waiting to happen. Perhaps it was overloaded or overheated or may be that just faulty, but had I remained there I could have been severely burnt. Anyway, I quickly switched off the electrical supply from the mains and extinguished the fire before it had gotten out of control and resulted in a conflagration.

Later that day, we went to a very poor village called Iree. This remote rural area had no electric lighting. The people depended mainly on the use of candles or torches at night and those who could afford it bought portable generators. Most people seemed to enjoy the slower pace of life. Many spoke only a little English. Toni was my interpreter, and his mum Bunmi made sure that I was well taken care of. The villagers were hospitable and welcoming to me. They also seemed to be overwhelmed with a sense of deep gratitude that I came all the way from the UK to visit them.

However, the only thing that took me to the village was the death of Toni's grandmother Emily, and I was there to support the family. A few months after returning to the UK, my mother died and Toni's dad sent him from Nigeria to support my family, for which we were very grateful.

The Demise of My Mother

Entombed in the devastation of grief, I thought my world was going to collapse and my dreams shatter, but God gave me strength and the grace to cope in my time of bereavement. "O death, where is your sting, O grave, where is your victory?" (1 Corinthians 15:55, NKJV.) "But thanks be to God, who gave us the victory through our Lord Jesus Christ" (verse 57).

I was engaged in praise and worship at Church on a Sunday morning when the LORD spoke to my spirit and said, "What are you doing here? Your Mom is going to die today. Normal people would be by their mother's side." Overwhelmed by emotion, I left the platform immediately and went to the back of the stage. As soon as I was out of sight, I wept profusely. Before going home, I left a message for my wife explaining the reason for leaving, and later my wife and I spent the afternoon with Mom. She went home to be with the Lord that very night.

My mother, Lucille Delphine Burrell (1918–2012), lived for the LORD and died in the LORD. It goes without saying that, "things come, and things go; so do our loved ones." The evolution of life, with all its changing circumstances, presents us with challenges, the finality of death being the ultimate – in this case a bittersweet experience. Losing my mother to death was very traumatic, but having had the honour of commemorating her life was a great privilege and a golden treasure. Mom combined her great characteristics with style and quality, immortalised as she was by her untiring Christian service and solid faith in the eternal God.

In this life, people fake a lot of things, including their "Christianity," but when I saw my 93-year-old mother on her deathbed, raising her feeble hand to the best of her ability and praising God audibly in English and in her heavenly language, I said to myself, "This is real." You cannot fake it at this age, especially in your final hour. By the time you reach this stage of life, the mask is off, the game is over and reality kicks in.

There's no doubt about it, Mom has gone home to be with the LORD. With the exception of *Irritable Bowel Syndrome (IBS)*, Mom enjoyed very good health for most of her life, but her health started fading in her late eighties. Following a bone marrow test, she was diagnosed with *Extensive Multiple Myeloma* at *Northwick Park Hospital, Wembley* on 5 April 2012, and passed away peacefully at Brook House on 21 May 2012.

Mom had no profound end-of-life revelation to give, but a couple of weeks before departing this life – after everyone else had left the room – she looked at me and said, "Don't worry yourself, we are going through a hard battle, but we must try and bear up." These encouraging words resonate in my mind and will be immortalised in our hearts. She epitomised a life well lived, an exuberant character and a magnetic personality, all of which radiated God's glory.

She has "fought a good fight. She has kept the faith and has finished the course." Mom will be greatly missed, but she is "absent from the body to be present with the Lord, and so shall *(she)* ever be with the Lord" – free from all pain, sickness and sorrow. She has left behind her a train of precious memories and an example which we are proud to emulate, as well as a vacuum that is hard to fill. Today, I miss her as much as I did the day she died.

Facing my mother's death was a major emotional crisis for me, and having survived that ordeal, I know there is no challenge in life that I cannot face. The Church was a tower of strength during my time of grief; the support of my family and friends, and my unwavering faith in God helped me to cope. Yesterday is past, today is present and tomorrow is future, but the future depends to a great extent on what I do today. All that I am and all that I will ever be in life, I owe to my Mom and my LORD and Saviour Jesus Christ.

Jesus emphatically states, "The thief [Satan] comes only to steal, kill and destroy; but I have come that they may have life, and have it more abundantly" (John 10:10, KJV). The word "but" in this verse is the most powerful conjunction in the entire Bible because it contrasts the supernatural negative with the supernatural positive in clearly defined terms.

Satan's primary objective is to kill us. Jesus' mandate is to restore life to its fullest dimension. He validates you, Satan intimidates and assassinates you. The fact that Satan wants to "steal" your life is a testament to the value and supremacy of life.

Mom at Ninety–three Years Old

L to R – Mom, Ivy and Eva (Three of Eight Sisters)

I was always a strong and healthy person, who seldom had a common cold or went to the doctor for any treatment. At one time, I was struck off the medical register because I had not been to the doctor for so many years. The tide turned in 2012 when my health started fading and a new chapter of my life began. God had showed me in a vision that I had major surgery and survived, but again I could not imagine this happening to me as I had never been hospitalised before.

However, as time progressed I began to experience an unusual tightening in my chest, shortness of breath and tiredness, which intensified during my mother's funeral arrangements. This prompted me to have a medical examination shortly after her burial, as suggested by my brother. A blood test showed that I'd had a heart attack without realising it, and simply carried on as though nothing had happened. An unrecognised heart attack is very common, and is sometimes called a silent heart attack, or medically referred to as silent ischemia (lack of oxygen) to the **heart** muscle.[11]

The difficult prolonged period of persecution and trials which Satan had orchestrated to impede my progress, had caused me undue stress, and may have contributed to my severe heart complications that triggered. Constant stress can cause your body to malfunction sporadically for days or weeks at a time, without you realising it. Furthermore, the body's involuntary response to stress can result in distress, which in itself can be fatal.

Although the link between stress and heart disease isn't clear, and according to the British Heart Foundation, "There is no evidence to suggest that **stress** causes **coronary heart disease** or heart attacks,"[12] research shows that chronic stress can increase your blood pressure (HBP or **hypertension**) and if untreated or not controlled, it may cause serious health problems including damage to the artery walls, which can lead to a heart attack or a stroke. Hence, there can be some correlation between severe hostility or chronic stress (whether it's job related or not) and cardiovascular disease. This is not to say that a heart attack cannot occur with normal blood pressure, but the risk is significantly decreased.

Invasive Heart Surgery 2012

This was the sixth deadly satanic attack on my life. Following a thorough examination at *Chase Farm Hospital,* including an electrocardiogram (ECG), a test that records the electrical activity of the heart, I was diagnosed with angina.

This led to further investigations, and a coronary angiogram at *Barnet Hospital,* which revealed five clogged coronary arteries due to calcification and the build-up of fatty deposits inside the arteries. Five of my arteries were simultaneously blocked: the two main arteries were 100 percent clogged, and others 90 percent, 75 percent, and 50 percent blocked, which restricted the blood flow and drastically reduced the supply of oxygen and blood to my heart.

The Cardiologist who carried out the above procedure advised me that an open-heart surgery was the preferred option, which involved a quadruple heart bypass. Medicines cannot clear blocked arteries, and I had never heard of a quadruple bypass operation before.

The condition was extremely dangerous, and so was the operation which could have been fatal. To me, it all seemed like a nightmare, and I began pondering how such an invasive operation would have changed my action-packed lifestyle.

Nevertheless, I told myself that I would not have died because my divine assignment was not yet accomplished.

In London, the cardiology hospitals have a long waiting list of usually around two to three months, but fortunately, I waited only about eight weeks for my surgery. During the interim, I had occasional hospital appointments and numerous blood tests, but the doctors inadvertently failed to give me any medication until I had my pre-admission examination.

Only God knows how I survived. I am a walking miracle, and a mobile reservoir of God's unmerited favour. When I consider the number of funerals that I have conducted, particularly of younger people than I, my heart rejoices in the God of my salvation. It's a wonder that I am still alive!

There was a great deal of anxiety from my immediate family, and the few colleagues and friends who knew the seriousness of my condition, but I was calm and cool as usual, and remained focused. I continued with my normal duties, which included preaching, counselling, visiting the sick, conducting weddings and funerals, having light workouts at the gym, swimming occasionally and even driving up and down the country to various events.

Toni and Nardia at Alexander Palace

One day while Toni and I were in the sauna, I overheard a man telling another man that his brother had died at the age of forty from a blocked artery. My ears popped open, and this brought home vividly to me how privileged I was to be alive, but nevertheless, my unwavering faith in God kept me going. It was business as usual.

In September 2012, I was preparing to conduct the wedding of Toni and Nardia, two young people from my Church. Toni was my "adopted/spiritual" son. My wife had booked to accompany her mother on vacation to Florida when she learned of my plight. Her natural reaction was to postpone the trip in order to be with me, but I insisted that everything would be alright and that she should not cancel the holiday. So she reluctantly went with my mother-in-law. The wedding passed off beautifully, and I was still awaiting my appointment for surgery.

While Toni and Nardia were on their week's honeymoon locally, they came and spent six to eight hours with me every day, ensuring that I was alright. I cooked dinner for them and Nardia did the washing up and tidied the house. Toni assisted with the shopping and lifting the heavy items. We made a great team, but for them it meant spending half of their special time with me. I appreciated their kindness, and I know their reward is guaranteed. There will always be a special place in my heart for them.

After my wife returned from the US, she was ministering in Birmingham when the hospital gave me one day's notice to be admitted for surgery. I telephoned her and she came home the same day. I began to brace myself for what now seemed inevitable except by a miracle. I read up on all that would take place once I was admitted to hospital, but I was never nervous or apprehensive because my life was in the hand of God. I had heard that the post-surgery pain was the worst part of the process, and of course, I don't like pain. So I decreed that I wouldn't have any pain.

I knew that my wife, my son, my brother, and my spiritual son Toni would be waiting anxiously at the hospital to hear how the operation went. So I declared that I would have early morning surgery so that they could confirm in the evening that all was well. I also told Toni the date on which I would return to Church after being discharged from the hospital, but he was not allowed to divulge it to anybody else. I was taken to *St Bartholomew's Hospital* in central London (also called Barts) on 29 October 2012. It was on a Sunday afternoon, and I had surgery the next morning.

Shortly after being admitted to the ward, a surgeon came to see me and said, "Mr Burrell, you are second on the list for surgery tomorrow." I am not certain how I responded to him because I was not at all pleased about this information. As soon as he left my bedside, I said, "God, you know I never wanted this," and I reminded the Lord of my request to be first on the list in my family's interest. About two hours later, the same surgeon returned and without giving any explanation said, "Mr Burrell, you are first on the list for surgery." I knew it was the work of Almighty God, and began to give thanks and praise to Jehovah.

On Monday 30 October 2012, I had *quadruple heart bypass surgery*. I got up at 6am, took the pre-op medication, and shaved the needed areas of my body in preparation for the theatre. I resigned myself to the fact that if God allowed this to happen to me, it must be for a great purpose. The feeling I had was of one who just wanted it over and done. I joked with the medical staff all along the way until I reached the theatre.

One of the doctors said, "Mr Burrell, I am going to give you some anaesthetics." Still feeling quite relaxed, I said, "Okay," and I was not aware of anything else for the next twenty-one hours when I found myself in the *Intensive Care Unit (ICU)*, also called the *High Dependency Unit (HDU)*. This is a unit where I was closely monitored by a doctor or nurse at my bedside continually for the first 24–48 hours.

The surgery that was expected to last for 4.5 hours took just about 3.5 hours. Bypassing the arteries involves a series of procedures which are repeated for each bypass that is performed during the surgery. The heart was stopped for about four hours, but my breathing was sustained with the aid of a heart-lung bypass machine (or "the CBP pump"), which temporarily takes over the function of the heart and lungs during surgery, maintaining the circulation of blood and the oxygen around my body. This "pump" was first used on humans in 1953, and may cause adverse effects on a patient's body and cognitive functions including complications of the inflammatory system, heart, lungs, kidneys, and brain. [13]

Following the operation, my family was granted the favour of God. A doctor took them to visit me in the *Post Anaesthesia Care Unit (PACU).* This was most unusual in the UK as family members are generally not permitted to accompany adult patients into the recovery room.

As a matter of fact, they helped the anaesthesia consultant to wake me up, and returned home thrilled to know that all seemed well, just as I had predicted. Nevertheless, the next few days were crucial and so everyone waited with anxious expectation. My son later told me that I did not wake up until he said, "Dad, if you don't open your eyes, I am going to take your car." Apparently, my eyes popped open immediately and I acknowledged them, and then fell asleep again.

When I woke up in the ICU early the following morning, I had to make conscious efforts to check whether the operation had already been done. I had no pain, and I felt no different than before, except for the tenderness of the wound, and I was hungry because I had not eaten for over twenty-five hours. So I requested breakfast; the nurses gave it to me without any hesitation, and began to express surprise about how well I was doing.

Their encouraging comments resounded in my mind all through the day, and the truth was that I felt great. When my family visited me that afternoon, everyone said how well I looked, and it seemed incredible that I had only just had such a major operation. I chatted and laughed with them, although I was still very sleepy and dozed off intermittently.

Critical Moments – Impending Death

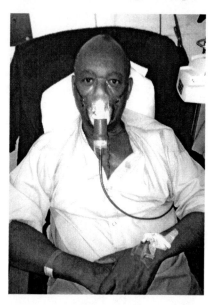

Everything went well until the third night when my blood pressure practically went out of control. It was over 200 systolic and kept escalating through the danger zone where I could have had a stroke or a massive heart attack. This was a breathtaking moment, as the awareness of death drew closer and the realisation hit home. The ICU doctors and nurses thought I was going to die. They were horrified and in a state of panic, but they did not want me to know what was happening. One of the nurses tried to console me "Just relax and sleep" she said, "Everything will be alright," but her expression was like an open book; I could have seen the horror on her face. By this time, their movements and body language had indicated to me the impending danger of my condition, and I had become concerned.

Although I was not having any pain or discomfort, I began to wonder what would happen to my family if I died. I considered the unfulfilled promises that God had made to me, and the work I still had to do. I now realised that only my faith in God could save me, so I prayed and told God "I couldn't die because my work was not yet finished!"

The other three patients in that ICU were also in a poor condition, and it seemed as if all four of us would die that night, but since I had already put everything in the hands of God, I redirected my focus to the others, who apparently were dying, and started to pray that God would ease their excruciating pain and spare their lives. It was after mid-night; no doubt my blood pressure was now under control, but I was still awake because my mind was preoccupied with many things.

To my great surprise, red lights were flashing and heart monitoring machines buzzing, but no doctor or nurse was on site to attend to the patients. This was a bit scary. I timed them to see how long it would be before anyone returned to the ward. Forty-five minutes had gone by when the staff nurse returned and started to rush around; then another nurse came about fifteen minutes later. This was totally unacceptable, but I felt sorry for the nurses because they had to work very hard, so I did not complain. This was my first time in hospital as a patient, and overall the treatment was excellent.

By the mercy of God, all the patients in that ICU survived to see the next day, and my blood pressure was back to normal. Thanks to Jehovah Ropheka, my wonderful Healer. One of the nurses, who had panicked about my high blood pressure, said to me, "You were saved by magic last night." I smiled and thought, "Lady, you don't know the power of God." Only His supernatural "magic" could save me. By midday, the amazing news that "I was saved by magic" had spread across the ward.

Providentially, I spent three weeks in the hospital because the potassium level in my blood was causing the doctors some concern, and they kept taking one test after another. A specialist was called in to see me, but he was equally puzzled. High potassium levels in your blood may lead to a condition called hyperkalaemia, which is usually caused by a kidney problem. This is serious and can be life-threatening.

Ironically, my kidneys' function was normal. The mystery was solved when a doctor discovered that the potassium in my blood was localised, and was the result of tiny veins in the back of my hand being damaged by the blood test needles. By the time I was discharged, I had gained enough strength in my "cardboard" legs (from which they had removed veins) to balance myself fairly well. Furthermore, the staples in my legs were removed before I was discharged – exactly what I wanted.

Another unusual thing occurred: I was discharged without seeing a physiotherapist. On leaving the ward, one of them said to me, "Mr Burrell, we did not come to see you because we have been watching you going up and down the ward on your own. You have been doing very well, so you didn't really need us."

One week after I was discharged (that's four weeks after surgery) I went to Church on the date I had pre-planned, which only Toni knew. Needless to say the entire congregation was shocked to see me, but nevertheless, they were pleasantly surprised. Initially, I continued going to Church every other Sunday morning and gradually increased my attendance.

My speedy recovery was evident right up to the time of writing, over two years later, and I have never had any related pain or ever felt sick. During this recovery period, I completed the writing of two books, *Love Sex and Marriage Volumes 1 & 2*, the second volume being a development of the philosophy in its predecessor, and symbolising accomplishment. In March 2013, I was awarded the degree of Doctor of Philosophy (PhD) in Theology, from Ashley University, USA.

During my recuperation, I continued to work closely with Rev. Earla Green to engage speakers and plan the services at COP, which she coordinated superbly with the support of the Church and Pastor's Council (CPC). In the meanwhile, I had to reduce or cease many of my ministerial duties, including regular preaching, and performing weddings, funerals, christenings, water baptisms etc.

These activities were delegated to able men and women of God, and the Church continued to deliver its vibrant and effective ministry. Most of these ministers were trained by me, and they understood the vision, mission and philosophy of the Church. We have a good ministry team, so whether I am present or absent the "Church" is still the Church.

In August 2014, my wife and I went to Jamaica for three weeks' vacation. We had a great holiday as per usual, but on our return journey from Kingston to Falmouth, the Knutsford Express caught fire in the centre of Ocho Rios – an alarming experience. The coach was literally blazing and a dark cloud of smoke ascending from underneath. Many passengers were screaming in panic and some swearing as they exited the bus. It wasn't long before the police and fire brigade were on the scene, but this was another potentially fatal incident, which Satan added to his onslaught.

On Sunday 5 April 2015, I invited Bishop Dr Eric Brown to preach at our Easter service. He and his wife Revd. Mrs Millicent Brown attended. We cordially welcomed them to COP and offered them our usual hospitality. They were both very impressed with the standard of worship and the growth of the Church, and commended us for the progress the Church had made.

Coincidentally, Bishop Dr Issachar Lewinson and Mrs I. Lewinson were also in attendance. Bishop Brown preached very well and the Church was blessed. Overall, we had an excellent day which concluded with a well-prepared meal and warm fellowship. We invited Bishop Brown back to our Fish Fry – a social, fund-raising, action-packed event on Easter Monday 6 April 2015. He accepted the invitation, but unfortunately was unable to attend. However, he is always welcome at COP.

Well-wishers have greeted me on various occasions with, "How are you?" "I heard you were very ill," or "I heard you were poorly." I have often had to pause and think, "When was that?" I honestly did not see myself as being sick, and I was not particularly bothered about my condition either. In retrospect, this seems crazy, but it is the truth. I saw myself as someone who had been wounded in an accident and had to take time off to recover. Others have been very anxious about my condition, but they were all amazed at my tremendous progress. How great is our God!

I resumed long distance driving and regular exercise at the gym and also swam two or three times a week. I was also preaching and teaching, and carrying out my regular day to day activities, but I was starting to feel discomfort in my chest which signalled to me that something wasn't right physically. I informed my doctor how I was feeling and he referred me to the hospital for further tests.

Three Angioplasty Procedures 2015

An "angioplasty" is a complex endovascular procedure, also called cardiac catheterisation and coronary angiography, and is used to widen narrowed or blocked coronary arteries (the main blood vessels supplying the heart). My condition has been described by my consultant as "always have been incredibly resistant, very diffusely diseased and heavily calcified." The term "angioplasty" means using a balloon to stretch open a narrowed or blocked artery. It is a less invasive procedure than a heart bypass surgery, but nevertheless a very difficult intervention.

This coronary procedure is performed by an interventional cardiologist (a cardiovascular invasive specialist with additional education and training in treating cardiovascular diseases through catheterisation techniques such as angioplasty and stenting). He is usually assisted by a team of cardiologists, nurse practitioners, nurses, radiographers, and cardiac specialists; all of whom have extensive and specialised training in these types of procedures.

Following my quadruple heart bypass surgery, an angiogram revealed that two of the grafts had been unsuccessful, and one had mysteriously disappeared. The fourth one was working successfully. However, I had begun to feel some tightness and slight chest pain under exertion or stress. This led to several medical investigations and two complex angioplasty procedures in March and June 2015 to unblock the right circumflex artery (one of the main arteries that was originally 100% blocked), but they were unsuccessful.

Another heart attack! **This was the seventh deadly satanic attack on my life**. Nothing can be more serious than a heart attack. I was rushed to the *Royal Free Hospital* by ambulance on 15 December 2015 with a mild heart attack. It just so happened that Dr Eliot Smith, my brilliant consultant was working there the following day. God gave me favour with this good gentleman. He has always acted genuinely in the best interests of my health, and I appreciate it. He is very determined and optimistic, and invariably had a few innovative medical practices up his sleeve. On the other hand, I too am inevitably very positive and cheerful. I think we make a good team.

I asked the duty consultant in cardiology if she thought my consultant would come to see me. She said, "No, I don't think so, he is very busy." When she left the ward, I smiled and said to my wife, "That's what she thinks, there's no way my consultant would know that I am here and not come to see me." By the afternoon, Dr Smith was by my bedside. He is always very cordial and helpful.

The next day, she returned and said to me, "I am going to suggest to Dr Smith that he operates on you here (at Royal Free) tomorrow." I should have kept quiet, but I said impulsively, "He won't!" She responded, "We never know what he may say, so let's wait and talk with him." Later she came back and said, "Mr Burrell, I have spoken with your consultant and he suggested that we send you to Bart's." I said, "Thank you," but that was a foregone conclusion."

On Wednesday 18 December, I was transferred to *St Bartholomew's Hospital*, where Dr Smith had reserved for my procedure the best Cardiac Catheterisation laboratory – a specially designed "operating" room called a cath lab (not the same as an operating theatre). The next day, after about five and a half hours in the cath lab, the blocked artery was eventually cleared. Following the three attempts and a total of fifteen hours in the cath lab, this angioplasty procedure was successful, but unprecedented in terms of the length of time it took to unblock the artery.

They gave me a local anaesthetic to numb the area. I watched everything on a heart monitor, and heard everything that my consultant said regarding the procedure. I could hear the horrendous buzzing sound of the electric drill and felt it drilling out the calcium, which mingled with the blood splattered on Dr Smith's apron. I felt drowsy sometimes, but not anxious. He occasionally asked me whether I was having any pain, but I was not.

Twice I heard him say to the medical staff, "His pressure is dropping, and I am very concerned; we have to hurry up now." Just at that moment, I felt as though the life was literally leaving my body. They gave me an injection to build up the pressure, and I felt better. After the second procedure, a cardiologist asked me, "How did you do it?" A cath lab nurse asked if I was from another planet, and said I deserved a medal.

The following evening, I was discharged from hospital without the knowledge of my consultant. Entering the ambulance, I collapsed and fell on the steps; a similar thing recurred when I reached my destination at about 9pm. By 1.00am I was in another ambulance on my way back to the hospital with a suspected heart attack. Again, I was rushed into the cath lab by about 2.00am and given an angiogram which fortunately did not confirm their suspicion. This was frustrating for me but devastating for my wife, who spent two whole nights by my bedside in the hospital.

Christmas was just a few days away, and although I was wearing breathing apparatus, and wired up to a heart monitor, I decided to write a Christmas message to my Church family and guests. My friend Professor Clinton Ryan had just written a helpful little booklet about Christmas, from which I have adapted relevant extracts that are incorporated in the following:

Hopefulness in a Time of Crises

Life is filled with many challenges and garnished with wonderful opportunities, especially during the Christmas season. These are precious moments that we often share with our loved ones and extended families. It is meant to be a time of happiness and celebration, but for people who are homeless, it can be one of the hardest times of the year.

During this adventurous season, stories of love, victorious testimonies and varied news have dominated the world of commerce, economics and politics. Many of these experiences have impacted particular areas of our country and the world at large. Where there is grief and confusion, war and poverty, our sympathy and prayers go out to the sufferers. None of us are immune from the overshadowing events that sometimes come our way during this festive season, but I am sure we understand why.

Whatever your crisis might be, whether financial, physical, emotional, marital, work-related, or to do with values or beliefs, I want you to know that there is a solution. Hope is the anchor that keeps your boat steady in the midst of a tempestuous storm, and enables you to make decisions that lead you to succeed in life. We were created with the capacity to overcome every test and adversity along life's journey.

Although we are separated from each other by distance and illness, I join with you in celebrating the Christ of Christmas. "Christmas" is undoubtedly one of the greatest events in the history of humanity – the Incarnation of Jesus Christ. Scripture says, "In the beginning was the Word, and the Word was with God, and the Word was God. And the Word became flesh, and dwelt among us, and we beheld His glory, the glory as of the only begotten of the Father, full of grace and truth" (John 1:1; 14, NKJV).

This is what Christmas meant to the fourth-century Christians, and this is how they celebrated it. We should do no less. We should not allow our rich Christian heritage or theological perspectives to be swept away by the tide of worldly cultures or pagan festivals, to such a degree that it ends up trivialising the Christ of Christmas.

Over the last few weeks, I have faced physical challenges, but through the saving grace and healing power of Christ, I will see you in the New Year. Continue to be strong in the faith; be unwavering in your commitment to Christ and love one another.

Thank you for your love, understanding, prayers and support to my wife during my absence. She has been a tower of strength and great aide to me. We love you all. Special thanks to Rev. Earla Green, Rev. and Mrs Ricketts, the CPC and all the ministering angels of the House. We wish you, and every one of our parishioners a Wonderful Christmas and a Happy and Blessed New Year (2016).

Signed: Bishop and Sister "B"
December 2015

It was not easy for me to write this message because my medical condition was unstable and I was having a number of issues. As a matter of fact, I was due back at the cath lab imminently for another procedure. The staff nurse passed by and looked at my heart monitor. She said, "Mr Burrell, are you writing a love letter? Your blood pressure has gone up." I smiled and told her that I was writing to my Church. My wife typed the message and it was read to the Church by a member of the Public Relations (PR) team on the Sunday before and after Christmas.

These procedures triggered a few more issues associated with my heart, but I was discharged from the hospital two weeks later, and my condition improved significantly. However, the tests, appointments and investigations continued. All of this was an education for me, and through it all I learned to trust in Jesus and to depend upon His Word.

A few months after the procedures, unbeknown to my consultant, I was driving over 120 miles (or 193.121 kilometres) to Birmingham, but on my way, I stopped at **Chase Farm Hospital** for an appointment with him. He said to me, "I have never seen another patient like you. Many people may not realise this, but it was your own attitude that pulled you through. Keep positive and focused."

I endorse the words of Paul who says, "Who shall separate us from the love of Christ? Shall tribulation, or distress, or persecution, or famine, or nakedness, or peril, or sword? "No, in all these things **we are more than conquerors through Christ,** who loves me" (Romans 8:35,37). Why has God allowed me to cheat death on various occasions while so many other people's lives have been wrecked, or have been curtailed prematurely? I don't have all the answers, but I know that God's purpose must be accomplished in my life.

Appreciation and Celebration

On Sunday 28 February 2016, my wife and I were picked up from our home in a chauffeur driven limousine bound for COP. Unbeknown to us, they had planned what turned out to be an excellent appreciation service and dinner. Normally we would access the Church building via the back door, but on this occasion, we were taken to the main entrance on the High Road. When we arrived, the head of protocol, Minoria Allen greeted us warmly in the car, and asked us to "wait a little," while she rushed back into the Church, I presumed to alert them to our arrival.

As we entered the sanctuary, the congregation was singing and we were greeted by many happy faces. Flashing lights from cameras sparkled in our eyes, and the ambience was captured on video cameras and phones. I noted happily that Bishop Donald Bolt, our new Administrative Bishop and his wife Mrs Joycelyne Bolt were on the platform.

Our son Robert and children were also in the congregation. I glanced at the morning's programme curiously under the watchful eyes of Rev. Earla Green, and caught on to what was happening. A very moving part of the service occurred when my eleven-year-old grandson Keran took the microphone from his dad and said, "I love you granddad." We were showered with gifts and flowers, but more surprises were still to come.

A spectacular afterglow followed the service. The back hall was elaborately decorated, and a sumptuous meal had been prepared for everyone to enjoy. The arrangement was fit for a king. We had an outstanding cake delicately decorated with our photos in the centre and our names written in blue across the white icing background. The atmosphere was electrifying, and amidst the excitement and laughter, members paid us beautiful oral tributes, which vividly and succinctly expressed their love, appreciation and genuine support, without any inhibitions or ulterior motives.

Scores of bottles of non-alcoholic wine were specially labelled for the occasion, with our photos perfectly positioned in the centre of each bottle. That took care of Sunday morning and afternoon; but a separate event was planned for the evening session, with our photos prominently placed on the front cover of the programme. More colleagues and friends joined us; Bishop Bolt preached, and the day's event concluded magnificently. We were overwhelmed by the excellent spirit which permeated such a lovely occasion.

The appreciation celebration was crowned with three weeks' vacation in sunny Jamaica – land that we love, all expenses paid. We were so grateful for this blessing. It was a kind of convalescence after a long period of illness and tedious work. The intention was that we would be well rested and pampered and would return home rejuvenated. Much effort was put into planning this magnificent event, and all in all it was a beautiful day that will be printed indelibly in our memories. We went to Jamaica and had what was undoubtedly our best holiday and returned to the UK as well as could be expected.

Another Deadly Satanic Attack

It seemed as if I was making a full or at least a significant recovery from my heart issues, and getting on with my life to the delight of everyone. I had started engaging again in pulpit ministry, and was involved in carrying out my normal day to day duties. In hindsight, I suppose that I may not have been as vigilant as I ought to have been and no doubt became complacent.

The 10 July 2016 was a typical Sunday on which I went to church as per usual, but I was having severe chest pain intermittently. Death apparently was written all over my face and it was quite noticeable. When my protocol team and others greeted me with their customary "Good morning Bishop." I didn't answer them and they knew it was serious. I was not playing this time.

I entered into the sanctuary assisted by members of my protocol team as usual, but had to leave momentarily. I couldn't cope with the music or the singing. Everything seemed all too loud. I returned to the protocol room and had first aid, but all remedial help failed. A paramedic, emergency medical technician (EMT) was at hand within minutes, and the ambulance crew arrived shortly after. The paramedics provided emergency medical treatment and transportation to the hospital.

They pushed me out of the executive board room strapped in a National Health Service (NHS) wheelchair, specially designed for emergency uses. While I exited through the Church hall, I saw expressions of shock and sympathy on the faces of onlooking Church members and children as I was once again whisked off to *St Bartholomew's Hospital* in an ambulance." I had had a mild heart attack. **This was the eighth deadly satanic attack on my life**.

It is one thing to watch the dramatic scenes of ambulances going by with screaming emergency sirens and flashing blue lights, but it's a different matter being a patient on board an ambulance. On our way to the hospital, while my wife was on the verge of fainting and I was on Entonox commonly known as "gas and air," I was writing my story mentally, which I transcribed on to paper in the emergency ward before I had any treatment. Why? Because I have learned to focus on purpose, not death; on solutions, not problems, and I knew that God had it all worked out. I had an angiogram and an angioplasty and was again on my way to recovery.

Before I was discharged four days later, I asked my consultant what I had done wrong that could have led to the last heart attack. He said "Nothing, it's not your fault; it's just that your body is not responding to the treatment. You look good on the outside, but not on the inside." To my surprise he added disappointedly, "The artery is not completely clear and there's not much more that I can do. I will see how you get on for the next couple of months, and maybe I could bring you back to change the stents every six months."

I listened to what he said, but I thought, "That's not going to happen." So I just decided to ask God to "take the case and give me the pillow." I know that nothing is impossible with God, and if He made me special, it is for a special reason. His will must be done! "**The LORD** will fulfil his **purpose** for **me**" (Psalm 138:8, NIV).

On Thursday 15 December 2016, I was readmitted to *St Bartholomew's hospital* for an angiogram followed by an angioplasty procedure, which took about three and a half hours in the cath lab. Again, God gave me His favour; my consultant and his medical team did an excellent job.

The procedure was successful and I was discharged the next morning. I arrived home before midday, and spent a good part of the afternoon and a few succeeding days completing my autobiography to meet the Christmas deadline, which I did. In the meantime, a young Christian brother named Donville Davis – one of my spiritual sons was extremely helpful in transporting me to and from various medical appointments and to go shopping. His kind assistance has been highly valued.

On a recent hospital appointment in January 2017, my consultant said to me, "You've been through a lot. It's amazing that you have pulled through such complex procedures." I told him that it was a miracle. He said, "I am very pleased for you, but I don't want to get too excited. It's early days yet, don't overdo it." I said to him, "I believe I'll be okay. There's even the possibility that I may grow new arteries." He agreed.

What is a Heart Attack?

Medically, a heart attack (also called a Coronary thrombosis) is bad news. It occurs when a coronary artery (or arteries) is narrowed or blocked so that the flow of oxygen-rich blood to a section of the heart muscle suddenly becomes restricted or blocked and the heart cannot get oxygen and other nutrients.

The lack of oxygen causes that part of the heart muscle to begin to die and this may result in other damage and even death. So a heart attack, whether minor or major, is a dangerous matter, and one's survival often depends on the speed at which medical attention is received.

From my experience, the symptoms of a heart attack are a crushing chest pain with severe discomfort, a burning sensation, shortness of breath, light-headedness, sweating, and a feeling of the life leaving one's body. It must be taken seriously and I would not wish it on my worst enemy.

Summary

My objective here is to emphasise a concern for health

and well-being. Since my attack of illness began in 2012, I have been admitted to hospital seven times. I have had quadruple heart bypass surgery, six angiograms, five angioplasties, and three heart attacks. I have had numerous tests, and have spent over twenty-seven hours in the cardiac catheterisation laboratory, but God has kept me safe in His hands. An angiogram is an X-ray photograph or test that shows up the coronary arteries when they are filled with a contrast dye. Arteries are tiny blood vessels which are normally invisible to X-ray, so the only way they can be seen is by filling them with dye.

My body does not like foreign bodies; it did not accept the heart bypass grafts and now it is not responding well to the stents – the last resort from a medical point of view. The doctors have done what they can, but only God can do the rest, and I know that I can trust Him with my health as I have done with other things. He made me a special person for a special reason! I don't understand everything about God, and I have unanswered questions, but His strength has been made perfect in my weakness and His grace is sufficient for me. (See 2 Corinthians 12: 8–10.)

At no time throughout the process did I ever worry. "Worry" is not in my vocabulary. It was introduced by the fall of Adam, and I never adopted it. I have often heard people say, "We have to worry because we are human beings." This has caused me to wonder where I fit in the equation, but I simply don't, and I am being modest. I am not just an ordinary human. I am born again. This means that through Christ, divinity now indwells humanity.

I have come to realise that I am not who I was; my life has been rearranged by the power of God. The new birth puts God at work in me. I have entered the realm of incarnational reality, and I have the mind of Christ. (See Philippians 2:56.) This gives me a new perspective of life. I do not any longer face my challenges simply as a human, but as a Christian.

Therefore, I don't worry. To worry is to dig your own grave with a dinner fork. Worry is unprofitable; it kills. When you worry, you are committing mental suicide. Why worry when you can pray? I have cried for my family and the Church when I saw their love, concern and worry, and I cried again for joy and with a deep sense of acknowledgement for God's grace and His mercy toward me, but never about my circumstances. God has it all under His control. Satan has often used Circumstances as the prelude to the downfall (loss of power, prosperity, status or victory) of many believers because they lack revelation knowledge.

Throughout every transformation that I have experienced – from birth to adolescence, conversion to manifestations, challenges to opportunities, there has always been a common denominator: the sovereignty of the LORD Jesus Christ. I have always been a beneficiary of His divine favour. There are no words in the human vocabulary adequate to express my profound gratitude to Almighty God for having chosen me and making me who I am, so I simply translated my thankfulness into tears because I know He understands.

The UK's Mortality Rate, Every Year:

- 160,000 people die from heart and circulatory disease.

- 73,000 people die from coronary heart disease (CHD)

- 40,000 people die from a stroke.

- 42,000 people die prematurely from cardiovascular disease (CVD).[14]

Interestingly enough, 60% of the above are males because men are more prone to heart attacks than women. According to the *World Heart Federation (WHO)* Causes of Death 2008 summary tables, the global number of deaths annually due to cardiovascular diseases total 17,327.000.[15] Researchers state that heart disease is causing more deaths every year in the USA than any other disease known to man. Even if you survive a heart attack, it will change your life forever. Men in particular need to take better care of their health, starting now. Don't wait until it's too late. "A stitch in time saves nine."

The "stitch in time" idiom simply describes the prompt sewing up of a small hole or rip in a piece of material, thus saving the need for more stitching later when the hole has become larger. It means that if you sort out little problems immediately, it may save you from bigger problems and harder work later on. "Procrastination is the thief of time." If you are having pain or discomfort in your chest, don't just assume it's indigestion, seek medical attention speedily; it could be a heart attack.

You can be days away from a heart attack without even realising. Now I believe strongly in the healing power of God, but there's not much point in praying for your health while ignoring your diet. Christians are quick to blame the devil for making them sick. While Satan is the primary source of sickness and disease, some ailments are self-inflicted. I heard about a man who dreamed that he saw the devil sitting on a wall sobbing, "Those church people, they blame me for everything."

Wisdom teaches us that we live and learn, but some people have to learn in order to live. As a young man, I was not fully aware of the importance of taking care of my health. The truth is that I used to actually abuse my health. I had a weakness for eggs and cheddar cheese and I often ate four eggs and cheese in sandwiches five days a week. In addition to that, I would put four teaspoons of sugar in my coffee and I loved sweet drinks. Some professing Christians smoke and indulge in drinking strong alcoholic beverages. These things all contribute to a build-up of calcium and cause blocked arteries.

Your health is your own responsibility. Responsibility is described as "responding to your ability. Neglect of one's health is one of the greatest tragedies of life; yet many people are guilty of this violation. Try and avoid coronary disease now by eating a healthy diet; stay away from greasy foods, meat fats and dairy products; cut out sugar, minimise your salt intake and if possible stick to a vegetarian diet. Do not procrastinate; take a proactive interest in your health. Ensure you:

- make exercise your daily habit

- watch your calories

- monitor your cholesterol levels (reduce your LDL and increase your HDL)

- keep a check on your weight

- get plenty of rest and learn how to relax

It is important the reader should understand that I am only writing what has been divinely revealed to me. One of the most amazing things is this: while God is dealing with me to bring healing and restoration to my life, He's using me to be an instrument of healing for others. Not every healing is the direct result of a miracle. A miraculous healing is usually instantaneous with no human effort or involvement, but sometimes healing is a gradual process or progression, and human effort or cooperation with God is required.

Because God is sovereign, and His ways and works are unfathomable. (See Romans 11:33.) He knows which method is best suited to our condition, and why. Your healing begins in your mind and soul. A clean healthy mind helps to generate a healthy heart and a healthy body. Some people cannot be healed until they receive counselling to help them find the root of their problems; some may have to confess and repent of their sins before the prayer of faith works for them. (See James 5:15.)

The First Lady Maxine

SECTION THREE

HEALINGS AND MIRACLES

The Bible says, "Jesus is the same yesterday, today and forever" (Hebrews 13:8). Indeed, God has kept His Word and blessed my ministry with hundreds and possibly thousands of miraculous healings. I can honestly say that since God began to use me in the realm of the miraculous, I have not been anywhere to minister without seeing miracles. In this part of my story, I wish to share a few testimonies with you for the glory of God.

Woman Healed of Floppy Heart Valve (Birmingham)

Rev. Mrs P. Brown suffered from a floppy heart valve, which caused palpitations if she was anxious or alarmed. She attended one of my healing sessions at a national convention and was instantly healed after ministry. That night the f ire alarm at her hotel went off, and inadvertently confirmed her healing. Ordinarily, if that had happened she would have had a feeling of panic and her heart would have palpitated rapidly, but on this occasion the alarm made no such impression on her. Over twenty years later, she is still rejoicing in her healing. Praise God for His miracle-working power.

Invalid Man Healed (Wood Green)

Donavan, a former member of Wood Green Church, had a road accident which incapacitated him and left him an invalid. He had sustained severe back injuries and after one or two operations, he refused more surgery. Unbeknown to me he came to Church one Sunday with the aid of his crutches.

I had a word of knowledge about a man with his condition that God wanted to heal. He came to the altar and I ministered to him. He was slain in the Spirit and when he got up, he could bend and touch his toes. He ran up and down the four steps to the lower part of the platform to demonstrate his healing. He said that whilst on the floor, he felt as though someone had poured a bucket of water over him and he began to sweat profusely. He went home and slept for several hours, and was completely restored to wholeness.

Woman's Leg Grew Two Inches (Wood Green)

One night in the School of Ministry, I had a word of knowledge that sister Edna had one leg shorter than the other, and I pointed her out. She came forward and confirmed it. I asked her how short was it, and she said two inches (5.08cm). I asked, "How do you know that?" She said that she had had it measured by the chiropractor. I invited a few of the other sisters to check the leg and make their own observations.

Everyone agreed that the left leg was about two inches shorter than the right leg. I asked the class to watch what was happening, and told them that God was going to cause it to grow. I said let's worship, and immediately the leg grew before our eyes to its normal length. I did not pray; I just spoke the rhema word "worship." The Greek term "rhema" means a word that is "uttered" or spoken directly by God rather than written down.

A Paralysed Woman Healed (Wolverhampton)

Tina was a totally crippled and helpless woman in a nursing home, whom God wondrously healed. Her condition was critical, and her hope was almost gone. The nursing home staff had to use a hoist to get her in and out of bed. She had to sleep sitting up in bed. She could not feed or wash herself, and was unable to move without the assistance of others.

She asked sister Schawsmith to take her to church one Sunday when I was preaching at the Harvest Temple, Wolverhampton, and she was brought along in a wheelchair. That morning, Tina came forward with the help of others to receive salvation. After the prayer, and when others had returned to their seats, she remained at the altar just staring at me.

I felt a deep compassion for her, and I asked her, "What's the matter?" She replied, "I can't walk." I was surprised to hear that and said, "You can't walk!" She said, "No." Still not knowing that she was completely crippled, I asked her if she believed that God could heal her. She said, "Yes." I prayed for her and she was healed instantaneously.

After the miracle, strength began to return to her body gradually. She walked down the aisle back to her seat without being aided by the wheelchair or anyone. Furthermore, after the service they folded up the wheelchair and she walked to the car park. Not only did God save and miraculously heal Tina, but He changed her countenance.

When she arrived at the nursing home, she rang the bell and one of the nurses came to the door, rather reluctantly. She said, "Please let me in; I am Tina, I live here." The nurse said, "No, the only Tina we have here is in a wheelchair." She said, "That's me, I am healed; please let me in." The nurse said, "No, and if you don't leave, I am going to call the police."

Again Tina pleaded with her and asked her, "Look at my face, don't you recognise me? Please call the manager." When the manager came and looked at her, she was astonished and exclaimed, "Tina, is that you?" They couldn't believe what God had done. Tina could walk around in the nursing home on her own. She tried to get in and out of bed without any aid, and started to wash herself. She was healed and she wanted to demonstrate it to everyone. "God is real; He can heal you!"

As time went on, she became stronger and stronger. She went into the City of Wolverhampton shopping, using her walking stick for support. She later went to Birmingham, and then to Africa with a relative, and elsewhere on holiday. Today, she is a totally independent person – sharing her miraculous testimony of the healing power of God to as many people as possible.

Woman Healed from Stroke (Farnham)

I went to Farnham Hospital Stroke Unit to visit a sister from the Aldershot Church. A few others were there talking with her. My eyes alighted on a woman who had no visitor and I gravitated towards her. I went over to her bed and started talking with her. She requested an unusual favour, which I was hesitant to grant any female patient. She asked me to lift up her bed cover and take out her hand. Well, I had to hear from the Spirit about this because I didn't know how she was dressed.

Anyhow, I did as she asked. I picked up her cold dead arm, and a deep compassion gripped my soul. I said, "Do you believe in God?" She said, "Yes." I asked her, "Do you know that Jesus can heal you?" and again she replied, "Yes." I prayed for her and the power of God surged into her body and healed her. It was not just her arm that was dead but her whole side. She was discharged from the hospital a couple of days later.

Constant Bleeding and Fibroids Healed (Nigeria)

Malomo suffered from abnormal uterine bleeding and fibroids for several months. After I ministered to her, God completely set her free. The fibroids shrank, the bleeding stopped and she had no more pain. God came true for her in a miraculous way.

Man Healed of Slipped Disc (Aldershot)

Walter came to Church one Sunday morning on his way from the local Military Hospital. Doctors had diagnosed a slipped disc, and advised him to wear a brace to support his back. They further instructed him to lay on his back on the floor at home. He came to Church to get my opinion on what he should do.

He believed that what the man of God told him was more important than what the doctors advised. I told him to do as the doctors had said, but also that he should return to the miracle service that evening; he complied. I prayed for him and he was slain in the spirit for a long time. He said that he felt as though someone had given him an injection in his spine, and he was instantly healed.

Crippled Woman Healed (Aldershot)

A planned miracle crusade was scheduled in Aldershot, but had to be cancelled. A crippled woman from Guildford had telephoned me to say that she was coming to the meeting. I rescheduled the meeting for her sake. She was taken to the crusade in a wheelchair. I prayed and told her to rise and walk in the name of Jesus. She got up and started walking strongly down the right aisle. Her family ran out to meet her and started to rejoice with her, some in tears of joy. God did it again! She told me that when I prayed for her, she felt as though electricity had surged through her hands and legs, and life re-entered her legs.

Woman Healed of Multiple Sclerosis (Bristol)

Sister Jennings had multiple sclerosis (MS) and was bedridden. I had just finished preaching in Bristol. Bishop W. Willis requested that on my way home I should pass by and prayer for this sister. We went to her house and I prayed for her and left immediately. Sister Willis told me that after I left she said, "Watch me, I am going to get up," and from that moment she began to walk and has been completely healed.

39 Years of Stomach Trouble Healed (Wood Green)

Everald Williams had a chronic stomach disorder from his early childhood. He was unable to drink milk or consume any milk based products without suffering stomach pain and diarrhoea. After ministry, I told him he should go and drink some milk and come back to testify what God had done for him. When he came back to Church in the evening I asked if he had the milk. His wife said to me, "Pastor, he can't drink milk." I said, "Don't tell me that," and insisted he should drink the milk. He drank it later that night and from then on he has been drinking milk, completely healed.

Man Restored from a Dustbin (Caribbean)

A woman asked me to pray for her backslidden son in the Caribbean so that he would return to the LORD. The next day he picked up a Bible leaf from a dustbin and read it. As a result, his life was miraculously restored to Christ, and he became a preacher of the gospel.

Woman's Leg Healed in My Office (Aldershot)

A very educated man and his wife came to Church to mock us. That Sunday morning, I preached on "The power in the Name of Jesus." He became convicted and couldn't speak. He said it was the first time he had ever been lost for words. I invited him and his wife to my office. After a brief chat, I prayed for them and they shook under the power of God. After what they had experienced that day they would never have wanted to mock us again. His wife said, "It's weird, it's going down my leg." I told her to kick with her leg, and she said "I can't." I repeated myself and she kicked with the leg. Unbeknown to me she was suffering from a bad leg, and God healed it instantaneously. Can God do that for a mocker?

Spiritual Air-conditioning (Luton)

I was the guest speaker for the Luton District convention, under the leadership of Bishop Headley Gayle. There was a general restlessness in the service because of the intense heat. The people were constantly fanning, and some were perspiring. When I got up to preach I prayed and asked God to send supernatural air-conditioning to extract the heat, and the people looked at me in a strange way. I said to them, "Don't look at me like that, that's exactly what is going to happen." Immediately, we all felt a cool wind blow through and everyone stopped fanning and relaxed for the rest of the service. That was the miracle-working power of God demonstrated.

Woman Healed of Deafness (Florida)

A woman in West Palm Beach, Florida was miraculously healed of deafness in one ear. She was seated in the second row of the Church, and I was preaching for only about ten minutes when she heard something pop in her ear, and her hearing was completely restored.

Severe Back Trouble Healed (Isle of Wight)

A man attended one of my crusades and saw many people falling under the power of God. He didn't think much of this because as he said, "They are all weak-minded." Nevertheless, the next day he and his friend attended another of my meetings and they sat together on the front row. His friend was suffering from chronic back pain. I laid hands on him in the name of Jesus and he too was slain by the Spirit and completely healed. The other man became convicted by the Holy Spirit, and became a committed Christian. He later gave me £1,000 for the Church and said, "Keep up the good work."

Woman with Incurable Disease Healed (Brussels)

A woman in Brussels was totally healed one Sunday morning of a so-called incurable disease. I was preaching and the Pastor was interpreting for me. I had a Word of Knowledge for a congregant in a blue dress. I pointed her out and asked the Pastor to tell her that she was healed.

While I was having dinner with the Pastor in the afternoon, she phoned to share her testimony, and was rejoicing in the miracle-working power of Jesus Christ. She said she hadn't believed in miracles previously. I said, "God how could you do that for an unbeliever?" He responded,

"She did not believe when she came to the meeting, but faith comes by hearing the Word."

Back Complaint Healed (Willesden)

A woman with severe back trouble was healed in one of my meetings. She had come for ministry, but left the service disappointed because nothing seemed to have happened. On her way home in the bus, she felt as though someone was pouring a kettle of boiling water down her back, and she was completely healed. She thought she had been healed on the bus, but the healing had actually taken place when the prayer of faith was offered, and the manifestation of what God had already done occurred on the bus. He knows best; we can't tell God His business.

Cancer Supernaturally Healed (Willesden)

A woman with cancer was healed after ministry. She left the meeting without any manifestation of her healing, but when she got home she passed the malignant growth in a stool, which was sent for laboratory tests to confirm the miracle.

Woman Healed of Breast Cancer (Willesden)

On my way from Aldershot to a crusade in Willesden, God gave me a Word of Knowledge about a woman who was coming to the meeting with cancer in her right breast. I shared that with my passengers in the car. During ministry, I felt the prompting of the Holy Spirit to call for her to come forth. As she got up and was walking down the aisle in agony, I stretched my hand towards her, and she fell to the ground. She got up miraculously healed.

Woman Healed of Cancer (Wood Green)

A woman who was dying from cancer in hospital said she wanted to go to church one more time before she died. A friend took her to Wood Green Church on a Sunday morning. She responded to the Word of God and came forward to the altar. She was saved and miraculously healed from the cancer. She came back to the evening service and was baptized with the Holy Spirit. She had no need for any further cancer treatment.

Deaf and Dumb Son Healed (Reading)

A Reading woman who attended a healing service asked me to pray for her deaf and dumb son in Italy. I told her to put her fingers in her ears and I prayed. Immediately, she felt a burning sensation in her ears, and believed her son was healed. Simultaneously, back in Italy the boy was having a meal and to the amazement of his family he began to hear and speak for the first time. God miraculously healed him!

Hindu Woman Healed of Cancer (Southall)

A Hindu woman responded to the altar call for healing. She was suffering from cancer. I prayed for her and God honoured His Word by healing her. As a result, her whole family came to Christ because they recognised that only Jesus could have performed such a miracle. No other god could do it for her.

Man's Short Foot Grew Instantly (Wolverhampton)

I was conducting a series of meetings at Wolverhampton. The previous night I'd had a vision in which I saw a man whose left foot was significantly shorter than the other, and I feared that this man might turn up to the meeting. I had never seen this condition in real life before, so it was a bit scary.

As I ministered the following night the Holy Spirit brought back this vision to my memory. I asked for the man to come forward, and there he was at the back of the Church. I watched in amazement as he moved toward the altar. I said to him, "Sir, have you got one small foot and a large one? He said, "Yes." He took his shoes off and when I saw his foot I was shocked; it was exactly what God had showed me.

I asked him if he believed that God could heal him. He smiled and said, yes. I asked him, "Do you want God to increase the small foot or to reduce the larger foot." He said he wanted the smaller foot to be increased. I laid my hand on him in the name of Jesus and he was slain in the Spirit. When the ushers picked him up the foot had grown to the exact size of the other.

40 Years of Total Deafness Healed (Leeds)

A woman was healed of forty years of total deafness in the tent meetings at Leeds. Medically, she had been advised to get a pair of hearing aids, which would cost her about £1,000, and she couldn't afford it. So she was wearing only one hearing aid. When she got home after ministry the television was too loud.

She told the children to turn the TV down, but they insisted that it wasn't loud. The next morning when she woke up she asked, "Why are the bird's singing so loudly this morning?" But the birds were chirping just as per usual, it's only that she hadn't been able to hear them before. At the bus stop on her way to work, for the very first time she heard the bus before seeing it, and the "penny dropped."

Woman Walked from Wheelchair (Wood Green)

A visiting preacher held a healing meeting at Wood Green one Saturday evening, and returned home. A Wembley woman who was wheelchair bound had the wrong date and turned up the following day for her healing. She was a little disappointed but I told her God could still heal her. I prayed for her and she walked out of the Church miraculously healed.

Prayer Stopped the Rain (Ilorin, Nigeria)

I was ministering for Pastor Joan Gamra in Nigeria. Most of the people including Pastor Gamra were already at the Church, but a few of us were still at home. It started to rain very heavily, causing so much flooding that we couldn't get to our vehicle that would take us to meeting and it was getting late. I got righteous indignation and opened the door while everybody else looked on. With my right hand raised towards heaven, I commanded the rain to cease in Jesus name! The rain stopped immediately and the sun came out.

Child Healed of Severe Stomach Problem (Willesden)

A mother brought her six-year old child to a healing meeting because he could not keep down anything he ate. He was weak and literally dwindling away. I took the child and threw him up in the air three times. He really enjoyed that – thinking I was playing with him. I told his mother to take him to the back hall and feed him at once. From that moment, he was able to keep down his food. God had healed him.

Man with Bad Leg Healed (Willesden)

A man who had a bad leg came before me for healing. I told him to jump on the leg. He said, "I can't." I repeated myself and again he said, "I can't." I gave him one slap on the leg, and he couldn't stop jumping. God healed him wonderfully.

God Paid the Mortgage (Wood Green)

A lady came to me one Sunday morning with a letter from her mortgage provider. She was in arrears of about £3,000, and had only a couple of days to pay it. I told her that I didn't have any money to help her, but I knew someone who could. I took the letter and held it before the LORD in prayer, and by the following day God miraculously provided the money.

Chronic Body Pain Healed (Aldershot)

One Sunday morning a young lady named Sara came to the altar and requested healing for her complaint. It was a rare and extremely painful condition that would cause her brittle bones to deteriorate until she ended up permanently in a wheelchair. I prayed and God healed her. She later made a statement that shocked me. She said, "I never knew what it felt like to live a pain-free life before."

Her dad was a scientist who did not believe in God or divine healing, but he could not deny his daughter's miracle. Hence, he and his wife came to check out our Church for themselves. They were overwhelmed by the spiritual atmosphere in the sanctuary.

So, they came to the back hall for refreshments after the service. I said to the young lady's mother, "The Spirit is speaking to me about you right now." She asked me, "What is He saying?" As I started telling her, she broke down in tears and begged me not to say anymore. She confessed that she had never seen a Church like this before, and her husband affirmed it.

Pastor Healed from Snake Bite (India)

There are many species of cobra. The Indian Cobra is one of the most venomous or deadly snakes in India and elsewhere. A bite from a cobra can lead to respiratory paralysis and cardiac failure. Obviously, death becomes imminent. Some victims die within minutes but others survive, especially if medical treatment is provided quickly.

A vibrant Indian pastor took a shortcut through the bushes to visit one of the members of his Church and was bitten by a cobra. He dwindled physically and was very sick when I was asked to pray for him. Immediately after prayer, his condition improved, a new infusion of life re-entered his body and God miraculously restored him to normal health.

Scary Hole in Arm Healed (Wood Green)

A woman with a hole in her arm received healing after ministry. Her flesh was eaten away by a sore so badly that it looked something like a pothole. I prayed and told her to take two photographs, a before and after healing. When she returned, the hole was completely closed and her skin was back to normal.

Why do more women seem to benefit from miracles than men? The reason may be probably because more women go to church than men, and women are generally more receptive. The truth, however, is that God wants all His people to live in the realm of his miracle-working power. Every provision that God made for Adam required a miracle.

CONCLUSION:

THE MAN, THE LIFE
AND THE MINISTRY

Who is this man? What's his vision, mission and philosophy of life? People will always have their own perception of you, and they may "frame you" or even lie about you, but the important thing is to never be persuaded by or base your life on the vociferous opinions of others. "Everyone is entitled to his own opinion, but not his own facts."[1] An opinion is not necessarily a fact, but fact is fact! You must recognise the difference and know yourself. The Apostle Paul writes, "Do you not know yourselves that Jesus Christ is in you? – unless indeed you are disqualified [good for nothing]" (2 Corinthians 13:5, NKJV). Know your value; know your position – know your purpose.

Before I address the questions regarding my identity and my mission, let me preface my comments by acknowledging that I am who I am through Jesus Christ. I am not on a cruise ship to the Caribbean; I'm on a warship with anti-Satan defense weapons of warfare to damage Satan's territories, depopulating hell and populating heaven.

Although I wear a big hat, sometimes, I am not a big-headed person, just someone with the ability not only to "dance in the rain," but to stay calm and "ride out the storm" – always maintaining a cheerful countenance.

When I was a teenager, my Pastor said to me, "Come what may, never take that smile off your face." With Christ, I am never alone! I am sure about this because I know who I am. Hence, I can smile through my tears and be strong in my weakness." My Master-Teacher taught me this principle. Jesus was not an eccentric or an arrogant person, but He was not afraid to tell people who He was. Several times throughout the New Testament He said, "I am…"

It has been said, "Your wife knows you best." True or false? That depends on several factors. However, when my wife and I renewed our wedding vows twenty-five years after our marriage, she wrote the following acronym, which I hope she still believes today; "With my man, my soul is content":

BARRINGTON MY MAN

Black, bashful, bearded, beloved

Astute, assertive, academic, adept

Righteous, refined, remarkable, renowned

Relentless, reliable, reassuring, relaxed

Imaginative, immaculate, intelligent, indefatigable

Natural, noble, notable, nutritious

Genuine, gifted, go-ahead, genial

Tolerant, tenacious, thoughtful, trustworthy

Observant, obliging, open-minded, open-handed

Non-violent, nice, noticeable, necessary

Magnetic, magnificent, mannerly, masterpiece
Youthful, yardstick, yogurt, Yorkshire pudding, yummy

Macho, masterly, militant, mature
Altogether, anointed, approachable, aplomb
Normal, non-toxic, muscular, nourishment

My character has been described variously as ambitious, enthusiastic, self-motivated, optimistic, confident, patient, reliable, cooperative, diligent, hard-working, honest, trustworthy and easy-going, and I am said to have a courteous and an extroverted personality. I am very passionate about the ministry, and I also try to be considerate of other people's time, so punctuality is crucial to me. I am usually methodical, conscientious, proactive, polite and even diplomatic without compromising the truth, but I try to be sympathetic, kind-hearted and supportive towards others.

I must admit that I have a natural tendency to react aggressively in the face of unfairness and injustice regardless of its source, but on the other hand, I am tender-hearted towards underprivileged and suffering people, especially children. This sort of thing has often brought tears to my eyes. When I see the sick and afflicted I am moved with deep compassion and want to heal everyone. I will go above and beyond the call of duty to render assistance to those who need my service.

I have knowingly ministered with love, patience and care to many criminals, top gang leaders and the morally depraved. They have all shown me respect, but more importantly they are somebody's children and God loves them. No doubt I have "Job's patience," but if I may confess: I detest most the behaviour of those who act rudely and have no manners or respect, especially to the elderly. Such behaviour is abhorrent and intolerable.

I have a warm, friendly disposition.; I'm not a contentious, arrogant or a mischievous person, but I am a no-nonsense, straightforward, impartial and assertive man. The good thing about all my friends is that they understand my personality and are always honest with me. My best friends from my early teens until now are John Kirby and Cecil Mullings in terms of longevity, but I am blessed with some other wonderful friends and colleagues in the ministry, which gives me a feeling of excellent comradeship and holistic support.

I have never had a fight or sought a quarrel with anyone, but I have always stood up for what is right and defended the cause in which I am persuaded. Of course, these characteristics make it easy to be misunderstood or misjudged, but that's who I am. I do not regard myself a perfectionist, but I do set high standards for myself and endeavour to be the best I can. I believe if we make God our priority, and not just an option, He will cause our efforts to stand out until they become outstanding (exceptionally good).

I am a person of integrity, and I do not like to see people suffer unfairness, injustice or abuse or to see the less privileged taken advantage of by those who think they are superior. Given the opportunity, I would be inclined to defend the "disadvantaged" free of charge. I believe all human beings, regardless of their status, colour, race or ethnicity, are equal in the sight of God, and therefore entitled to respect and equitable treatment.

I can get angry, but never lose my temper. Once you lose your temper, you lose your equilibrium and can no longer make intelligent or rational decisions. That is why drunkenness is such a bad thing. I manage my anger and stay in control regardless of the circumstances. Don't always follow your feelings because feelings can lead you to wrongdoing, which can get you into trouble.

When a vacuum is created in your life, that void will be filled by some external force contrary to your wishes. If you are not in control, you are out of control and Satan will take control. Emotional, relational, marital and financial issues, feelings of emptiness, unfulfilled dreams, fatigue, lack of enthusiasm and purpose make life seem meaningless at times, and you may be tempted to wallow in self-pity or seek fulfilment in drink, drugs, immorality or some other vice, which will only compound the problem. Instead, take positive action, manage your life and don't allow the circumstances of life to manage you.

If you don't manage your anger, it will manage you. No matter how angry you are, think before you speak, and look before you leap. Count to ten first or don't say anything. In the heat of the moment, you may say something that you regret later. Find techniques for venting your anger in healthy ways: play music, take a walk, engage your energy into positive activities and wholesome leisure pursuits or just take timeout and relax. I like to sit on the floor and just relax or enjoy a good clean joke.

My favourite hobbies are fishing and cooking, and my best-loved sports would be shooting birds and running. If I have a preferred colour, it would be sky blue or wine. The dish I enjoy most is fish and plain rice. Nowadays, I mainly eat steamed fish with okras and green bananas, yam and vegetables to help me keep my weight down and to enhance my health. Taking 30–60 minutes' walk in the fresh air is also added benefit.

I have a profound passion and anointing for writing, which has sometimes led me to write for several consecutive hours, even almost all night. I cannot tell anyone how long it has taken me to write any book because I have written two to four books simultaneously. I am very seldom not writing because I am always getting inspirations, new aspirations and fresh revelations.

Walking along the road, I have written on brown-paper bags and cigarette boxes, and I have even stopped my car to write down things that have been revealed to me. The Holy Spirit has taught me "writing." It is not unusual for me to wake early mornings between 2 and 5am to write what God has unveiled to me in the night season. My wife has often asked me, "Why don't you sleep?" I replied, "Honey you don't understand. I have to empty my mind on paper before I can sleep."

I love being in the company of people and interacting with them. I am a fun-loving person, who enjoys clean hilarious jokes. (I never make the same mistake twice; I make it ten times to make sure – only joking.) I always look forward to travelling and taking holidays abroad, which is an education in itself, and I especially enjoy being by the beach – for me this is the icing on the cake.

BOB Leaning on a Boat by the Beach

A Beach in Montego Bay, Jamaica

I cherish the times I have spent by the majestic waves, and crystal, clear blue-green waters of the Caribbean Sea – a Luxurious and carefree existence with its fresh air of relaxation and timeless comfort. This is where I have meditated on several occasions and received many great inspirations and revelations for my books and sermons. I enjoy life, but I don't believe in wasting my energy in non-productive ways. I am destined to occupy my time doing the Master's business.

Irie Spot, On Seafront, Trelawney, Jamaica

Reflecting on my experiences, I have concluded that the best thing I ever did was to serve God faithfully throughout my life. I have no regrets, and if I had to do it all over again, I would serve Jesus Christ every day of my life. If anyone asks me, "What was the greatest thing that happened in your life?" I would reply, "Being born again." This is the most amazing and phenomenal experience one could have.

One's spiritual life begins with faith in Jesus Christ of Nazareth, the Son of the Living God. This is fundamental to Christianity. As water and air are indispensable to natural life (we need them to survive), so is Jesus to spiritual life. We just can't live without Jesus! He is the originator – the fountain and source of life. "In Him we live and move and have our being… For we are also His offspring" (Acts 17:28).

Some who started in the ministry with me fell by the wayside. They were broken and crushed by the bewilderment of lies, and the tyranny of unscrupulous people. To those who ask me, "What is it that has kept you going over the years?" My response would be threefold: "My sense of the divine call, the power of the Holy Spirit and my personal responsibility to God."

Along with the call to the ministry comes a tremendous responsibility for which I am not only indebted, but accountable to God. (See Acts 20:28.) In fact, the reason I was born and came into the world is to worship God and serve His people.

The Profile of an Apostle
~ A Man Sent by God ~

I envisage a glorious church in the Spirit realm, yet to be manifested on Planet Earth, which has inspired and influenced my philosophy of ministry. Furthermore, I believe that I have been chosen and sent by God as one of His end-time apostles. God has commissioned me to preach the gospel and heal the sick. Christ has appeared to me on eight occasions and reaffirmed this mandate.

I began preaching at the age of eighteen – believing that the Holy Spirit would demonstrate in my ministry the reality and power of God, as experienced by the early prophets and apostles. This ministry which I have received has taken me to Ghana, Nigeria, Brussels, Switzerland, Belgium, France, Germany, India, Canada, U.S.A, Nevis, Jamaica and across England and Wales, bearing witness to the resurrection power of Jesus Christ the Son of the Living God.

God has given me a harvest of souls for His Kingdom, and I have seen and experienced hundreds of outstanding miracles. Some have testified to financial breakthroughs, and many so-called incurable cases have been healed by the power of God and for His glory – leaving the medical profession baffled at times.

I have been in the ministry of the New Testament Church of God (UK) for over forty-seven years with an impeccable track record, and I have worked under all five National Overseers. I became a pastor at twenty-two years of age, and was appreciated as the youngest pastor in the organisation. It was quite challenging at the time because many older people did not feel comfortable with a young person as their leader, and there were always those who thought they knew more than the Pastor.

Over the years, I have pastored six congregations. Wood Green is the last Church I have pastored and where I'm still pastoring. It will possibly be my last pastorate. During my ministerial tenure, I have served the Church indefatigably

– engaging at local, district and national levels in various capacities including as:

- Sunday School Teacher

- President of the Young People's Endeavour (YPE)

- District Youth and Christian Education Director

- Local Pastor

- Bible School Teacher

- Overseer for three Districts

- National Youth and Christian Education Board Member

- National Evangelism and Home Missions Board Member

- National Executive Council Member (NEC)

- National Evangelist

In addition to the pastoral duties in the local church communities, I have executed the ministry of Bible school teacher, counsellor, and advisor; and been keynote speaker at many family enrichment seminars, conventions, crusades, and other events. This has given me a comprehensive exposure to many aspects of the ministry, and the opportunity to interact with diverse cultures within the wider context of the Church for which I am highly honoured, and extremely grateful to God and the Church. It has not only uncovered my vulnerabilities and weaknesses, but strengthened my character.

Furthermore, my ministry is immortalised through the seven books that I have written (six already published), and the many lives I have invested in. My book "Christianity and Culture" will help many people to interact with each other and appreciate cultural diversity. I believe all people are equal in the sight of God and have the right to be loved and respected and be treated equitably.

My innovation and personal contributions regarding analytical changes in the churches' infra-structures and ministries, have had an impact on and transformed the aspirations of many believers to move on to another level in terms of their relevance, faith, worship and ministry in the twenty-first century and beyond.

Some may perceive me as controversial and radical. If. need be, I can demonstrate these characteristics and deal with situations in peaceful confrontation, but ideally, I would prefer to distance myself from that approach.

I consider myself very down to earth and people-orientated, and am always cheerful, optimistic and hopeful. Some of my enduring qualities are that despite my busy schedule, I make time for people; actively dispensing my energy in service: encouraging, empowering, giving them opportunity, talking and listening to anyone in need, and showing strength of character through my deeds and the example of God's love and care toward others, even in the face of adversity. The paradox of Christian love is that we love even those who are unlovable. In my humble way, I have also done much to promote a multi-cultural approach to Christian witness, and a radical unity without uniformity.

I have devoted many precious years to serving unreservedly the elderly, young people, alcoholics and drug addicts, and supported local, national and international projects for orphans and the underprivileged in countries like Ghana, India and in parts of the Caribbean. By God's grace, I will continue to dedicate my life to serve the Church and its wider community to the best of my ability.

The Life and The Ministry

As I navigate this life, clinging to the majestic promises of God, "**I press toward the mark** for the prize of the high calling of God in Christ Jesus" (Philippians 3:14). I have many friends and family members in the church. Throughout the years, I have always looked forward to going to church. It is my life. I love the singing, the preaching and the fellowship. One of the main problems with the church, though, is that it is composed of too many unbelieving "believers," who quote the Scripture, but don't believe it; they preach it, but do not practice it; and they profess what they don't possess. This kind of "spirituality" makes a mockery of the church.

I am not a perfect person because absolute perfection in this life is impossible. Often, I have been tested and there were times when I felt discouraged. I have tried to imagine what it feels like to backslide and start smoking, drinking, fornicating and doing the things that sinners do. That's like lying on your back with stiffened limbs and closed eyes trying to imagine what it feels like to be dead when rigor mortis occurs. Well, that's an ugly picture. For me, it's harder to backslide than to live for Christ by the sustaining grace of God. I often say, if God keeps the fish fresh in the salty sea, He can keep us holy in this sinful world.

This Christian lifestyle is what I know and what I love and I am unreservedly committed to it, not to the worldly life and its fashions. You can have the whole world, but give me Jesus. The Bible says, "And **do not be conformed to this world**, but be transformed by the renewing of your mind, that you may prove what is that good, and acceptable, and perfect will of God" (Romans 12:2, NKJV). I know it's easier to talk the walk than to walk the talk. In other words, it's easier to preach than to live what we preach. Nevertheless, we should practice what we preach.

I don't wilfully or deliberately sin against God because I don't know how I could live with that, but I have failed God time and time again, and had to bow before Him in wholehearted repentance. The Church has failed me many times; relatives and friends have failed me too, but I can tell the world that Jesus Christ never fails and I have an excellent relationship with Him, which neither time nor eternity can change. Enoch is profiled, "The man who walked with God and never died." (Genesis 5:24.) God remunerates the faithfulness of His people.

Noah is also described as "a righteous man, with a standard of morality and justice that was high among the people of his time, and he **walked** with **God**" in a perverse generation that God said was evil and violent. (Genesis 6:9,11.) The phrase "walking with God" is used often in the Bible. It is a metaphor – a figure of speech indicating the manner of our life or how we conduct ourselves. It implies dedication and commitment to our spiritual calling. For instance, Abraham's walk with God was one of obedience and faithfulness. My **walk** with God is crucial to my existence; it has been a profound, personal and productive one.

I have never prayed long prayers of petitions for hours, sweating and wailing, but I have had meaningful times of reflective, meditative and intercessory prayers. Except for our corporate all–night prayer meetings, the longest I can remember praying at any one time was just over an hour, and my longest time of fasting and prayer (without food or water) has been ten consecutive days and nights.

(A word of caution: it is not ideal for us to fast for more than three days without water. This can be damaging to one's health, and may ultimately lead to death. If you are new to fasting do talk to your elders about this.) But sometimes you have to pause for the cause. Take time out for prayer and fasting; it's good spiritual discipline.

I have always felt closer to God because of these cherished moments in His presence. This is really about worship – having fellowship, communion and an intimate relationship with God. I believe the purpose of prayer is not just to practise a routine habitually, as good as this may be, but to get results. If we don't get a positive outcome when we pray, it nullifies our prayers. God wants to answer our prayers!

"God is not a man, that He should lie, nor a son of man, that He should repent *[change his mind]*. Has He said, and will He not do? Or has He spoken, and will He not make it good?" (Numbers 23:19, NKJV.) As believers, and especially as leaders, we need a vision, a plan, a strategy and a Bible-based ministry. Once these have been firmly established, pray and pray again consistently in light of the Word until God produces the miracle needed. Prayer moves the hand of God in favour of His people.

I understand that God deals with everyone differently, and I do not wish to pontificate or to impose my opinions or my life experiences as a standard for anyone else. I am not always right, it's just that I am never wrong when I follow where the Holy Spirit leads me. But I think we need to examine what we do, how we do it and why. What makes some prayers ineffective?

Why does God answer some prayers and not others? Does God have favourites? Well, if He does, I must be one of them, but He doesn't."

James says, "The effective fervent prayer of a righteous man avails much" (James 5:16, NKJV). In other words, this kind of prayer is productive. What's important here is that our prayers are effective. It's not how long or how loud one prays, but how effective it is – the quality, the fervency, the frequency and the sincerity of one's prayer.

There is something that I want the world to know, which means a very great to me. It is just that no words are adequate to express it. But here it is: the reason why I have surmounted, not just survived, my great struggles in life is not due to my own strength, but because God has orchestrated an army of believers, nationally and internationally with a specific mandate to fast and pray for me. Even though this was unknown to me for many years, and I have never met most of these prayer-warriors, I constantly experience the power of their prevailing, persistent prayers.

God is not a hard task master, and He will always respond to faith. He cannot deny faith. God assures us in His Word that "the prayer of faith" (or "the prayer offered in faith") produces a favourable result. (See James 5:13–16.) Of course, all this is subject to the righteous life of the person praying.

Righteousness fuels the power of our spiritual engine. Righteousness is the condition for answered prayer. The word "condition" here means the circumstances or factors which determine the manner or outcome of something. A covenant is based on terms and conditions. If we are not right with God, we violate the covenant and the promise of His Word is made null and void.

John affirms, "This is the confidence we have in approaching God: that if we ask anything according to his will, he hears us" (1 John 5:14). Isn't it wonderful to know that our prayers don't fall on deaf ears? When John says "hears us" he means that God is in agreement with our prayers and answers us. But our approach is equally important; our prayers must always be offered in humility, faith and total submission to the will of God.

The Apostle Peter admonishes us, "As new born babes, desire the sincere milk of the word, that you may grow thereby" (1 Peter 2:2). Reading and internalising the Word of God has been one of the great keys of my success. I believe that what God says is true, even when there is evidence to the contrary. God's Word is settled for eternity and neither time nor circumstances can alter what He has established.

I have found that living by the principles of God's Word has been my strong tower and bedrock in life because there's no failure in God. The Word of God is my anchor in the ocean of life. God and His Word are one. The Word releases God to work in you. You cannot walk in the supernatural if you try to separate God and His Word. Speak the Word in faith; it will neutralise the power of Satan and produce miracles, signs and wonders for your benefit and God's glory.

Is God in your life? I have discovered through experience that it is a contradiction to pray for God's blessings and protection upon your life if you have closed the door on God. God is standing at your door; He needs your attention! He is seeking to come in and minister to your needs, but He is not an intruder. Great blessings are awaiting you, but God wants you to open the door and invite Him in – just open the door! Never give up on Him!

Another very important lesson that I have learned and am still learning is that of obedience to God. He wants us to have a communicative relationship with Him. He doesn't store up malice even if we offend Him. A lady told a ministerial colleague that the LORD said he should marry her. My colleague replied, "Sister, I'll have to ask the LORD if He is keeping malice with me, for He didn't tell me that."

Talking is easy; it's cheap, but communication is hard. Poor communication affects all levels of relationships: friendships, family relationships, romantic relationships, business relationships and spiritual relationships. Prayer is one of the ways we communicate with God – we talk with Him and He with us. God also speaks to His children by His Word and through the Holy Spirit, but we need to listen and respond to Him. Effective communication has two sides – listening and talking. I wonder why God gave us two ears and only one mouth, could it be that He intended us to listen twice as much as we speak?

Listening is crucial to effective communication, which in turn is key to successful relationships. Our relationship with God is first and foremost, and He requires obedience, not conformity. Salvation is about transformation, not conformation. Some people refer to what others say or quote some well-known proverbs as an excuse for not doing the will of God. We must throw away the proverbial garbage on the scrapheap of life and obey God.

Obedience is a decisive action of the will, carrying out the instructions of someone in authority. This may necessitate a change on our part, which results in obedience to the divine will, whereas conformity is mere compliance to impress others, in which case we remain fundamentally the same. Some of us are too stagnated and old school. We are not moving with the flow, but simply going through a prolonged period of lack of growth and development – still doing the same old thing the same way and expecting different results.

If we keep on doing the same old thing, we'll get the same results, but "if we want something we've never had we've got to do something we've never done."[2] It intrigues me to see how many times we pray and fast for God to move mightily at our national events and when He shows up there is no room to accommodate Him, because our programmes are too full. Something must be done expeditiously.

We need to update our methods and optimise our resources – get the most out of what we have. When we optimise a computer, for example, we modify it for a specific function or programme so as to maximise efficiency and speed in retrieval, storage, or execution. We, ourselves, need to change so that we can become God's instruments of change in the twenty-first century. Our effectiveness greatly depends on our willingness to make necessary and appropriate adjustments. God wants to optimise our lives so He can use us to be channels of blessings to our world.

Through obedience, we obtain great blessings and avert many impending dangers – we can't go wrong. Obedience is conducive to our eternal security, growth and development. Scripture admonishes us, "but grow in the grace and knowledge of our Lord and Saviour Jesus Christ" (2 Peter 3:18, NKJV). The believer must grow. When we don't grow, we stay at the last place we met God, and eventually start dying. The little knowledge we have acquired perishes with us because we lack wisdom. Wisdom may be defined as the right application of acquired knowledge.

However, there is a difference between knowledge and revelation. To put it another way, we may differentiate between acquired knowledge and revelation knowledge, and the two different levels of knowledge have different sources. One is learned information and the other is spiritual revelation. Information comes via our natural senses, but revelation is from above. Mere information without transformation is simply intellectual stimulation.

The Holy Spirit had to teach me this because I never heard it taught in church. I have known some truths for many years, but it was not until this knowledge became internalised (moving from my head to my spirit) and burst forth in my innermost being that the truths were manifested externally. At this point I became one with the Word. In other words, knowledge must be translated into revelation before there can be a transformation and a manifestation.

Furthermore, I have learned that if I live by sense knowledge, I will never know my purpose or fulfil God's plan for my life. It is true that we were created superior to the animals with the capacity to reason, but God's original intention was for mankind to live by revelation knowledge, which can come from no other source but the highest – God Himself.

Man is the crown of God's creation, made in the image and likeness of God, so that God can relate to him in a manner otherwise impossible with any other species on this planet. Hence, if I want to know God, I don't necessarily have to study theology, pneumatology or Christology, but I must have communion and fellowship with Him and listen to what His Spirit says to my spirit.

My Two Greatest Revelations:

1. One afternoon when I was prostrated on my face praying in my lounge, the Holy Spirit said to me, "When you are born again, you enter into incarnational reality – God comes again in human flesh." The incarnation is divinity coming into humanity in order to bring humanity into divinity. Wow! As I mentioned earlier, this was again revealed to me when I was praying in my Church office and the Spirit said to me, "You and Christ are one." I have a union anointing, which constantly reminds me of my interconnection with Christ. And my body is the temple of the Holy Spirit.

2. Speaking about the immaculate conception and incarnation of Jesus Christ, Scripture says, "The Word became flesh and dwelt amongst us, and we beheld His glory" (John 1:14). The invisible Word (Logos) became the Living Word and manifested Himself for all to see. What a tragedy for Jesus to appear among us and for sin to blur our vision! Sin causes our spiritual eyesight to malfunction and obscure the glory from us, so that we cannot see Him.

    Is there a difference between **sight** and **vision**? Yes! You can drive or control your life either by your sight or your vision. Sight is seeing with your physical eyes; vision is what you see in your mind (heart) before seeing it with your natural eyes. So, you can have a good eyesight and a poor vision. Many people who are physically blind can see with their minds – the biblical heart. On the other hand, there are those who can see with their natural eyes, but are blind in their hearts. They lack vision.

Helen Keller was an American, born a physically normal child with the ability to see and hear. At the age of nineteen months she was stricken by an illness (now believed to have been scarlet fever) that left her blind and deaf. Yet she became an author, a political activist, and a lecturer and crusader for the handicapped – particularly becoming an important influence on the treatment of the blind and deaf.

She was the first blind-deaf person to earn a bachelor of arts degree. To the question, "What is worse than being blind?" Helen replied, "The only thing worse than being blind is having **sight** but no **vision**.[3]" That is an apt description of many in our generation. Generally speaking, sight is the ability to see the visible; vision has the super-ability to see beyond what is seen.

Jesus began by saying to those assembled in the synagogue, " Today this Scripture is fulfilled in your hearing" (Luke 4:21), and before your eyes as God intended it – a fulfilment of Isaiah 42:7; 61:1–2. Here, Christ revealed Himself as the embodiment or personification of **prophecy**.

The Scriptures *[the Word]* were "oracles of God" (see Romans 3:2), which meant the "many ways" or "various modes" by which God spoke to His prophets. Hence the prophets themselves came to be defined as "oracles" and their messages **(or** prophesies) from God were also called "oracles" (2 Samuel 16:23). Peter affirmed, "For no prophecy [or oracle of God] was ever produced by the will of man, but men spoke from God as they were carried along by the Holy Spirit." (See 2 Peter 1:21.) Which prophecy do you fulfil?

As an oracle of God, you cannot preach your own ideologies, philosophies, traditions or cultures, or your likes and dislikes, or what you heard from your associates. Your mandate is to preach what "thus says the LORD." Paul says, "**Preach the word!** Be ready in **season** and out of **season**. Convince, rebuke, exhort, with all longsuffering and teaching" (2 Timothy 4:2, NKJV).

3. One day as I was driving down the A406 North Circular road, God said to me, "Your greatest discovery in life is not an oil well or a gold mine, but who you are." This is powerful and revolutionising. It's not what you do that determines who you are, but who you are that determines what you do."

When you don't know yourself, you have to seek the confirmation of others for what you do, and you tend to go through life reacting to circumstances, needing the approval of others and just surviving rather than living. The level of the anointing on your life defines who you are, not your birth certificate. When you know who you are, you will know your purpose.

In summary, the greatest discovery is the discovery of who you are. The greatest investment is the investment of yourself in people, and the greatest reward is to hear God say on that great day, "Well done, you good and faithful servant" (Matthew

25:21, 23). I always knew that I was destined to preach, and I knew that my two role models were Evangelist Billy Graham and Rev. Jeremiah McIntyre, but I wish that I knew fifty years ago who I was. One thing I will never forget is that I am who I am by the grace of God. Important lessons can be drawn from our past mistakes.

I am driven not by money, prestige or accolades, but by a passion for service in the Kingdom of God. My personal motto is "Reaching people, changing lives, advancing the Kingdom of God," which we have adopted at COP as the mission statement of our Church. If I can achieve this goal, then my living shall not have been in vain.

The minister of God must have a consecrated motive. He or she must seek God's will and glory, the salvation of lost souls and the best interests of the church and mankind in general. Jesus said to His disciples, "If any man will come after me, let him deny himself, and take up his cross, and follow me" (Matthew 16:24). This implies that the Christian ministry calls for dedicated service and whole hearted commitment regardless of the colour of one's skin, ethnicity, race or geographical background.

One should avoid rushing into the sacred office unprepared; it's not for intruders or amateurs. Prioritise your options, and optimise your priorities (or productivity). Jesus says, "Seek first the Kingdom of God and His righteousness and all these things shall be added to you" (Matthew 6:33, NKJV). The notion is that we should seek the heart of God and not His hand. Too many people seek the things that should be added, and missed out on the Kingdom blessings and opportunities.

If it is money you want, the ministry is not for you – there are higher paid jobs. If it's popularity you are seeking, you would be better off being a pop star. But you could own the world and its money, if you don't have Jesus Christ in your life you have nothing. In spite of how intellectual you may be, if you don't know God and His love, you know nothing.

The ministry is a specific calling – a divine assignment, which requires the unreserved dedication of a man or woman's entire life to the work of God's Kingdom. Some ministers are forced by necessity to have secular employment, but that is not the ideal; the sooner you get out of it and commit your life to fulfil the divine calling, the more effective your ministry will be.

Sometimes the sins of pride, greed and selfishness become major obstacles in our lives and bring the ministry into disrepute. They are like little foxes that spoil the vines by gnawing and breaking them (Song of Solomon 2:15), and the non-productive vines or suckers that suck the sap or life out of the fruit-bearing vines. (See John 15:1–2.)

When Adam and Eve sinned against God, they lost God-consciousness and gained sin-consciousness, from which came self-consciousness (they saw their nakedness). They subjugated the tendency to do good to the power to do evil. Their flesh took control as the first person singular was enthroned and that little "I" became the centre of man's problems, and everything came to be about "I, me and myself."

There is a force in every man called the carnal flesh, and an agent in redeemed man who is the Spirit of God. Both are in opposition to one another, and only one can rule over the same territory at one time. If king "I" is on the throne, then the flesh is in control. "Flesh" cannot please God. Therefore, Christian ethics demand that king "I" be dethroned and King Jesus, who the Spirit represents, be crowned as the reigning monarch of our lives.

Which king is reigning in our hearts determines how we live, and the kind of leadership we give to those we serve. One of the reasons why many churches are dying is because there are too many ministers standing behind the sacred pulpits, who have slipped through the net. These are men and women who are neither called nor commissioned by God, and the wrong king is on their throne. They are imposters, who merely profess what they do not possess – playboys or monkeys in suits, who have no idea what ministry is all about.

There are some things in life that will either break you or make you. They will either bring the best out of you or the worst, depending on how you handle them. My experiences as a senior pastor have been my school of theology. Through it all, I have learned to trust in God, whose hand has been evident upon me from the time I was in my mother's womb. Although I am very friendly, and often joke a lot, there's no playing around when it comes to ministry. The ministry has no room for phonies.

I have learned in the school of life that not everyone who smiles at you wishes you well; so choose your company carefully. It is better to be alone than in the wrong company, because you become like those with whom you closely associate. Your association says much about you. Avoid negative and toxic people. Only keep friends that will add value to your life. With some people, you spend an evening, with others you invest it.

The Two Things I Dislike Mostly in the Ministry

I enjoy the ministry and wouldn't exchange it for anything. I do ministry because that's what I am called to do, and I serve because of who I am – a servant, and for love, not money. Today, the godly use of servanthood has been corrupted and degraded to servitude. I will retire from the pastorate at the appropriate time, but never from the ministry (energetically and actively engaged in Christian service as I am.) It's a lifetime commitment to God, but there are two things that have been required of me that I would rather not have had to do:

- **Conduct funerals** – these are a big responsibility, which gives the pastor a great opportunity to minister to families during their time of grief, but I find them too sad, and I hate to see people grieve. Often, I am myself close to tears. I have always maintained that if I could assign the funerals to someone else I would. God knows my heart!

- **Exclude erring and unruly members from the Church** – this is like a spiritual burial, but sometimes you are left with no option. After you have entreated an erring or sinning adherent as a brother or a sister, and he or she refuses to take counsel, then you should follow biblical principle and exclude them from the fellowship of the Church; not in anger, but to give them an opportunity to repent. (See Matthew 18:15–17; 1 Corinthians 5:1–13.) This may break one's heart, but it is the right thing to do. This is one of those times when you must follow your head and not your heart.

Oftentimes people ask, " Where is your love and forgiveness?" My response is this: it is where it has always been. I love people, but that love must never be abused or compromised our values. Practising the biblical procedure for church discipline does not violate Christian principles. Furthermore, love and forgiveness should be the motive for church discipline, not punishment.

God created you as a special unique YOU. You can still have unity in diversity, but the crucial thing is never to lose your identity. A person without an identity is disconnected from their true self. Remember, it's not a crime to be different! If God had intended us all to be the same, mankind would have been mass produced, but "God made each one from a single mould, and disposed of it." He did not want to replicate any human being. Your genes are matchless. That is why out of over 7.4 billion sets of finger prints on earth, there is not another one like yours. You are an original.

The best way to be is to be the best as yourself, not having a false intellectual perception. When you no longer think, talk and act as yourself, but as the misleading images you visualised, the danger is that you may fall prey to your own fabricated illusions. Be yourself, and strive for excellence in whatever you do. Don't imitate any preacher's voice or style. God wants you as you, not somebody else.

If you are a preacher, evaluate your own preaching. Is it contemporary and relevant to your congregation? Preach the unadulterated gospel of the exalted Christ in an apostate world. Maximise your potential, and enjoy life to its maximum! You are not an afterthought; you were in God's original plan before the creation of the world, and He created YOU as a gift to this planet. You have significance, acceptance and purpose. The world needs You!

I have reached a stage in life where I don't have to wear a mask and parade around as if I was at a masquerade, I can be real and transparent without fear of intimidation or retribution. I am not in the habit of telling people what they want to hear instead of what they need to hear. I am very outspoken and I like others to be frank with me. It takes a man to say what he means, and mean what he says. One can be a Christian in theory, and a hypocrite in practice. As a rule of thumb, people prefer honesty over hypocrisy.

A Jamaican proverb says, "Boiling water can't hurt a dead pig." I speak and write as a dead man, "nevertheless I live; yet not I, but Christ liveth *[lives perpetually]* in me" (Galatians 2:20, KJV). A dead man holds no grudges and has no insecurities. He does not insist on his own way, and negative criticisms have no effect on him.

When you are alive, your body's immune system will launch massive attacks on viruses and diseases, but when you are dead these things will have no more impact on you. You are dead to them. Jesus Christ came to the tomb of my sins, breathed His breath of life into my dead spirit, and resurrected me to a new life in Him. Now, I am a new creation in Christ, but paradoxically, I am dead to the things of this world.

I have deduced that a great number of church customs to which we have cleaved over the years are not right. Sometimes, even the way we pray is unbiblical. For instance, there are times we try to "pray out demons" and speak in tongues over them; whereas the Bible says we should "cast out demons." How many people pray for the Lord to make them humble? The Bible says, "Humble yourself." Therefore, I don't take things at face value anymore. I question, evaluate and explore the traditions we practice.

Few funerals I have gone to and have not heard the minister say that God has taken the deceased home, or that they have fulfilled their earthly assignment or their time on earth has expired. That would no doubt have comforted the bereaved families, but is it always true? How does the minister know that? Does death always imply that the deceased's time to be with the LORD has come? Has God called every dead believer home? "The LORD gave, and the LORD has taken away; blessed be the name of the LORD" (Job 1:21). Is this verse applicable to every funeral? My answer to all these questions is, "No!"

It is God's good pleasure that we live a long healthy life here on earth, but the problem is that most of us believe the devil's lie instead of God's truth. "I have no pleasure in the death of anyone," says the Lord God. "Therefore turn and live!" (See Ezekiel 18:32, NKJV.) In the model prayer, Jesus teaches us to pray for the will of God to be done on earth as it is in heaven. (See Matthew 6:10.) but God's will is not always done on earth. On the other hand, if God's will be done on earth as it is in heaven, what is the will of God in heaven? Sickness? Premature death? Are these things not a part of the curse? Are we not redeemed from the curse of the law? (See Galatians 3:13.)

Many have said, "If your time hasn't come yet you can't die." The implication is that you cannot die contrary to God's will or in other words before your time. But that's not true, many people have died prematurely. Hence the Bible says, "Do not be overly wicked, nor be foolish: Why should you die before your time?" (Ecclesiastes 7:17, NKJ)

What do you think: when a person is murdered, is it God's appointed time for that individual to die? If someone commits suicide, is that God's timing for him or her to die? If a serial killer kills eight people from one family over a period of six months, is that God's appointed time for them to die? What about babies who were illegally aborted, was that God's timing for them? "No, not necessarily."

The most terrible funeral I have had to conduct was of a young man who threw his two-year-old son from the sixteenth story of a Building in Stockwell, Southwest London and then jumped to his death. Was that God's time for them to die? When a suicidal killer bombs a shopping mall and kills many innocent people, has their time come to die, and God's plan for them come to fruition? Have they lived to their full potential? It's very unlikely.

Some people die unnecessarily because of their careless or wayward lifestyles. Others die because their life is curtailed by a fatal accident or injury. Many lose the battle with an illness or disease, and many others simply give up and lose the will to live. Some die because they become victims of demonic forces or evil powers, but the LORD is blamed for their demise. "He has taken them home," it is said, but has He? If my time has come and God wants to call me home, does He need to depend on any of the above circumstances to terminate my life?

When I am conducting a funeral, I keep uppermost in my mind the bereaved families, not the deceased. My philosophy is that the purpose of a funeral is to comfort, support and strengthen the mourners, and a memorial is for the dead. A eulogy is for the living, and an obituary for the dead.

Give me the for-get-me-nots when I am alive, while I can appreciate and enjoy them. Too late the roses when the soul is gone! In point of fact, you can eulogise someone when they are alive, and if you fail to do so, why exhibit a show when they are dead? All the flowers we lay on the coffin or casket and the grave are really for our benefit, not the deceased, who can't see or smell them. Do the dead ones miss us? No, but we do miss them. They will not come back to us, but we will have to go to them. (See 2 Samuel 12:23.) So, everything we do at the funeral is summed up in this: we celebrate the life and mourn the loss.

I don't understand why any Christian minister would tell the grieving families at a funeral, "we are not here to mourn, but to rejoice because our deceased loved one has gone home." That's not biblical, and it really doesn't make sense. It is simply false piety. Of course, we do not mourn as those who have no hope, and our grief is tempered by the fact that he or she knew the LORD, but it is necessary to grieve.

Grief is the reaction we have in response to a death or loss. Let's not spiritualise it. The grieving process is natural and healthy. It goes without saying that the more significant the loss, the greater the grief. Most people find the death of a loved one very difficult to cope with, and this is normal. If people supress their feelings and don't grieve their loss, it may affect them physically, mentally and emotionally.

I don't try to push the deceased into heaven with a long stick. That's not my prerogative. I sing, preach, pray, and read the Holy Scriptures, but I don't determine their destiny. That's God's and the individual's business. The finality of death on this planet provides an exit to the next life, where everyone must be accountable to God.

The Bible says, "The days of our years are threescore years and ten; and if by reason of strength they be fourscore years, yet is their strength labour and sorrow..." (Psalm 90:10). This means that after the **curse**, our lifespan was fixed at 70 or 80 years. Above and beyond that we are living on borrowed time. So what happens when a young person dies at 25 or 40 years old? I say that death has "cheated" them. Conversely, the believers should **"cheat death."**

We are no longer under the curse; why should we die before our time?" God says, "You shall walk in all the ways that the Lord your God has commanded you, that you may **live**, and that it may go well with you, and that you may **live long** in the land that you shall possess" (Deuteronomy 5:33). It is well with you by God's grace!

"You shall serve the Lord your God, and he will bless your bread and your water, and I will take sickness away from the midst of you *[or from among you]*. No one shall suffer miscarriage or be barren in your land; I will fulfill the number of your days" (Exodus 23:25–26, NKJV). "No good thing *[including **long life**]* will He withhold from those who walk uprightly" (Psalm 84: 11).

God further promises His faithful **redeemed** children: "He *[you]* shall call upon Me, and I will answer him: I will be with him in trouble; I will deliver him, and honour him. With long life I will satisfy him, and show him My salvation" (Psalm 91:15–16, NKJV). The term "long life" implies living to a ripe old age. How old can humans live? I don't know, but I believe God desires us to have long life. Well, how long is long life? Only God knows. However, before Adam fell into sin, God's original intention for mankind was immortality.

What is the Psalmist really telling us in this verse? He is primarily saying six things:

- I will answer him. Our duty is to pray. The answer to our prayers is guaranteed by God.

- I will be with him in trouble. God will not leave us comfortless, but He will be a constant help in times of trouble.

- I will deliver him. God assures us protection or deliverance from evil, sickness, disease accidents and even death.

- I will honour him. God will not despise us, but He will honour us with righteousness and nobility; He will grant us privilege and favour.

- I will satisfy him with long life. God will extend your life and fill it with abundant grace. You will not live an empty, miserable life but goodness and mercy will follow you all the days of your life.

- I will show you my salvation. God will rescue you and save you. No weapon that is formed against you will prosper, and God will favour you with eternal life.

Child of God, not only will your heavenly Father bless you with long life, but He will fill up your life with good things and you will not die before your time. Now, will death cheat you or will you cheat death? You cannot walk in what you do not know, and you cannot know what you do not practice. You believe only what you act upon.

You may say, "I believe God will heal me." But do you trust Him to heal you? Or you may have heard that God can heal, but do you know that He will heal you? Faith is based on knowledge, and all things are possible to those who have faith. The Words of God are settled in heaven concerning your deliverance and circumstances; demons, time or eternity cannot change them. I rest my case!

My Victory in Jesus

~A Life in The Realm of The Spirit~

I am redeemed from the kingdom of darkness, and I have been translated into the Kingdom of God's dear Son. What a miracle! Satan was my master. I was bound, condemned, and doomed for eternity in hell. But thank God, Jesus came and broke the bonds, loosed my soul from eternal damnation and gave me His life. I have the eternal life of God in my mortal body right now. I am a partaker (meaning a sharer) of His divine nature.

I am now a part of the Kingdom of God – where Christ reigns as Lord of lords and King of kings. He invites me to join Him on His throne of majesty and power. I reign as king in life through Jesus Christ. His Kingdom is within me. I have the ability of God within me. I live by the faith of the Son of God in me. God has faith in me. His presence is within me, and His glory is upon me. I am anointed by the Holy Spirit to do the works of God. The will of God is being done in my life as it is in heaven. God is working within me both to will and to do His own good pleasure. He is building me up and making me strong in faith by His own Word. Nothing happens to me by chance; everything is for a divine purpose.

Once I lived in bondage to Satan. I was enslaved to sin. But now in this new Kingdom, sin has no more dominion over me. I am not any longer a sinner, that was my background. I am who God says that I am, and I can do what He says I can do. I am a new creature. My life has been transformed and rearranged by the power of God. I am now the righteousness of God in Christ. I am complete in Christ. I am free from the old inferiority complex, failure syndrome and low self-esteem that held me in captivity. **Hallelujah!** I am free! There's no more condemnation now! No more degradation! Glory to God! Whether I live or die, I have the victory; so, Satan can't win.

In the old kingdom of darkness, I lived under the weight of oppression, depression, sickness, fear, poverty and failure. I was bound by unclean powers. But now, through the precious blood of Jesus Christ the Son of the Living God, I am delivered. I am free! I declare it emphatically; goodbye Satan, goodbye sickness, goodbye fear, goodbye poverty, goodbye weakness and demonic oppression!

I am born again; this puts God in me. His miraculous power is working in me. I am a son of God. Jesus Christ is my elder brother. Satan has no stronghold on my life. The Greater One lives in me and He is greater than any force that can rise up against me. I cannot be defeated by demons or circumstances because **Christ is my victory.** In Him, I am more than a conqueror. No weapon that is formed against me shall prosper. The Word of God abides in me. My mind is renewed and I am pre-programmed by His Word.

Therefore, the words coming out of my innermost being where the Greater One lives have the same creative, miracle-working power as though He has spoken them Himself. Hence, the words that I speak are spirit and life. God sees through my eyes, and with my hands He reaches to others. His love has been poured out into my heart through the gift of the Holy Spirit. Therefore, it impacts on my personality, builds my character, motivates my actions and encompasses me.

I am an heir of God and joint heir (joint owner) with Christ. He took all that I was and gave me all that He is and has – a marvelous exchange. I have received a rich inheritance. My victory is guaranteed. I am empowered to prosper. I am blessed with every spiritual blessing in heavenly places in Christ Jesus. I am blessed with heaven's best. Thank you, God, for having given me the victory through Jesus Christ my wonderful LORD! All that I am and will ever be, I owe to Him.

This book ends here, but I live on, and death is not the end of my story. If I had been born dead (Job 3:16), I would have been buried and no one would have heard of me, but thank God I was born alive and I have lived a full life. The Christian hope of life beyond the grave attests to the perpetuation of my journey and to my eternal life in Christ. May my life continue to speak for me when I am gone.

Jesus has conquered death, and He will have the last word. I prophesy to you that when the sunset and the time of my departure comes, people will look at my remains in the casket and say, "He looks good" – a testament to the authenticity of this book and the faithfulness of God. I live good, look good and will die good. One of my friends has asked me, "Why end the book with you in a casket rather than in the arms of Jesus?" My corpse will be enclosed in a container called a casket, but I won't be in the casket; I'll be gone. Being "in the arms of Jesus" is not the end, but the beginning of a new life, a new journey and would require a new autobiography. It is an awesome experience for believers to relish in the age to come.

Death is simply the exit of my spirit from this earthly life to the eternal abode in my heavenly home – forever in the immediate presence of God. Paul says, "We are confident, yes, well pleased rather to be absent from the body and to be present with the Lord" (2 Corinthians 5:8, NKJV). I know that this Scripture will not be fulfilled the moment I die, but it guarantees my immortal destiny with the Lord – an exodus from the curse to the cure. Goodbye to this unfriendly, sin-cursed world – contaminated by evil, sickness, disease, war and disasters of all types.

Relaxing with my wife at the 2015 Christmas banquet at COP

REFERENCES

Preface

1. 102 Motivational Quotes by Peter G. James Sinclair <https://www.motivationalmemo.com/102-motivational-quotes-by-peter-g-james-sinclair>

2. Benjamin Franklin Quotes, <http://www.goodreads.com/quotes/460142-if-you-fail-to-plan-you-are-planning-to-fail> Retrieved 27 July 2016.

3. By Bertha V. James, <http://reporter.blogs.com/thresq/2009/11/tyler-perry-jesus-copyright-song.html> Retrieved 30 August 2016.

Section One: The Early Beginnings

1. Boy Attacked by Ghost: <https://www.youtube.com/watch?v=ChTgIvi98l4>

2. The Cost of Absent Fathers, <http://jamaica-gleaner.com/gleaner/20130526/focus/focus3.html>

3. President Obama's Father, <http://www.npr.org/2011/07/11/137553552/president-obamas-father-a-bold-and-reckless-life> Retrieved 30/7/2016

4. Hurricanes that affect Jamaica over the years, <http://www.discoverjamaica.com/gleaner/discover/weather/weather.htmRetrieved> 30/7/2016.

5. History Notes - The National Library of Jamaica

6. <https://www.google.co.uk/#q=By+1930%2C+there+were+four+thousand+Chinese+immigrants+in+Jamaica.5+> Retrieved 3/12/2016.

7. National Library of Jamaica, http://www.nlj.gov.jm/history-notes/history-notes.htm Retrieved 30/7/2016.

8. Jamaican Nicknames, <https://lifeofajamaican.com/2015/06/14/jamaican-nicknames/> Retrieved 15/7/2016.

9. Author/source unknown.

10. "JAMAICAN HISTORY I". Discover Jamaica. Retrieved 21/7/2016.

11. "History of Jamaica's Legislature". *8 October 2008.* Japairlament.gov.im Retrieved 6/12/2016.

12. The Jamaica Observer, Tuesday 6 December 2016: <http://www.jamaicaobserver.com/news/National-Anthem-co-authors-finally-have-their-day_9943009> and <http://jis.gov.jm/information/anthem-pledge/> Retrieved 6/12/2016.

13. <https://www.google.co.uk/#q=who+was+the+first+prime+minister+of+jamaica> Retrieved 6/12/2016.

14. The Story of the SS Empire Windrush is available at: <http://www.icons.org.uk/theicons/collection/ss-windrush/biography/windrush-biography> Retrieved 19/7/16.

15. <https://www.google.co.uk/#q=resulting+in+an+estimated+172%2C000+West+Indian+born+people+living+in+the+UK+by+1961> Retrieved 22/7/16.

16. United Kingdom Population, <https://www.google.co.uk/#q=the+population+of+britain+in+1963> Retrieved 20/7/2016.

17. Swinging Sixties, <http://corporate.uktv.co.uk/news/article/swinging-sixties/> Retrieved 20/7/2016.

18. <https://www.theguardian.com/commentisfree/2016/may/08/marvin-rees-bristol-mayor-racist-past> Retrieved 22/7/2016.

19. <https://www.theguardian.com/commentisfree/2016/may/08/marvin-rees-bristol-mayor-racist-past> Retrieved 22/7/2016.

20. A history of the pill | Society | The Guardian

21. <https://www.theguardian.com/society/2007/sep/12/health.medicineandhealth> *Retrieved 30/7/16.*

Section Two: Ministerial Opportunities and Challenges

1. Parliamentary debate, quoted by *The Times Newspaper* on 4 July 1967.

2. Apollo Mission Overview, <https://www.nasa.gov/mission_pages/apollo/missions/apollo11.html> Retrieved 24/7/2016.

3. NASA's Moonwalking Apollo Astronauts: <http://www.space.com/17317-nasa-apollo-moon-astronauts.html> Retrieved 24/7/2016.

4. Literary Devices, <http://literarydevices.net/heavy-is-the-head-that-wears-the-crown/> Retrieved 24/8/2008

5. Minutes of the 2006 General Assembly (Supplements to the Minutes) P.196, Sec. lll. Rights and Authorities. Retrieved 27/8/2016

6. The 2006 Supplement to the Minutes p. 169, S41, 111. Retrieved 25/7/2008.

7. Church's Book of Discipline, Church Order and Governance (2008), page 117, S41 iii. Retrieved 6/12/2008.

8. NTCG Administration Governance Manual 2008, chapter 3, 3.1.2. Retrieved 29/12/2008.

9. 2006 Minutes of the General Assembly S66, 7. Retrieved 22/11/2008.

10. What Causes a Storm? <https://www.google.co.uk/#q=what+creates+a+storm> Retrieved 3/4/2016.

11. Silent Heart Attack: <https://www.goredforwomen.org/about-heartdisease/facts_about_heart_disease_in_women-sub-category/silent-heart-attacksymptoms-risks/> Retrieved 15/4/16

12. British Heart Foundation: <https://www.bhf.org.uk/heart-health/preventing-heart-disease/stress> Retrieved 20/5/2016.

13. Heart Bypass Machine: <https://www.google.co.uk/webhp?sourceid=chromeinstant&ion=1&espv=2&ie=UTF-8#q=heart+lung+machine+side+effects&*> Retrieved 20/5/2016.

14. Heart UK, <https:heartuk.org.uk/press-kit/key-facts-figures> Retrieved 9/7/2016. 29

15. Global facts | World Heart Federation <www.world-heart-federation.org/cardiovascular-health/global-facts-map/> Retrieved 9/7/2016.

Conclusion

1. Daniel Patrick Moynihan, <https://www.google.co.uk/webhp?sourceid=chrome-instant&ion=1&espv=2&ie=UTF-8#q=Daniel+Patrick+Moynihan+Everyone+is+entitled+to+his+own+opinions+but+not+his+own+facts> Retrieved 4/12/2016.

2. Thomas Jefferson, <https://www.monticello.org/site/research-and-collections/if-you-want-something-you-have-never-had-spurious-quotation> Retrieved 12/02/2017.

3. 3. <https://www.google.co.uk/webhp?sourceid=chrome-instant&ion=1&espv=2&ie=UTF-8#q=what+causes+Helen+Keller++to+say+The+only+thing+worse+than+being+blind+is+having+sight+but+no+vision>. Retrieved 12/02/2017.

Barrington and Maxine

OTHER BOOKS BY
BARRINGTON O. BURRELL

PROCLAIMING THE POWER OF GOD

~~~~~~~~~~~~~~~~~~~~~~~~~~

African-Caribbean Church Culture in Britain:

The Evolution of Black Majority Churches in Britain

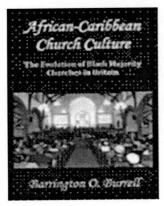

ISBN: 978-1-908447-54-8

Trade ~ 265 pages

Phone = 44 (0) 7878-615-686

Email: Barrington ob@ yahoo. co.uk

This is a practical, though provoking book in which the author takes a straightforward and fascinating approach to the evolution of "Black Majority Churches in Britain," Calling a shovel a shovel and a spade a spade, it provides a radical, critical perspective on its subject matter – giving a valid and meaningful counterbalance to the current debate on African Caribbean Churches in the United Kingdom. As a valuable, educational, motivational and spiritual resource, this book will significantly inspire and impact its readers. It will be particularly beneficial to those who seek a greater understanding of the Black Churches' experience, passion, culture and diversity in the UK.

Love, Sex & Marriage Volume 1: The Growing Years

ISBN: Hardcover 978-1-4797-9954-1

Softcover 978-1-4797-9953-4

EBook 978-1-4797-9955-8

Trade ~ 123 pages

In this fascinating and insightful book, Barrington Burrell explores the beginnings and early lives of new-born babies along with their subsequent growth and development over the years to puberty and adolescence. Teenagers exist in a world of their own. They are like strangers in a foreign country. Most are experiencing a difficult period of transition between childhood and adulthood.

This is also a time of progression from school to college, university or employment. At this crucial stage of their development, young people have a keen interest in fashion, music and sex. This book provides positive guidance to teenagers about how to cope with the biological changes they face, and how to keep themselves sexually pure until marriage. It also gives adults powerful insights into the world of youth and young people's constant struggles with emotional, physical spiritual and sexual issues.

Love, Sex and Marriage Volume 2: Maximised Adulthood

**ISBN: Hardcover
978-1-4836-0332-2**

Softcover 978-1-4836-0331-5

Ebook 978-1-4836-0333-9

Trade ~ 281 pages

This is a meticulously researched and comprehensive book. It is undoubtedly one of the most informative, educational and insightful work of its kind for the global audience. Using ancient Scriptures combined with modern in sight, Barrington Burrell explores the theology of love, sex and marriage from a hermeneutical and practical Christian perspective. He draws from his many years' experience as a Christian minister and counsellor, and from his extensive research to address some of the most potent topics in human existence.

The book will open the readers' mind to the realities of love, sex and marriage, and give them incredible insights on how to keep love and intimacy alive within the context of marriage. It also addresses various marital problems, including proper communication, insecurity, incompatibility, unfulfilled expectations, jealousy, impotence, premature ejaculation, sexual misconceptions, role conflicts, divorce and remarriage.

Secrets of Greatness

~Soaring from Survival to Success~

ISBN: Hardcover 978-1-4990-8613-3

Softcover 978-1-4990-8611-9

EBook 978-1-4990-8612-6

Trade ~ 348 pages

In Secrets of Greatness, Dr Burrell provides us with a route map to success of the very highest order, consistent with the greatest model of success known to us, Jesus Christ.

Based upon an intimate study of the Old and New Testaments, and a lifetime's work as a pastor and drawing together such disparate threads as psychology, biology, history and motivational dynamics, Dr Burrell gives his readers a meticulous and definitive explanation of the essence of greatness and how it is within the capability of each and every one of us to achieve more than we ever thought possible.

In each chapter and section, the author shines a light on a different aspect of the process of becoming what we are destined to be in the Creator's great plan for us, and illuminates the spaces through which we all must travel on our journey to greatness.

Dr Burrell explores his subject with the keen mind of a scholar, the compassion of a man of God and the tenacity of a warrior: and has written a book which is as uplifting as it is useful. It is a book which can only fill us with hope for the future. Secrets of Greatness is a corrective for our secular age – a spiritual book in materialistic times – and a tonic for all those who thirst for a different measure of success than is commonly presented in our media.

Lightning Source UK Ltd.
Milton Keynes UK
UKOW03f0614290517

302223UK00001B/180/P